MULTICULTURAL EDUCATION SERIES
James A. Banks, Series Editor

Sustaining Disabled Youth:
Centering Disability in Asset Pedagogies
Federico R. Waitoller &
Kathleen A. King Thorius, Eds.

The Civil Rights Road to Deeper Learning:
Five Essentials for Equity
Kia Darling-Hammond &
Linda Darling-Hammond

Reckoning With Racism in Family–School
Partnerships: Centering Black Parents'
School Engagement
Jennifer L. McCarthy Foubert

Teaching Anti-Fascism: A Critical Multicultural
Pedagogy for Civic Engagement
Michael Vavrus

Unsettling Settler-Colonial Education: The
Transformational Indigenous Praxis Model
Cornel Pewewardy, Anna Lees, &
Robin Zape-tah-hol-ah Minthorn, Eds.

Culturally and Socially Responsible Assessment:
Theory, Research, and Practice
Catherine S. Taylor, with Susan B. Nolen

LGBTQ Youth and Education:
Policies and Practices, 2nd Ed.
Cris Mayo

Transforming Multicultural Education Policy and
Practice: Expanding Educational Opportunity
James A. Banks, Ed.

Critical Race Theory in Education: A Scholar's Journey
Gloria Ladson-Billings

Civic Education in the Age of Mass Migration:
Implications for Theory and Practice
Angela M. Banks

Creating a Home in Schools: Sustaining Identities for
Black, Indigenous, and Teachers of Color
Francisco Rios & A Longoria

Generation Mixed Goes to School:
Radically Listening to Multiracial Kids
Ralina L. Joseph & Allison Briscoe-Smith

Race, Culture, and Politics in Education:
A Global Journey from South Africa
Kogila Moodley

Indian Education for All:
Decolonizing Indigenous Education in Public Schools
John P. Hopkins

Racial Microaggressions: Using Critical Race Theory
to Respond to Everyday Racism
Daniel G. Solórzano & Lindsay Pérez Huber

City Schools and the American Dream 2:
The Enduring Promise of Public Education
Pedro A. Noguera & Esa Syeed

Measuring Race: Why Disaggregating Data Matters
for Addressing Educational Inequality
Robert T. Teranishi, Bach Mai Dolly Nguyen,
Cynthia Maribel Alcantar,
& Edward R. Curammeng

Campus Uprisings: How Student Activists and
Collegiate Leaders Resist Racism and Create Hope
Ty-Ron M. O. Douglas, KMT G. Shockley,
& Ivory Toldson

Transformative Ethnic Studies in Schools:
Curriculum, Pedagogy, and Research
Christine E. Sleeter & Miguel Zavala

Why Race and Culture Matter in Schools: Closing the
Achievement Gap in America's Classrooms, 2nd Ed.
Tyrone C. Howard

Just Schools: Building Equitable Collaborations
with Families and Communities
Ann M. Ishimaru

Immigrant-Origin Students in Community College:
Navigating Risk and Reward in Higher Education
Carola Suárez-Orozco & Olivia Osei-Twumasi,
Eds.

"We Dare Say Love": Supporting Achievement in the
Educational Life of Black Boys
Na'ilah Suad Nasir, Jarvis R. Givens,
& Christopher P. Chatmon, Eds.

Teaching What *Really* Happened:
How to Avoid the Tyranny of Textbooks and
Get Students Excited About *Doing* History, 2nd Ed.
James W. Loewen

Culturally Responsive Teaching:
Theory, Research, and Practice, 3rd Ed.
Geneva Gay

Music, Education, and Diversity:
Bridging Cultures and Communities
Patricia Shehan Campbell

Reaching and Teaching Students in Poverty: Strategies
for Erasing the Opportunity Gap, 2nd Ed.
Paul C. Gorski

For a complete list of series titles, please visit www.tcpress.com   *(continued)*

MULTICULTURAL EDUCATION SERIES, *continued*

Deconstructing Race
JABARI MAHIRI

Is Everyone Really Equal? 2nd Ed.
ÖZLEM SENSOY & ROBIN DIANGELO

Teaching for Equity in Complex Times
JAMY STILLMAN & LAUREN ANDERSON

Transforming Educational Pathways for Chicana/o Students
DOLORES DELGADO BERNAL & ENRIQUE ALEMÁN, JR.

Un-Standardizing Curriculum, 2nd Ed.
CHRISTINE E. SLEETER & JUDITH FLORES CARMONA

Global Migration, Diversity, and Civic Education
JAMES A. BANKS, MARCELO SUÁREZ-OROZCO, & MIRIAM BEN-PERETZ, EDS.

Reclaiming the Multicultural Roots of U.S. Curriculum
WAYNE AU ET AL.

Human Rights and Schooling
AUDREY OSLER

We Can't Teach What We Don't Know, 3rd Ed.
GARY R. HOWARD

Engaging the "Race Question"
ALICIA C. DOWD & ESTELA MARA BENSIMON

Diversity and Education
MICHAEL VAVRUS

First Freire: Early Writings in Social Justice Education
CARLOS ALBERTO TORRES

Mathematics for Equity
NA'ILAH SUAD NASIR ET AL., EDS.

Race, Empire, and English Language Teaching
SUHANTHIE MOTHA

Black Male(d)
TYRONE C. HOWARD

Race Frameworks
ZEUS LEONARDO

Class Rules
PETER W. COOKSON JR.

Streetsmart Schoolsmart
GILBERTO Q. CONCHAS & JAMES DIEGO VIGIL

Americans by Heart
WILLIAM PÉREZ

Achieving Equity for Latino Students
FRANCES CONTRERAS

Literacy Achievement and Diversity
KATHRYN H. AU

Understanding English Language Variation in U.S. Schools
ANNE H. CHARITY HUDLEY & CHRISTINE MALLINSON

Latino Children Learning English
GUADALUPE VALDÉS ET AL.

Asians in the Ivory Tower
ROBERT T. TERANISHI

Our Worlds in Our Words
MARY DILG

Diversity and Equity in Science Education
OKHEE LEE & CORY A. BUXTON

Forbidden Language
PATRICIA GÁNDARA & MEGAN HOPKINS, EDS.

The Light in Their Eyes, 10th Anniversary Ed.
SONIA NIETO

The Flat World and Education
LINDA DARLING-HAMMOND

Diversity and the New Teacher
CATHERINE CORNBLETH

Educating Citizens in a Multicultural Society, 2nd Ed.
JAMES A. BANKS

Culture, Literacy, and Learning
CAROL D. LEE

Facing Accountability in Education
CHRISTINE E. SLEETER, ED.

Talkin Black Talk
H. SAMY ALIM & JOHN BAUGH, EDS.

Improving Access to Mathematics
NA'ILAH SUAD NASIR & PAUL COBB, EDS.

"To Remain an Indian"
K. TSIANINA LOMAWAIMA & TERESA L. MCCARTY

Education Research in the Public Interest
GLORIA LADSON-BILLINGS & WILLIAM F. TATE, EDS.

Beyond the Big House
GLORIA LADSON-BILLINGS

Teaching and Learning in Two Languages
EUGENE E. GARCÍA

Improving Multicultural Education
CHERRY A. MCGEE BANKS

Education Programs for Improving Intergroup Relations
WALTER G. STEPHAN & W. PAUL VOGT, EDS.

Teaching Democracy
WALTER C. PARKER

Transforming the Multicultural Education of Teachers
MICHAEL VAVRUS

Learning to Teach for Social Justice
LINDA DARLING-HAMMOND ET AL., EDS.

Learning and Not Learning English
GUADALUPE VALDÉS

The Children Are Watching
CARLOS E. CORTÉS

Multicultural Education, Transformative Knowledge, and Action
JAMES A. BANKS, ED.

Sustaining Disabled Youth

Centering Disability in Asset Pedagogies

EDITED BY

Frederico R. Waitoller
Kathleen A. King Thorius

Series Foreword by James A. Banks

TEACHERS COLLEGE PRESS
TEACHERS COLLEGE | COLUMBIA UNIVERSITY
NEW YORK AND LONDON

Published by Teachers College Press,® 1234 Amsterdam Avenue, New York, NY 10027

Copyright © 2023 by Teachers College, Columbia University

Front cover photo by FG Trade / iStock by Getty Images.

All rights reserved. No part of this publication may be reproduced or transmitted in any form or by any means, electronic or mechanical, including photocopy, or any information storage and retrieval system, without permission from the publisher. For reprint permission and other subsidiary rights requests, please contact Teachers College Press, Rights Dept.: tcpressrights@tc.columbia.edu

Library of Congress Cataloging-in-Publication Data

Names: Waitoller, Federico R., editor. | Thorius, Kathleen King, editor.
Title: Sustaining disabled youth : centering disability in asset pedagogies / edited by Federico R. Waitoller and Kathleen King Thorius ; foreword by James A. Banks.
Description: New York : Teachers College Press, [2022] | Series: Multicultural Education Series | Includes bibliographical references and index.
Identifiers: LCCN 2022031498 (print) | LCCN 2022031499 (ebook) | ISBN 9780807767689 (Paperback : acid-free paper) | ISBN 9780807767696 (Hardcover : acid-free paper) | ISBN 9780807781395 (epub)
Subjects: LCSH: Students with disabilities—Education. | Youth with disabilities—Education. | Culturally relevant pedagogy.
Classification: LCC LC4015 .S88 2022 (print) | LCC LC4015 (ebook) | DDC 371.9—dc23/eng/20220727
LC record available at https://lccn.loc.gov/2022031498
LC ebook record available at https://lccn.loc.gov/2022031499

ISBN 978-0-8077-6768-9 (paper)
ISBN 978-0-8077-6769-6 (hardcover)
ISBN 978-0-8077-8139-5 (ebook)

Printed on acid-free paper
Manufactured in the United States of America

To our families, and with appreciation and in memory of Tom Skrtic, who has and will continue to shape who we are and the way we think and act.

Contents

Series Foreword ix

Acknowledgments xiii

Disability and Asset Pedagogies: An Introduction to
the Book xv
    Kathleen A. King Thorius and Federico R. Waitoller

PART I: CENTERING DISABILITY CULTURE AND IDENTITY IN SCHOOLS AND SOCIETY

1. Disabled Lives: Worthiness and Identity in an
Ableist Society 3
    Anjali J. Forber-Pratt and Bradley J. Minotti

2. Cultivating Positive Racial-Ethnic-Disability Identity: Opportunities in Education for Culturally Sustaining Practices at the Intersection of Race and Disability 17
    Seena M. Skelton

3. Smooth and Striated Spaces: Autistic (Ill)legibility as a Deterritorializing Force 31
    Sara M. Acevedo and Robin Rosigno

4. Luring the Vygotskyan Imagination: Notes for a New Bridge Between Disability Studies in Education and Asset Pedagogies 46
    Federico R. Waitoller

PART II: SUSTAINING DISABILITY IDENTITIES WITHIN PEDAGOGICAL APPROACHES

5. Black Deaf Gain: A Guide to Revisioning K–12 Deaf Education   59
   Onudeah D. Nicolarakis, Akilah English, and Gloshanda Lawyer

6. Disability Critical Race Theory as Asset Pedagogy   74
   Subini Annamma, David Connor, and Beth Ferri

7. Krip-Hop Nation Puts Back the Fourth Element of Hip-Hop: Knowledge with a Political Limp   86
   Leroy F. Moore Jr. and Keith Jones

8. Breaking Down Barriers: Hearing from Children to Learn to Teach Inclusively in Bilingual Education   95
   Patricia Martínez-Álvarez and Minhye Son

PART III: ON NURTURING TEACHERS AND EDUCATIONAL LEADERS

9. Of the Insubstantiality of "Special" Worlds: Curricular Cripistemological Practices as Asset Pedagogy in Teacher Education   111
   Linda Ware, David Mitchell, and Sharon Snyder

10. Mothers of Color of Children with Dis/abilities: Centering Their Children's Assets in Family as Faculty Projects   126
    Cristina Santamaría Graff

11. Practicing for Complex Times: The Future of Disability Studies and Teacher Education   144
    Srikala Naraian

12. Curriculum Theorizing, Intersectional Consciousness, and Teacher Education for Disability-Inclusive Practices   156
    Mildred Boveda and Brittany Aronson

13. Leveraging Asset Pedagogies at Race/Disability Intersections in Equity-Expansive Technical Assistance   169
    Kathleen A. King Thorius

Notes   183

References   185

About the Editors and the Contributors   222

Index   228

Series Foreword

The major theoretical argument of this book is that it is imperative to implement *asset pedagogies* (APs) in schools to actualize educational equality and social justice for disabled students. Waitoller and Thorius define asset-based approaches "as an umbrella for various pedagogical approaches that privilege, value, and sustain the cultural and linguistic practices of minoritized students" (p. xv). Culturally responsive pedagogy (Gay, 2018), culturally relevant pedagogy (Ladson-Billings, 2021), funds of knowledge (Moll & González, 2004), third space (Gutiérrez, 2008), and Culturally Sustaining Pedagogy (Paris & Alim, 2014) are examples of pedagogies that the editors categorize as asset-based. These teaching approaches build upon the home cultures and languages of students from diverse groups. Waitoller and Thorius contend that APs, which have not been widely developed or used to teach disabled students, should be utilized to enhance their academic achievement and social experiences in schools. The chapters in this book, which give comprehensive and sometimes poignant accounts and descriptions of the schooling experience of disabled students, detail the ways in which they experience systemic ableism and assaults on their dignity and identities in schools. The editors state that this book creates "a dialogical space for placing disability into conversation with asset pedagogies centering how disability intersects with other markers of difference to create unique cultural repertoires to be valued, sustained, and utilized for learning" (p. xvi).

In a seminal article, Robert K. Merton (1972), the distinguished sociologist, constructs a typology that describes the roles of insiders and outsiders in knowledge construction. Insiders view reality from the perspective of their cultural communities; outsiders view cultural communities as detached and dispassionate observers. Merton contends that both insider and outsider perspectives are needed to give a comprehensive depiction of social reality. Outsider and insensitive perspectives on people with disabilities, including the views of eugenics advocates who argued for their sterilization, are well-known and have been institutionalized within the academic community and the popular culture since the late 19th century (Bashford & Levine, 2010). A cogent strength of this book is that it includes engaging and compelling chapters by scholars who are insiders within disability communities. These scholars illuminate personal and powerful perspectives that depict living with disabilities and dealing with ableism on a daily basis. Anjali J. Forber-Pratt, the coauthor of Chapter 1, is a brown disabled woman Indian adoptee; Bradley J. Minnott, Forber-Pratt's coauthor, is a disabled white man. Seena M. Skelton, in Chapter 2, describes her experiences as an African American scholar and former student with a disability; Leroy F. Moore Jr. and Keith Jones, the authors of Chapter 7, are Black disabled hip-hop artists and community activists. These authors provide complex, engaging, and comprehensive perspectives of the ways in which they are both victimized and agents for change and transformation within disabled communities.

The major purpose of the Multicultural Education Series is to provide pre-service educators, practicing educators, graduate students, scholars, and policymakers with an interrelated and comprehensive set of books that summarizes and analyzes important research, theory, and practice related to the education of ethnic, racial, cultural, and linguistic groups in the United States and the education of mainstream students about diversity. The dimensions of multicultural education, developed by Banks and described in the *Handbook of Research on Multicultural Education* (Banks, 2004), *The Routledge International Companion to Multicultural Education* (Banks, 2009), and in the *Encyclopedia of Diversity in Education* (Banks, 2012), provide the conceptual framework for the development of the publications in the series. The dimensions are content integration, the knowledge construction process, prejudice reduction, equity pedagogy, and an empowering institutional culture and social structure. The books in the Multicultural Education Series provide research, theoretical, and practical knowledge about the behaviors and learning characteristics of students of color (Conchas & Vigil, 2012; Hopkins, 2020; Lee, 2007; Pewewardy et al., 2022), language minority students (Gándara & Hopkins 2010; Valdés, 2001; Valdés et al., 2011), low-income students (Cookson, 2013; Gorski, 2018), multiracial youth (Joseph & Briscoe-Smith, 2021; Mahiri, 2017), and other minoritized population groups, such as students who speak different varieties of English (Charity Hudley & Mallinson, 2011), and LGBTQ+ youth (Mayo, 2022).

This book is an important contribution to the Multicultural Education Series because it describes ways in which disability is related to important concepts described in other books in the series that focus on race, gender, social class, language, and sexual orientation. The chapters in this book explicate *intersectionality* by revealing the ways in which disability interacts and interconnects with concepts such as race, social class, and identity. The discussion of disability and identify described in this book is informative, comprehensive, and incisive. Disability identify is an individual's connection to and solidarity with a disability community. This book describes how disabled individuals must negotiate and navigate the institutions in which they function to acquire a healthy identity within their disabled community because of the ableism that is institutionalized within schools and society writ large.

This book is significant not only because of the timely concepts about teaching and schooling disabled students that it explicates but also because disabled students make up about 14% of the student population in the United States (U.S. Department of Education, 2019). It also merits the serious attention of all educators because most individuals will acquire a disability as they age—such as impairments related to hearing, sight, thinking and memory, walking, self-care, and independent living. A report published by *Health Day* (Preidt, 2014), which is based on data from the U.S. National Institute of Aging, indicates that 40% of seniors have a disability. The population of senior citizens is increasing substantially in the United States and in other nations in the Global North. Consequently, the information and perspectives about educating disabled youth in this book are not only timely and important for enhancing the teaching and learning of disabled students, they contain knowledge, insights, and explanations for enriching the personal lives and journeys of all educators and other citizens. I hope it will attain the influence and audience that it deserves.

—James A. Banks

REFERENCES

Banks, J. A. (2004). Multicultural education: Historical development, dimensions, and practice. In J. A. Banks, & C. A. M. Banks (Eds.), *Handbook of research on multicultural education* (pp. 3–29). Jossey-Bass.

Banks, J. A. (Ed.). (2009). *The Routledge international companion to multicultural education*. Routledge.

Banks, J. A. (2012). Multicultural education: Dimensions of. In J. A. Banks (Ed.), *Encyclopedia of diversity in education* (Vol. 3, pp. 1538–1547). SAGE Publications.

Bashford, A., & Levine, P. (Eds.). (2010). *The Oxford history of eugenics*. Oxford University Press.

Charity Hudley, A. H., & Mallinson, C. (2011). *Understanding language variation in U.S. schools*. Teachers College Press.

Conchas, G. Q., & Vigil, J. D. (2012). *Streetsmart schoolsmart: Urban poverty and the education of adolescent boys*. Teachers College Press.

Cookson, P. W., Jr. (2013). *Class rules: Exposing inequality in American high schools*. Teachers College Press.

Gándara, P., & Hopkins, M. (Eds.). (2010). *Forbidden language: English language learners and restrictive language policies*. Teachers College Press.

Gay, G. (2018). *Culturally responsive teaching: Theory, research, and practice* (3rd ed.). Teachers College Press.

Gorski, P. C. (2018). *Reaching and teaching students in poverty: Strategies for erasing the opportunity* gap (2nd ed.). Teachers College Press.

Gutiérrez, K. D. (2008). Developing a sociocritical literacy in the third space. *Reading Research Quarterly, 43*(2), 148–164.

Hopkins, J. P. (2020). *Indian education for all: Decolonizing Indigenous education in public schools.* Teachers College Press.

Joseph, R. L., & Briscoe-Smith, A. (2021). *Generation mixed goes to school: Radically listening to multiracial kids.* Teachers College Press.

Ladson-Billings, G. (2021). *Culturally relevant pedagogy: Asking a different question.* Teachers College Press.

Lee, C. D. (2007). *Culture, literacy, and learning: Taking bloom in the midst of the whirlwind.* Teachers College Press.

Mahiri, J. (2017). *Deconstructing race: Multicultural education beyond the color-bind.* Teachers College Press.

Mayo, C. (2022). *LGBTQ youth and education: Policies and practices* (2nd ed.). Teachers College Press.

Merton, R. K. (1972). Insiders and outsiders: A chapter in the sociology of knowledge. *The American Journal of Sociology, 78*(1), 9–47.

Moll, L. C., & González, N. (2004). Engaging life: A funds-of-knowledge approach to multicultural education. In J. A. Banks, & C. A. M. Banks (Eds.), *Handbook of research on multicultural education* (pp. 699–715). Jossey-Bass.

Paris, D., & Alim, H. S. (2014). What are we seeking to sustain through culturally sustaining pedagogy? A loving critique forward. *Harvard Educational Review, 84*(1), 85–100.

Pewewardy, C., Lees, A., & Zape-tah-hol-ah Minthorn, R. (Eds.). (2022). *Unsettling settler-colonial education: The Transformational Indigenous Praxis Model.* Teachers College Press.

Preidt, R. (2014). 40 percent of seniors report having a disability. *HealthDay.* https://consumer.healthday.com/senior-citizen-information-31/age-health-news-7/40-percent-of-seniors-report-having-a-disability-694261.html

U.S. Department of Education. (2019). *2015–16 Civil rights data collection: school climate and safety.* https://www2.ed.gov/about/offices/list/ocr/docs/school-climate-and-safety.pdf

Valdés, G. (2001). *Learning and not learning English: Latino students in American schools.* Teachers College Press.

Valdés, G., Capitelli, S., & Alvarez, L. (2011). *Latino children learning English: Steps in the journey.* Teachers College Press.

Acknowledgments

First, we acknowledge the thoughtful work of the authors of this edited volume, who despite the current pandemic, family, and political circumstances have continued to work with us. We are extremely grateful to all of them. This book is as much theirs as it is ours. We also thank the external reviewers for the chapters—Saili Kulkarni and María Cioè-Peña—as well as all the chapter authors who also contributed a peer review to the volume.

We acknowledge the leadership of many senior and mid-career colleagues and mentors (those who are still with us and those who are not) in the fields of DSE and critical special education who have contributed critiques of special education that continue to push the field across its borders and boundaries into conversation with and reimagination through the lens of disability studies. These people include but are not limited to Alfredo Artiles, Susan Baglieri, Wanda Blanchett, Ellen Brantlinger, Alicia Broderick, David Connor, Scot Danforth, Curt Dudley-Marling, Beth Ferri, Paul and Diane Ferguson, Susan Gabel, Deb Gallagher, Elizabeth Kozleski, Tom Skrtic, Jan Valle, Subini Annamma, and Linda Ware.

We also acknowledge the work of scholars in the field of APs who have provided us the tools to interrogate and improve the teaching and learning of students with disabilities: Gloria Ladson-Billings, Geneva Gay, Luis Moll, Norma González, Carol Lee, Django Paris, Sami Alim, and Kris Gutiérrez. We thank James Banks for giving us the opportunity to publish in his Multicultural Education Series, in which many ground-breaking works have been published. We are honored and humbled to be part of the series and hope that this edited volume book can expand the development of APs, like the books in this series have.

Finally, we thank the institutions and institutional colleagues that have supported us throughout the last 10 years in our careers: the University of Illinois at Chicago, the Indiana University School of Education–IUPUI, and the Great Lakes Equity Center.

Disability and Asset Pedagogies

An Introduction to the Book

Kathleen A. King Thorius and Federico R. Waitoller

Since the late 1990s, asset pedagogies (APs) have continued to challenge and disrupt the deficit ideologies that have informed most U.S. teaching and curriculum. We use the term APs as an umbrella for various pedagogical approaches that privilege, value, and sustain the cultural and linguistic practices of minoritized students, including but not limited to Black, Indigenous, Latina/x, and Asian students. Well-known APs include culturally relevant pedagogy (Ladson-Billings, 1995), culturally responsive pedagogies (Gay, 2002), funds of knowledge (Moll & González, 1994), third space (Gutiérrez, 2008), and cultural modeling (Lee, 2007). More recently, Paris and Alim (2012) argued for a Culturally Sustaining Pedagogy (CSP) that is not only responsive to the cultural and linguistic repertoires of Black, Indigenous, People of Color (BIPOC) students but that also sustains and perpetuates these repertoires as necessary for realizing multilingual and multicultural participatory democracies. APs undoubtedly have improved the educational experiences of BIPOC students and have challenged the normative curriculum that has historically informed school practices.

Despite the positive impact of APs on the education of minoritized youth, aspects of education related to students' learning, identities, cultures, and lives remain erased, untheorized, and underdeveloped: those related to disability (Andrews et al., 2019; Waitoller & Thorius, 2016). With some exceptions (Gutiérrez & Stone, 1997), AP scholars have left the development and implementation of pedagogies for disabled youth to the purview of the field of special education, which by and large has focused on remedial, behavioral, and cognitive approaches toward fixing the so-called educational deficits of disabled students (Thorius, 2016).

Before we go any further, the issue of "naming" merits a pause and consideration. Most chapter authors in this book, including the two of us, use the term *disabled students* or *disabled youth* rather than the term more conventionally utilized in education scholarship: *students with disabilities or youth with disabilities*. We acknowledge intense and ongoing debates about identity-first language (i.e., disabled students) and person-first language (i.e., students with disabilities) (Ferrigon & Tucker, 2019; Sequenzia, 2016). Following the lead of most of the chapter authors for whom disability is a central aspect of their identities, we use identity-first language. The term disabled is neither discriminatory nor pejorative, and in relation to the purpose of this volume it denotes disabled identity/ies and culture/s as those to be sustained and affirmed, rather than eliminated or fixed. Identity-first language highlights the wide range of cultures, cultural repertoires, ways of being, bodyminds, and languages of disabled people (Brown, 2002); contributes to the development of positive identity; and promotes a shared consciousness (Liebowitz, 2015). Furthermore, it signals that people are disabled by oppressive structures, practices, and discourses—disability is not only biological; it is a social and political experience that occurs in a world arranged by and for nondisabled people. We also acknowledge that disability is an individual experience. The extent to which people identify themselves as disabled varies according to their own identity development (Gill, 1997), and students and families may avoid identity-first language due to the history of oppression and stigmatization they experience in institutions like schools.

The purpose of *Sustaining Disabled Youth* is to expand APs though a cross pollination of ideas and practices across fields, as well as theoretical and practical arenas, with an emphasis on disability studies in education (DSE). The book curates a collection of works that situate disability as a key aspect of children and youth's cultural repertoires and identity constructions, and thus, a necessary pillar for developing and practicing pedagogies that sustain them. The book creates a dialogical space for placing disability into conversation with APs, centering how disability intersects with other markers of difference to create unique cultural repertoires to be valued, sustained, and utilized for learning. In *Sustaining Disabled Youth*, established and emerging community and university scholars and activists, many of whom identify as disabled, engage with the following critical questions:

- How can disability culture, identity, and anti-ableist teaching and learning develop and sustain APs that attend to intersecting forms of oppression?
- How can understandings of cultures of disablement in schools serve to interrogate and/or complement the production and implementation of APs that attend to intersecting forms of marginalization?
- How can disability culture, identity, and anti-ableist teaching transform teacher education programs?

As we engage with these questions, a description of our own positionality as non-disabled scholars merits a careful description. Federico R. Waitoller is a white Latino immigrant, heterosexual, cisgender male whose first language is Spanish and who does not identify as a person with a disability. He was born and raised in Buenos Aires, Argentina, until he was 21 years old, when he came alone to the United States with little to no English. He was a preschool teacher and a special education teacher until he started a doctoral program focusing on preparing culturally responsive special education professors. Since then, he has worked with teachers, researchers, and activists to dismantle intersecting forms of oppression in schools and district policies, particularly in the city of Chicago. He acknowledges that it has been, and continues to be, a learning journey that includes an interrogation and dismantling of his own ableism, racism, and patriarchism.

Kathleen A. King Thorius is a white, cisgender woman who identifies as nondisabled, yet continues to explore her identity in relation to disability, including in her own experiences with schooling and as a sibling and goddaughter of individuals who have experienced disability-related institutionalization. Among her roles, she is the executive director for one of four educational Equity (formerly Desegregation) Assistance Centers funded by the U.S. Department of Education's Office of Elementary and Secondary Education. Previously, while an Office of Special Education Program (OSEP)-funded fellow in a PhD program to prepare culturally responsive special education professors, she worked within a national technical assistance and dissemination center focused on the elimination of racial disproportionality in special education. Prior to that, Kathleen was an urban public school psychologist; many of the approaches to locating and responding to disability that are critiqued throughout this volume are those she reproduced and engaged over her time in this role. However, over the years, she has continued to receive and appreciate critique from family, colleagues, and friends of color and with disabilities, particularly related to how her white nondisabled privilege has shaped her belief that she could rightfully engage in race and disability justice work across topics, spaces, and groups, with few exceptions. Kathleen has learned from these generous individuals that to engage in antiracist, anti-ableist work with nondisabled white people like her, and with the same accompanying intersectional privilege, is the space within which she has the most responsibility. She also has learned from critical and sociocultural learning theorists in the fields of disability studies in education, critical race theory, and cultural historical activity theory that her technical assistance work is a vehicle for confronting two historical legacies contributing to symbolic and enacted violence against students of color/with disabilities "and that people like me have engaged for centuries and continue to reproduce: our roles as oppressors with positions of superiority and roles of appraisal within intersecting systems of white supremacy and ableism," (Thorius, 2019, p. 327).

We hope that this edited volume contributes to answering the difficult questions to which our chapter authors so beautifully, powerfully, personally, and authentically respond. In what follows, we briefly introduce disability studies in education (DSE), identify seven areas of convergence where disability studies can contribute to a more inclusive expansion of APs, and finally, provide descriptions of each chapter.

DISABILITY STUDIES IN EDUCATION

Disability studies in education emerged as part of the interdisciplinary disability studies (DS) (e.g., Davis, 1997a, 1997b; Linton, 1998) and disability rights movements, and as a response to and critique of U.S. special education. The history of this field has been developed and well-documented by scholars and activists who have worked collaboratively and persistently to bring DS into the field of education (Bogdan & Biklen, 1977; Connor et al., 2008; Taylor, 2006). DS emerged in the United Kingdom, where disabled activists introduced a social model in which disability is constructed in relation to oppressive social and environmental contexts, and thus, identifies disabled people as among those groups that are minoritized (Union of the Physically Impaired Against Segregation, 1975). As the work of DS and DSE scholars is deeply described and widely cited throughout this volume, here we offer only an introduction.

Drawing from the larger field of DS, DSE strives for deeper understandings of disability, and the daily experiences of disabled people across educational contexts, throughout societal arenas, across diverse cultures, and within various temporal and historical contexts. These DSE foundations are applied in theory and practice toward creating and sustaining inclusive and accessible schools (Connor, et al., 2008). One of the major contributions of DS is its understanding of disability as a social, cultural, and identity-related construct: a stark contrast to the medical models of disability that pervade educational settings.

Over time, DS and DSE have forwarded, debated, and critiqued several models for defining disability, including minority, social, relational, and cultural models. The "minority" and "social" models of disability were related and foundational contributions of the field of DS in the United Kingdom and the United States, respectively. Both models respond to the fact that, despite disabled people account for the largest minoritized group across global contexts, their experiences of segregation, exploitation, and other forms of oppression-based violence have been left out of larger civil rights movements (unlike race, ethnicity, sex, and gender). In other words, disability rights have not been considered a civil rights imperative (Davis, 1997a, as cited in Baglieri et al., 2011).

The minority and social models further pose that systemic barriers, degrading attitudes, and social exclusions are what limit people with impairments from full, valued, and inclusive participation in society. The social model of disability does not deny the reality or impact of impairment for disabled individuals. Rather, it counters ableist (i.e., oppressive toward disability and disabled people) environments and contexts to accept and account fully for impairment as another aspect of human diversity (Gallagher et al., 2014). Extensions and critiques of the social model have pointed out that it does not adequately account for the complexities of disability experiences across sociocultural contexts (Siebers, 2010). That is, disability identity is complex and intersectional, and as such, social barriers and experiences are equally complex and varied.

DSE has a complicated relationship with special education, as the latter takes for granted a medical model of disability, the predominant model of disability across contexts, and as such conceptualizes disabled youth as in need of diagnoses, cure, remediation, and other "fixes" that define their personhood as deviant (Fitch, 2002), abnormal (Dudley-Marling & Gurn, 2010), and pathologic (Annamma, 2017). Moreover, special education's distinct focus on fixing the disabled child excludes acknowledgment of societal and structural educational barriers that contribute to the negative consequences of inequitable access, participation, outcomes, and related stigma for disabled youth (Shifrer, 2013), and places the onus for navigating these barriers on students and their families (Skrtic, 1995). Significant tensions remain between DSE scholars, critical special education scholars, and traditional special education scholars who continue to rely on medical models and separate, intervention-based approaches to teaching disabled youth.

Other tensions have emerged within the field of DSE itself, where scholars and activists have critiqued the field as being too white (Bell, 2011). As a response, over the last 2 decades DSE and critical special education scholars have drawn from intersectionality to examine the intersections of disability and other forms of social difference in education (e.g., Annamma et al., 2013; Artiles, 2011). Arguably the most prominent example of a continually developing theoretical framework at these intersections is disability critical race theory (DisCrit) (Annamma et al., 2013), which accounts for "the ways that racism and ableism are interconnected and collusive normalizing processes," (Annamma et al., 2018, p. 47). Providing new opportunities to investigate how intersecting patterns of oppression target students at the margins of whiteness and the "tyranny of ability" (Parekh, 2017), DisCrit has since been taken up by scholars to expose and dismantle entrenched inequities in education (e.g., Kulkarni et al., 2021). Annamma, Connor, and Ferri provide a more detailed history of the lineage of DisCrit in their chapter within this volume.

EXPANDING ASSET PEDAGOGIES WITH DISABILITY STUDIES

In this section, we identify seven areas of convergence where disability studies can contribute to a more inclusive expansion of APs: (1) disability culture(s), (2) disability identity, (3) disability as content, (4) disability epistemology, (5) disability as critical consciousness, (6) disability justice, and (7) disability in teacher education.

Disability Culture(s)

APs foreground the cultural nature of learning and human development. They are informed by a cultural historical view of learning (Cole, 2005), in which learning involves a lifelong acquisition of cultural practices and tools that occur as individuals participate with others in joint activity. Culture, from this vantage point, can be defined as "a historically unique configuration of the residue of the collective problem-solving activities of a social group in its efforts to survive and prosper within its environment" (Gallego et al., 2001, p. 12). In APs, students' and families' cultural repertoires are positioned as valuable tools for learning. For example, teachers adopting funds of knowledge (Moll & González, 1994) pedagogy utilize what they learned from their ethnographic work with families to develop rich educational activities that privileges students' cultural tools and language. In such activities, instruction expands the roles, forms of participation, and resources available for learning, including the funds of knowledge of teachers.

Despite this emphasis on culture and language, APs have not accounted for disability as culture(s) to be valued and sustained through pedagogy. We use the term disability cultures(s) to recognize the plurality of cultural repertoires within disability communities. Disabled people have developed diverse cultural patterns and identities in response to social, economic, and cultural contexts and struggles. Disabled people have shared cultures, values, norms, and beliefs (Devlieger, 2000; Gill, 1995; Mindess, 2000; Pfeiffer, 2004), though there is little agreement of what these cultural aspects entail, and it is difficult to unify one disability culture (Brown, 2002; 2015; Galvin, 2003).

To conceptualize disability culture(s) in a more general form, Brown (2002) describes it as "a set of artifacts, beliefs, [and] expressions created by disabled people ourselves to describe our own life experiences" (p. 50). Gill (1995) also identifies some commonalities across disability cultures that "include, certainly, our longstanding social oppression, but also our emerging art and humour, our piecing together of our history, our evolving language and symbols, our remarkably unified worldview, beliefs and values, and our strategies for surviving and thriving" (p. 18). Forber-Pratt (2019) also indicates that despite the heterogeneity within disability cultures, there are shared values and characteristics unique to disabled people that makes them distinct from cultures of other social groups such as LGBTQ+ or people of color (POC), among others. Forber-Pratt (2018) for instance found that disabled college students shared some key values such as fighting for independence, social justice, and giving back to others. Such insights on disability culture(s) raise important questions for APs, including *How can the cultural repertoires, language, values, and ways of being of disabled youth be utilized for learning, extended, and sustained in schools, universities, and other social institutions?*

Further, as disability intersects with other social markers of difference (e.g., race and gender), these intersections are points of cultural hybridity. Leroy F. Moore Jr. and Keith Jones's chapter in this volume and the work of bloggers and activists such as Talila A. Lewis and Mia Mingus are powerful examples of such cultural hybridity. Thus, APs need to account for how disabled youth's cultural repertoires can be the result of hybrid practices based on racial, ethnic, and language backgrounds, among others. An important question to engage with is *How does cultural hybridity serve as a source for innovative learning and for guiding disabled youth to address complex social justice conundrums?*

Disability and Identity

Identity has been a key concept in educational research since the mid-20th century applied to examine the challenges minoritized youth face in schools as well as the development of learning spaces that support their positive and healthy identity development (Langer-Osuna & Nasir, 2016). Valuing and sustaining minoritized students' identity is a critical component of APs (Paris, 2017). Paris and Alim (2014), for instance, compel us to sustain both traditional and evolving youth cultural identities to contribute to a just, multicultural, and multilingual democracy.

Unfortunately, APs scholars and educators have dedicated limited attention to a key component of many students' identities: disability. Dunn and Burcaw (2013) define disability identity as "sense of self that includes one's disability and feelings of connection to, or solidarity with, the disability community" (p. 148). Disability identity, thus, can be conceived as a unique phenomenon that molds an individual's self-image and the way they relate to the world (Forber-Pratt, 2017). We must acknowledge that disability identity varies according to the extent people identify themselves with disability culture at different points of their lifespan (Gill, 1995), which poses a challenge for developing a consensus on one disability identity development model. Children and youth may not identify themselves as disabled people during their schooling years but may do so later in life.

Disability identity can support disabled people to adapt to and to challenge social barriers, stressors, and prejudice that affect them (Forber-Pratt et al., 2017; Forber-Pratt & Zape, 2017). Disability identity development relies on critical reflection and the development of self-narratives as one faces disability-related struggles that lead to self-change (Charmaz, 1995). Through this development, disabled people negotiate visible or invisible impairments and the social meanings that nondisabled people assign to their disability (Forber-Pratt et al., 2017). Healthy identity is crucial for disabled people's mental and physical health, and to develop the capacity and strength to address ableism, reaffirming their individual and personal growth (Campbell, 2008; Mpofu & Harley, 2006). The stronger the identification of one's disability identity, the less likely one will desire a cure (Hahn & Belt, 2004) or experience depression and anxiety (Bogart, 2015). Research suggests that such positive aspects of disability identity occur also when other identities intersect with disability such as LGTBQ+ (Valeras, 2010; Whitney, 2006). Yet disability offers a unique contribution to identity development independent from other social locations. Such uniqueness exists because disabled people develop an identity shaped by experiences that most likely their families and friends do not share. Disabled people shape their identity through interactions with health professionals, teachers, and other caregivers who do not share their disability experience. We must note as we briefly highlight these aspects of disability identity that research on disability identity has mostly included white participants (Forber-Pratt et al., 2017).

Such insights on disability identity development have direct implications for APs. APs must explicitly attend to disability as a constitutive and essential component in the construction of fluid cultural identities that youth develop in interaction with race and gender identities. Important questions emerge from this pedagogical implication: *How do APs contribute to sustain and critically examine disabled youth identities even when they may not yet identify as disabled person? How can APs account for the development of youth disability identities as they intersect with other forms of social identity such as race and gender?*

Disability as Content

To the extent that most curricula, even those that can be considered APs, continue to signal and construct the "normal" body (Erevelles, 2005) as nondisabled, such content contributes to the erasure of disabled students as full members of school communities. Cultural aspects of disability, including disability identity construction, need to materialize in school curricula. By centering disability—specifically, ability pluralism—within existing APs' goals of "linguistic, literate, and cultural pluralism" (Paris & Alim, 2014, p. 88), disability as content can extend APs' challenge to assimilationist educational goals through which curricula seek to normalize students (Erevelles, 2005).

Disability as content also can contribute to innovative approaches to learning, many of which require collaboration, collective action, and multiple technologies relevant to disabled youth. Disability as content reimagines disability as it pervades popular media, books, music, and movies wherein disabled people continue to be positioned as inspirational (Schur et al., 2013), charity recipients, evil (Charlton, 2006), superpowered (Clare, 1999), and asexual (Kim, 2011). Rather, disability content in APs counters and provides realistic accounts of disability identity and experiences, including those related to oppressions and to accomplishments. It simultaneously addresses those cultural aspects of disability experience and identity that should be eliminated (e.g., ableism and disablement, stigmatizing labels and violent treatment) and which should be sustained (e.g., access, innovation, affiliation, and identity).

Disability as content also serves as a strong counter-narrative to dominant messages about body-minds and builds understandings and affirmation of the various ways of being in the world. Several DSE scholars and BIPOC disabled activists provide us with instruction on how to situate disability as content and aesthetics in curriculum (e.g., Chrysostomou & Symeonidou, 2017; Siebers, 2010; Symeonidou & Damianidou, 2013), and at intersections of race, such as Leroy Moore Jr.'s Black Disabled Art History 101 (2016). An important question emerges for APs scholars and teachers when disability content is considered: *How do APs thoughtfully select and use disability as content in instructional areas such as social studies, STEM, and literacy?*

Disability as Epistemology

APs call educators and researchers to value and privilege the epistemologies of BIPOC communities. Yet disability as epistemology has received little acknowledgement. Disability epistemologies offer powerful tools for understanding the meaning of the human body for all human beings at all identity intersections (Flynn, 2021). Disability epistemologies resist traditional understandings of epistemologies—positivist approaches to generating theories of knowledge that seek to eliminate biases that could invalidate such knowledge (Jensen, 2004) and that locate some potential biases as connected with the embodiment of knowledge, along with the preferences and partisanships of knowledge producers. Disability epistemologies explicitly challenge positivist epistemologies, first because the knowledge of disabled people is embodied, and second because the goal of knowledge production is to address and advance the situation of disabled people in society (Michalko, 2002).

DS and DSE scholars and activists have identified disability experience as its own epistemological stance that requires disability to be established as a critical category of analysis (Linton, 1998) within which disabled ways of being and knowing can serve as resources for healing the physical, social, and spiritual harm enacted upon disabled students at the intersections of special and general education (Hernández-Saca & Cannon, 2019). Disability epistemologies include ways of navigating and countering social and physical barriers, innovative practices toward access and participation, and collective alliances against exclusion, all of which contribute disabled people's emic epistemological view of their disability labels on the development of curricula that challenge views of disabled students as incapable (Chávez et al., 2003). Other disability epistemologies inform understandings of time and physical space (Nijs & Heylighen, 2015) and simultaneously resist ableist and white supremacy cultures of binary, individualism, quantity over quality in productivity, and urgency (Davis, 2017; Okun, 1999). Considering disability as epistemology, APs scholars and teachers should reflect: *How can disability as epistemology can inform how students are asked to interrogate and learn about the world around them?*

Disability as Critical Consciousness

Via culturally relevant pedagogy, students develop critical consciousness through which they challenge the status quo of the current social order, including how racism functions across contexts and people to oppress BIPOC students. Just as culturally relevant teaching asserts that it is not possible for students to achieve academic excellence and remain culturally grounded if their excellence represents only individual achievements, APs informed by DSE involve students' broader sociopolitical consciousness about dominant and nondominant constructions of disability, which allows them to critique the cultural norms, values, mores, and institutions that produce and maintain ability hierarchies at the intersection of other minoritized identities including disability (Waitoller & Thorius, 2016). That is, at the intersection of DSE and other APs, students develop critical consciousness to understand and critique how ableism and other oppressions such as racism work in tandem, and collectively develop goals and activities toward deconstructing ability and other identity hierarchies (e.g., in early childhood approaches to teaching about bodymind diversity and disability) (Lalvani & Bacon, 2019).

Moreover, critical consciousness afforded by DSE allows educators and students, disabled and nondisabled, to recognize the ableism structured into otherwise critical pedagogies. For example, in a study of ableism enacted within Theatre of the Oppressed (Boal, 1979) pedagogy, Ray (2017) locates how certain participatory expectations and rhetoric, including how the common directive, "Get on your feet!" assumes a particular embodiment of participants. Analysis of the assumptions about students' embodiments as communicated through certain expectations for participation can contribute to students' critical consciousness about ableism, even at the intersection of other APs. APs scholars and teachers should grapple with the following question: *How can we nurture student's critical consciousness at the intersections of disability, race, gender, and class?*

Disability Justice

Notions of social justice inform the foundations of APs. First, APs draw from a redistributive notion of justice as they call for equitable access to rigorous academic instruction that yields positive educational outcomes for BIPOC students (Ladson-Billings, 1995). Second, APs are also based on cultural aspects of social justice as they call for recognizing and valuing BIPOC students' cultural tools and forms of participation. Last, APs adopt a political dimension of social justice, requiring teachers to nurture students' sociopolitical consciousness so that they not only learn about academics but also learn to understand and critique social institutions, structures, cultural norms, and practices that create and maintain social injustices.

Despite this heavy focus on social justice, APs have incorporated no insights from disability activists and DSE scholars, who have also identified ways to think about justice. For example, Sins Invalid (2015), a disability justice–based artist collective, advanced a framework for disability justice that can enrich APs. The framework has ten principles: (1) base social justice efforts in intersectionality, (2) center the leadership of those most affected, (3) defy capitalist principles that define people in terms of their economic production, (4) create cross-movement solidarity, (5) recognize people wholistically, (6) engage in long-term sustainable action, (7) foster cross-disability solidarity, (8) value interdependence, (9) expand collective access, and (10) foster collective liberation. Mingus (2017) proposes a justice model based on liberatory access, interdependence, and access intimacy that replaces the myth of independence and individualism. Mingus (2017) defines access intimacy as the comfort that one has when someone deeply understands accessibility needs without having to explain or fight for them. Annamma and Handy (2021) and Waitoller and Annamma (2017) argue for an intersectional justice in education that encompasses disability. That is, efforts to bring social justice into education need to examine and dismantle forms of oppression and privilege experienced by multiply marginalized students.

A full review of disability activists' and scholars' work on social justice is beyond the scope of this chapter (for examples, see Annamma et al., 2013; Artiles et al., 2016; Christensen & Rizvi, 1996; Lewis, 2016). Yet the insights discussed above have important implications for the future of APs. APs, for instance, need to account for the intersectional forms of injustice experienced by disabled students, including but not limited to normative parameters of learning in the classroom, segregation, and stigmatization and prejudiced. APs need to closely engage with issues of interdependence, solidarity, and access intimacy as defined by disability activists and centered by the voices and experiences of disabled students.

Disability in Teacher Education

APs have shaped and continue to shape teacher training. Yet APs teacher-educators' and scholars' work will benefit from their peers in DSE. DSE and critical special education scholars who have brought DSE into teacher education programs have done so by reorienting the goal of teacher preparation toward inclusive education: an education grounded in the social and disability justice goals described in previous sections. Indeed, scholars such as Blanton et al. (2018), Boveda and Aronson (2019), Naraian (2016), Thorius (2016), Ware (2013), and their colleagues have posed and studied the generative tensions created by socializing pre-service and in-service special and general educators into DSE (Naraian & Schlessinger, 2018) and at intersections such as CRT and DisCrit (Annamma, 2015) whereby educators work to develop practices that counter the normalizing and intervention-based focus of traditional special education approaches. Recently, Kulkarni (2021) has documented these processes in relation to special education teachers of color, and in particular their counternarratives of smartness and goodness about their BIPOC disabled students. The last section of this book also offers powerful chapters to cross-pollinate APs and DSE in teacher education programs.

BOOK ORGANIZATION AND CHAPTER DESCRIPTIONS

Our rationale and discussion of significance of this volume, alongside our constructive critique of existing APs, lead us to organize the book into three parts. Part I, titled "Centering Disability Culture and Identity in Schools and Society," is composed of four chapters that provide the theoretical and practical foundations to expand APs with disability studies and the lived experiences and epistemologies of disabled people. In Chapter 1, Anjali J. Forber-Pratt and Bradley J. Minotti engage with a question we wish we did not have to pose but put forth in relation to the residues of eugenics in medical and social practices that seek to eliminate the existence of disability, and of disabled people: *Are disabled lives and identities worth nurturing and sustaining?* In this "unwanted chapter," the answer is an absolute yes! Of course! Forber-Pratt situates herself as a brown, disabled, woman Indian adoptee, who is a disability activist and scholar. Her experiences in school are marked by a lack of APs to sustaining her intersecting identities. She writes, "My disability was met with such angst and negativity that not only did I sue my school district in federal court as a teenager, but I also believe that experience made me critically reflect on worthiness and my own disability identity." Minotti describes himself as a doctoral student in school psychology with cerebral palsy. Recalling his experiences throughout his education, he states, "I always felt like my disability was something I had

Disability and Asset Pedagogies xxvii

to mitigate as much as possible in order to fit in." The chapter provides a brief history of underpinnings that have served to devalue the worthiness of disability and those that have contributed to honor it. The chapter ends with concrete recommendations to foster the worthiness of disabled identities and disability pride in schools. Forber-Pratt and Minotti leave the reader with a direct and powerful message: "We must build an asset-based approach that supports the development of a positive and healthy disability identity, honors the lived experiences of disabled students, and affirms their worth as valued members of their school community."

In Chapter 2, Seena M. Skelton discusses disability as culture at the intersection of race more generally, and in relation to her childhood experiences as a Black student with a disability who attended a segregated elementary school for students with disabilities in Detroit, Michigan, and received special education services up through her graduation from high school. Skelton examines how her racial and disability identities were both sustained and marginalized in school and provides readers with rich descriptions of troubling as well as transformative experiences. Skelton also frames and describes pedagogical practices for cultivating students' ethnic-racial-disability identity development, drawing from aspects of identity frameworks developed in relation to race/ethnicity and disability separately.

Sara Acevedo and Robin Roscigno write as autistic activists and scholars in Chapter 3. Using an interdisciplinary approach, Acevedo and Roscigno assert that "autistic illegibility is an asset to autistic people and the key to collective liberation." The authors review the neurodiversity movement, along with critical disability and autism studies as epistemological and hermeneutic tools, concluding that autistic ways of being "are fundamentally disruptive to hegemonic notions of education, and thus neuroqueer the very notions of both "asset" and "pedagogy." Drawing from Deleuze and Guatari's notions of nomadology and smoothness and striation, they examine vignettes from their own embodied experiences. They take the reader on a journey of interrogation of their own views on autism and consider potentials for expanding what we understand as "assets" in APs.

Waitoller, in Chapter 4, aims to lure the Vygotskyan imagination of the reader by focusing on the cultural nature of learning and human development. Waitoller draws from cultural-historical activity theory (CHAT) and more specifically from Vygotsky's (1993) work with disabled youth to extend a bridge between APs and DSE. He offers a brief overview of Vygotsky's insights about disability and utilizes them to expand (1) APs' accounting for disabled youth's dynamic biocultural repertoires, and (2) the social model of disability to forge a better understanding of disabled youth learning and development. Waitoller concludes that a "Vygotskian bridge offers exciting possibilities for a new generation of APs that account for and sustain disabled youth learning and identity development."

In Part II, titled "Sustaining Disability Identities Within Pedagogical Approaches," the volume moves from educational and social foundations to teaching and learning practice. The chapters engage with the following question: *How can disability culture, identity, and anti-ableist teaching and learning develop and sustain asset pedagogies that attend to intersecting forms of oppression?* In this section, authors offer different approaches to cross-pollinate APs with disability studies and activism.

In Chapter 5, "Black Deaf Gain: A Guide to Revisioning K–12 Deaf Education," Onudeah D. Nicolarakis, Akilah English, and Gloshanda Lawyer pose the construct of Black Gain, describing the vibrant Deaf, DeafBlind, DeafDisabled, Hard of Hearing, and Late-Deafened (DDBDDHHLD) community along with its unique cultures and languages. The authors assert that the use of the DDBDDHHLD acronym is a critical step toward intersectional inclusivity in this community to locate the different oppressive experiences of this community (Ruiz-Williams et al., 2015) as related to race, ability, and language, among other characteristics, and to identify these identity intersections as spaces of "gain." Inspired by Deaf-Latinx critical theory (Deaf LatCrit) as a theoretical framework (García-Fernández, 2014), Black Deaf Gain is a frame through which teachers can examine and reorient deficit-based pedagogical practices and "identify and respond to antiblackness, racism, ableism and linguicism in deaf education and in the formation and implementation of asset- and strength-based pedagogies."

Few theories in education have experienced proliferation such as that accomplished by disability critical race theory (DisCrit) (Annamma et al., 2013) over the past 8 years. In Chapter 6, Subini Annamma, Beth Ferri, and David Connor continue to contribute to the intellectual growth of this theory to assert DisCrit as an AP. Their chapter presents a framework to guide a preschool-to-college DisCrit classroom ecology composed of three elements: curriculum, pedagogy, and solidarity. The authors present concrete examples of how these three elements of the framework have been taken up by emerging research informed by DisCrit and remind us that educational research needs to account for classroom practice to tune up existing theory.

Leroy F. Moore Jr. and Keith Jones write as Black disabled hip-hop artists and community activists in Chapter 7. They carefully critique hip-hop's absence of a disability framework: its erasure of Black, Brown, and Indigenous disabled people, artists, and communities—as well as hip-hop's reproduction of ableism. Moore and Jones describe the history and politics of their movement in hip-hop called Krip-Hop Nation: an international collective of hip-hop musicians with disabilities. They detail Krip-Hop Nation's mission to not only uplift their Black disabled community but to correct hip-hop and APs scholars and the hip-hop industry and culture about the absence of disability. Finally, Moore and Jones describe ways in which teachers and students can bring Krip-Hop Nation politics into schools and classrooms to sustain Black Disabled youth, by claiming space, reclaiming language, and seeking Black Disabled liberation.

Bilingual education has been an important focus of APs, and yet, as Martinez-Alvarez and Minhye Son discuss in Chapter 8, limited attention has been given to bilingual students with disabilities. Titled "Learning from Children to Cultivate Inclusive Bilingual Education," the chapter examines how to sustain and support the multilayered identities of bilingual students identified with disabilities. Drawing from CHAT and inclusive education research and practice, Martínez-Alvarez and Son argue that children's funds of knowledge need to be incorporated into the curriculum through nurturing their volitional efforts to assert their agency. The chapter presents two classroom interactions from a project in which Spanish- and Mandarin-speaking children with and without disabilities give feedback to student teachers about their lesson. The authors recommend that classroom practice foster spaces to be "in-between," where children are supported to take risks and utilize their intersecting forms of cultural repertoires based on culture, language, and ability/disability.

The last section of the book focus on teacher and leadership education. Titled "On Nurturing Teachers and Educational Leaders," this section highlights different efforts to bring a disability-informed APs to teacher and leadership education. The chapters engage with the following question: *How can disability culture, identity, and anti-ableist teaching transform teacher and leadership education programs?*

In Chapter 9, "Of the Insubstantiality of 'Special' Worlds': Curricular Cripistemological Practices as Asset Pedagogy in Teacher Education" David Mitchell, Sharon Snyder, and Linda Ware offer *curricular cripistemologies* to inform teacher education programs. The authors point out that deficit-based approaches and remediation frameworks informing special and general teacher education curricula deliver students with disabilities into the "shadowy worlds of insubstantiality" and, therefore, cannot nurture future teachers into APs. According to Mitchell, Snyder, and Ware, what needs remediation is the teacher and teacher education programs itself. They propose that teacher education programs adopt curricular "cripistemologies" that reimagine the ways disability informs the curriculum, rewriting disability as a way of understanding the world (i.e., an epistemology) and supporting students with disabilities in recognizing and understanding their experiences as a source of expertise.

In Chapter 10, Cristina Santamaría Graff demonstrates how to bring BIPOC parents of students with disabilities and their cultural and linguistic repertoires to inform teacher preparation programs. Santamaría Graff describes her research and teaching partnership called Family as Faculty, in which she works alongside families of children with dis/abilities, and, specifically with many Latina mothers who have, "with gentle force, guided (her) unlearning of what counts as knowledge within . . . special education."

Santamaría-Graff shares the stories of four Black and Latina mothers who instruct us all, with particular relevance for preservice special education teachers, about their children's assets at the intersections of disability, race, language, and other identities.

In "Practicing for Complex Times: The Future of Disability Studies and Teacher Education" (Chapter 11), Sirkala Naraian reminds us that teaching is never only an idealized phenomenon, but also one based on practice. Naraian presents a compelling argument that to nurture and develop teachers in APs' principles that account for disability, teacher education needs to be grounded in teachers' knowing. Naraian grapples with the following question: *How can an asset-based approach to students' learning also subsume an asset-based approach to teachers' learning?* She takes the reader through her own theoretical journey informed by U.S. Third World feminism (Sandoval, 2003) and posthumanist thought, with examples from her own teacher education research to illustrate these theories. Naraian underscores the importance of examining teacher narratives of "becoming" to understand how teachers are part of broader assemblages of actors and tools that coevolve together.

In Chapter 12, "Curriculum Theorizing, Intersectional Consciousness, and Teacher Education for Disability-Inclusive Practices," Mildred Boveda and Brittany Aronson explore the importance of theorizing in inclusive education and special education teacher education research, practice, and transformation. The authors demonstrate the pitfalls of educating disabled students in the two distinct systems of "special" and "general" education that inform teacher education programs. They reflect on their own histories of collaboration and intersectionality within university teacher education programming that prepares educators to promote disability-inclusive education, highlighting how understandings of curriculum theory can contribute to more powerful preparation and capacity building for pre-service and in-service teachers who work with disabled students. The authors identify important aspects of curriculum theorizing needed to bring disability-inclusive APs into teacher education programs, including assumptions about disability and disabled students inherent or implied in existing curriculum, curricular acknowledgement of intersectionality, and the ways in which disabled knowledge and individuals are centered.

In the final chapter, "Leveraging Asset Pedagogies at Race/Disability Intersections in Equity-Expansive Technical Assistance," Kathleen A. King Thorius considers her history of encountering and perpetuating the intersection of ableism and racism in her own practice as a school psychologist and technical assistance provider, including the reproduction of racial and ability hierarchies in her professional and personal life. She describes coming to learn more about how her individual and collective actions can contribute to systemic transformation toward equitable, just schools for students at the intersection of race, disability, and other minoritized identities through the framing and praxis of equity-expansive technical assistance. She applies what she continues to learn toward a technical assistance approach that aims to mediate technical assistance partners' (often school, district, and state department educators and administrators) learning toward innovative action and equity-driven systemic goals. Informed by CHAT (Engeström, 1987) and within the expansive learning cycles (Engeström & Sannino, 2010) characteristic of equity-expansive technical assistance (TA) (Tan & Thorius, 2019), TA providers like Thorius develop and/or introduce artifacts into partnerships in order to "(a) mediate educators' examination of local conditions for in/equities; (b) stimulate contradictions between this status quo and partners' desired outcome of the partnership; and (c) support partners' development and refining of innovations toward equity-focused systemic changes in policy, practice, and belief systems" (Thorius, 2019). Thorius applies this framework and describes examples of TA specifically aimed at developing educators' knowledge about APs toward and at eliminating ableism and racism in education.

Part I

CENTERING DISABILITY CULTURE AND IDENTITY IN SCHOOLS AND SOCIETY

CHAPTER 1

Disabled Lives
Worthiness and Identity in an Ableist Society

Anjali J. Forber-Pratt and Bradley J. Minotti

The purpose of this chapter is to describe and interrogate the concepts of merit and worthiness in the context of disability. The underlying premise of this chapter is that all disabled lives are worth living. It is important to look at the history and development of disability culture to understand merit and worthiness and their significance to the community. The history of the disability movement related to disability and worthiness can be traced to the eugenics movement. Importantly, much of the history surrounding the eugenics movement is grounded in the medical model of disability and led by nondisabled individuals asserting their beliefs about worthiness and the quality of life of disabled individuals. Disabled activists, scholars, and other disabled community members have critiqued the problematic notion of eugenics (Garland-Thomson, 2017) and have demanded agency over their own lives, using the mantra of #NothingAboutUsWithoutUs. Further, the concept of *disability pride* expands on the notion of worthiness of one's disability and is a strong marker for the development of one's disability identity.

This chapter seeks to link the historical concepts surrounding merit and worthiness of disability to more forward-thinking, modern notions of disability identity and disability pride. Promoting positive disability identity in youth is important because students with disabilities are often stigmatized. This stigma may be internalized by disabled students, and teachers may notice this being surfaced in a variety of ways (i.e., decreased academic achievement, increased involvement in bullying or victimization experiences, and increased psychological needs). While less is known about disability identity development in youth, the implications for educators are important because of their ability to promote positive disability identity development and potentially help to reduce these negative outcomes with students with disabilities. For this reason, some logical theoretical conclusions will be presented to highlight the ways in which teachers and educators can and should incorporate ways to foster a positive and healthy development of disability identity into their pedagogical style and illustrate why and how adopting asset-based approaches is crucial for student development.

In the following pages, we first frame our positionality as authors, including our relationship to disability and education. Then we provide an overview of key terms related to the construction of disability, including the ways in which disabled youth's identity and worthiness have been neglected and erased in schools and society due to ableism. Finally, we provide a discussion and examples of how to sustain disabled youth/disability identity through asset-based curricula and instruction with tangible suggestions for educators.

POSITIONALITY STATEMENTS

Anjali Forber-Pratt: I am a brown, disabled, woman Indian adoptee. I use a manual wheelchair due to transverse myelitis from infancy. I have a service dog who helps me with everyday tasks like carrying empty boxes to the dumpster and picking things up. Related to education, I spent time in schools as a graduate student in speech-language pathology, cotaught a preschool class, and then earned my PhD in education from the University of Illinois at Urbana-Champaign. As faculty, I conducted research largely focused on disability identity and bullying/victimization of students with disabilities. I have a complicated relationship with schooling due largely to the lack of asset pedagogies (APs) I encountered throughout my schooling. My disability was met with such angst and negativity that not only did I sue my school district in federal court as a teenager, but I also believe that experience made me critically reflect on worthiness and my own disability identity. For context, I was asked in front of my peers my 1st day of class my sophomore year, "What are you doing in an honors-level English class, it's not like you can go to college anyway?" More is written elsewhere on that saga (Forber-Pratt, 2016, 2019). As pivotal as becoming an activist to obtain an education was, it was also my early exposure to disability sport and culture that afforded me with the positive support and allowed for me to develop confidence and strength. Disability sport gave me a community to develop skills to challenge the deficit-based models I faced in my own formal education. It is my hope that more of these asset-based approaches can be intertwined into our educational systems to help support the growth and development of a healthy disability identity. All students deserve to feel worthy, not worthless as I did.

Bradley Minotti: I am a disabled white man. I was born with cerebral palsy and use a power chair or walker. I am currently a PhD student in the school psychology program at the University of Florida. Additionally,

I received my bachelor's degree in psychology from the University of Florida. During my time as an undergraduate student, I was able to live with and form a community with other disabled students. I began to develop a positive disability identity through my friendships with other disabled people and by working to improve the lives of students with disabilities on campus through the Disability Resource Center. These experiences helped me to feel comfortable with my disability and empowered me to advocate for myself to receive the accommodations and supports I needed to succeed. As a student in a K–12 public school system, I was frequently told I would not be able to succeed academically. Furthermore, my parents had to fight numerous times to get me the accommodations I required to attend school. I was also the only student who was open about their disability in my classes. I always felt like my disability was something I had to mitigate as much as possible to fit in. Therefore, I often felt isolated from my peers. My hope is that teachers, principals, and other school staff will work to create a positive school climate where disabled youth are valued and able to thrive in their schools without having to fight for access or inclusion.

Our positionalities are included to better understand our emic and etic perspectives (Bhattacharya, 2017) and how those lenses frame the further discussion. Specifically, we share an emic status of being cultural insiders to the disability community and draw from experiences within schools, yet this is also balanced with an etic perspective as school-based and disability researchers with the abilities to draw from this broader literature. Next, a brief history of relevant underpinnings that both question and devalue disabled students' worthiness as well as those which honor and promote disability pride are presented. This contextual framing is important to understand why asset-based approaches that are affirming and promote the development of disability identity and pride are needed for a more just and inclusive education.

A BRIEF HISTORY

Models of disability are common frameworks used to talk about disability, but they also tell some of the story of important history as well (Mackelprang & Salsgiver, 2016). The medical model of disability centers on the impairment itself (Albert, 2004). This prevailing approach to disability has existed for hundreds of years. The connotations associated with the medical model are often negative toward people with disabilities. According to this model, disability is a problem to be kept out of mainstream society (Gill, 1995). The eugenics movement was an unfortunate trend that paralleled this mindset. This movement blatantly and violently made it known that disabled lives were not worthy. Supporters of the eugenics movement sought to sterilize those with cognitive impairments to "cleanse" the human gene pool of "undesirable traits." This resulted in some doctors, caregivers, and/or family members deciding to forcefully sterilize adults and children with disabilities without their consent to stop reproduction. This action was sanctioned by many state governments, as well as by the U.S. Supreme Court in a 1927 case (*Buck v. Bell*, 1927). According to the American Baby & Child Law Centers, "to the surprise of many, this Supreme Court ruling has never been formally overturned" (American Baby & Child Law Centers, 2018). Even today, the practice of nonconsensual sterilization of people with disabilities remains legal in many parts of the United States. These forced sterilizations are usually at the request of a disabled person's parents/guardians, who believe that sterilization (i.e., hysterectomies, vasectomies) will improve their child's quality of life and/or make them easier to care for. Yet as more disabled children become adults and choose (and are allowed) to become parents, they provide role models for fellow parents with disabilities as well as disabled people considering parenthood (see DisabledParenting.com).

More recently, advances in genetic testing and orphan drug testing have made strides to minimize the effects of achondroplasia, which Little Person advocates fear will eradicate this disability and erase their rich history, sense of pride, and identity (Saner, 2020). "People like me are endangered," an activist for Little People of America, the largest advocacy organization in the United States for individuals with dwarfism, told *The Guardian*, "and now they want to make me extinct" (Saner, 2020). Eugenics ideology is not only historical—it is still well alive and operating in current times.

The importance of this history is that, for decades, *the majority nondisabled society decided that disabled lives were not worthy*. It was through empowerment and the birth of the disability rights movement that disabled individuals began to advocate for their rights to become parents and to change the eugenics narrative. The implications for disabled youth are tremendous, because for some adults this messaging rooted in eugenics still prevails.

As evidenced by this practice of eugenics, the crux of the medical model of disability is the perception of disabled individuals *by* the nondisabled majority—hence, the voices and opinions of people with disabilities are not included; rather, they are minimized by the viewpoints of the dominant culture. This mindset is prevalent in many educational processes and systems as well as deeply embedded in many special education teacher training models (Brantlinger, 2006a). For example, the special education services eligibility determination processes and diagnosis processes are rooted in the medical model (Triano, 2000). The embodiment of the medical model of disability is reinforced when students with disability are not fully included alongside their peers in, for instance, physical education class, choral concerts, or on field trips, and such exclusionary decisions are justified by blaming the students' disability.

The medical interpretation of disability was fiercely rejected during the birth of the disability rights movement in the late 1960s and 1970s (Shapiro, 1994; Zames-Fleischer & Zames, 2001). The main premise of the movement was and still is that people with disabilities should be afforded the opportunity to live in the community with whatever supports are needed. The focus is on a term used by activist Ed Roberts: *interdependence along with community-based living with necessary supports in place* (Forber-Pratt, 2019; White et al., 2010).

The social model of disability, conceptualized by Oliver in 1983, posits that disability exists due to society's failure to remove social, economic, and environmental barriers, which then alienate people with disabilities and deny them basic civil rights (Barnes & Mercer, 2001; Finkelstein, 1980; Oliver, 1983; Shakespeare & Watson, 2002). Disability in this context means individuals are socially disadvantaged as opposed to physically disadvantaged.

A more recent model, in alignment with asset-based thinking, is the diversity model of disability. The diversity model centers on the sociopolitical experience of disability (Altman, 2001). According to this perspective, disability is thought of as an individual difference within the spectrum of human diversity, a unique cultural identity like other demographic identities such as gender and ethnicity, and a central and valued aspect of identity (Andrews, 2019; Andrews & Forber-Pratt, 2021; Olkin, 2017). Attitudinal and social injustices are the most profound difficulties faced by the disability community according to the diversity model. These barriers are a result of discrimination against and prejudice toward disabled people, also called *ableism* (Mackelprang & Salsgiver, 2016). Furthermore, continued education about the different models of disability and the role of ableism are vital, given that many students in special education teacher training programs still endorse harmful deficit-based views about disability (Broderick & Lalvani, 2017).

DISABILITY IDENTITY

The prevailing constructions of disability have traditionally focused on negative aspects of impairments, such as pain, muscle weakness, inability to complete tasks, or difficulty breathing. These aspects often elicit fear and discomfort among nondisabled people, and so the celebration of a disability identity can seem strange to many outsiders (Andrews & Forber-Pratt, 2021). No matter the societal changes that occur, there are some aspects of disabled life that remain difficult or impossible in some cases, and accommodating disability involves tangible efforts not required to establish equality for other marginalized groups (Andrews & Forber-Pratt, 2021; Asch, 2017; Morris, 1993).

Disability identity is defined as a sense of self that includes one's disability and feelings of connection to, or solidarity with, the disability community (Dunn & Burcaw, 2013). A coherent disability identity is believed to help individuals adapt to a disability, including navigating related social stresses and daily hassles (Forber-Pratt & Zape, 2017), just as other social identities have been linked to numerous health outcomes (Haslam et al., 2009). Despite this, disability identity is relatively understudied compared to other social identities, and the literature focuses mostly on adults with disabilities (Forber-Pratt et al., 2017), not school-age students.

Yet the most recent U.S. Department of Education's Civil Rights Data Collection reported that students with disabilities make up 14% of the student population nationally, or approximately 7.1 million students (U.S. Department of Education, 2019). Of these, 12% served under the Individuals with Disabilities Education Act (IDEA) and 2% served under Section 504 (U.S. Department of Education, 2018). Further, the influence of being in school may also shape the identity development of disabled youth, especially when schools are the institutions where students receive disability diagnoses. Yet viewing disability simply as a diagnostic label ignores the psychosocial processes at play and the social implications that having a disability has on the individual and how that individual navigates their world (Mueller, 2019).

This is further complicated by the prevailing negative attitudes of the nondisabled majority regarding disability and worthiness. In response such negative views of disability, and to promote human rights, disability pride emerged within the disabled community. Disability pride is the idea that people with disabilities can be proud of their disabled identity. There is, however, no homogeneity among the disability community; therefore, disability pride means different things to different people (Qadri & MacFarlane, 2018). For some, it means understanding one's own limitations, including chronic pain or illness, while accepting and loving who you are. For others, it means taking pride in your whole self, including one's disability. For still others, it means the inability to separate one's disability from their identity, though it is just a core part of who they are. From empirical work with adults, Bogart and colleagues (2018) found that personal and environmental factors (stigma, social support, and being a person of color) predict disability pride. Further, disability pride has been shown to be a way to protect self-esteem against stigma (Bogart et al., 2018). One impetus for disability identity and disability pride was the shared experiences of oppression by disabled people due to ableism.

ABLEISM

A broad definition of ableism is "a system that places value on people's bodies and minds based on societally constructed ideas of normality, intelligence, excellence, desirability, and productivity" (Lewis, 2022). Bogart and Dunn (2019) describe this as "stereotyping, prejudice, discrimination and social oppression toward people with disabilities" (p. 650). More specific to the education space, Hehir (2002) describes ableism as "the devaluation of disability that results in societal attitudes that uncritically assert that it is better for a child to walk than roll, speak than sign, read print than read Braille, spell independently than use a spellcheck, and hang out with nondisabled kids as opposed to other disabled kids" (p. 1). Nario-Redmond (2019) takes this further by characterizing different types of ableism as hostile, benevolent, or ambivalent. These ableist notions range from the outwardly hostile—such as hate crimes that are committed because of one's disability (Sherry, 2016)—to more subtle expressions such as paternalistic overprotection or praise for everyday activities (Nario-Redmond et al., 2019). Although less is known about the experiences of ableism from disabled youth, implications of these trends for disabled youth will be discussed next.

The passage of the Americans with Disabilities Act (ADA) in 1990 and the Americans with Disabilities Act Amendments Act in 2008 (ADAAA) enshrined greater legal protections for Americans with disabilities (U.S. EEOC, 2021). While these laws represent a positive development and have expanded access to many areas of life for adults and youth with disabilities, disabled youth continue to experience systemic ableism.

Victimization

Many disabled youth experience violence, neglect, and other mistreatment from their families and caregivers. According to a report from the Bureau of Justice Statistics in the U.S. Department of Justice, people with disabilities age 12 and older are 2.5 times more likely to be a victim of a crime than nondisabled people (Harrell, 2017). Several studies report that youth with disabilities are more likely to be victims of many forms of violence, including physical and sexual victimization, than their nondisabled peers (Jones et al., 2012; Sullivan, 2009). Tragically, some disabled youth are victims of murder at the hands of parents and caregivers (filicide). The number of filicides committed against disabled youth are difficult to track as they are often underreported (ASAN, 2021). However, a report by the Ruderman Family Foundation attempted to gather data on filicides against people with disabilities in the United States between 2011 and 2015 using media reports. Their analysis found that there were 219 media reports of filicide against people with disabilities between 2011 and 2015 (Perry et al., 2017). Moreover, disabled youth between the ages of 0 and 18 had the highest number of reported filicides (Perry et al., 2017). The disproportionately high rates of violent victimization and filicide committed against disabled youth highlights how ableism threatens the health and well-being of disabled youth. Moreover, the way society discusses and reacts to these events demonstrates how disabled youth are marginalized and devalued. The media often focuses on the perpetrator of the violent action instead of reporting on the life of the disabled victim. Furthermore, the disabled victim is portrayed as having suffered because of their disability or are discussed in terms of their perceived limitations (ASAN, 2021; Perry et al., 2017).

This narrative is ableist, is rooted in historical eugenic thinking, and is harmful to disabled youth because it depicts their lives as constantly difficult and perpetuates the stereotype that disabled youth are suffering and are a burden because of their disability. This reinforces the societal view that the lives of disabled youth matter less than their nondisabled peers, which helps to continue the cycle of violence against youth with disabilities. Therefore, disabled youth who are victims of filicide need to be reported on in a manner that highlights the positive value of their lives to challenge the ableist narrative commonly found in the media. Furthermore, educators should teach students to recognize ableism in society and how to support their disabled peers to reduce the ableism that fuels violence against disabled youth. Furthermore, ableism impacts broader societal structures, which often hinders the ability of disabled youth to receive a quality education and access the services they need to survive. It is essential that these current manifestations of ableism are addressed because they negatively impact the quality of life for disabled youth.

Education

The graduation rate for students with disabilities in the 2017–2018 academic year was 72.7%, which is significantly lower than the 85% graduate rate for students without disabilities (NCES, 2020a; NCES, 2020b). Students with disabilities have a legal right to a free and appropriate education under the IDEA. Students with disabilities rely on accommodations from their IEP or 504 plans to fully participate and succeed at school. However, students with disabilities experience barriers due to ableism that hinder their ability to access a quality educational experience. One example of systemic ableism in the schools is the ongoing disciplinary gap between disabled students and their nondisabled peers. Research shows that students with disabilities are much more likely to receive an out-of-school suspension than their nondisabled peers, especially once they reach middle school (Losen et al., 2015). Moreover, it is important to note that Black students with disabilities experience far more disciplinary punishments in comparison to their white peers with disabilities (Green et al., 2019). Therefore, is essential that educators and other school staff work to confront the dual problems of racism and ableism in schools. This systematic removal of students with disabilities from educational environments at disproportionate rates due to ableism robs disabled students of the right to receive a quality education. Moreover, a U.S. Government Accountability Office (GAO) report found that two-thirds of schools had physical accessibility issues, including inaccessible classrooms, unsafe ramps, and doors that were inaccessible to wheelchair users (Nowicki, 2020). These barriers demonstrate the perception of students with disabilities as unworthy of a free and appropriate public education, which they are entitled to by law. Further, these barriers have been exacerbated by the COVID-19 pandemic.

The COVID-19 pandemic created many additional barriers for disabled students, highlighting the systemic ableism present in schools. During the seismic shift to online learning, many school districts requested waivers from IDEA requirements, which began to negatively impact the ability of disabled students to access a quality education. After sustained pressure from parents and disability advocacy organizations, the U.S. Department of Education decided against granting the waivers (Green, 2020). Despite this, many districts failed to provide disabled students the services required under the law. This led to many negative academic and socio-emotional consequences for students with disabilities. Therefore, various districts nationwide and even the Department of Education for the state of Indiana are currently under investigation by the Department of Education's Office of Civil Rights for civil rights violations against students with disabilities (Grove & Longnecker, 2021; Kamenetz, 2020).

This unfortunate series of events is one example of how systemic ableism harms disabled youth. Despite modest increases in dollars from congressional stimulus packages, disabled students were left behind— having not received the necessary supports—and may be disproportionately impacted after the pandemic ends due to learning loss (Gilman, 2021; Hanson, 2020). This reality underscores that fact that the needs of disabled students are not prioritized by the education system. Further, many students with disabilities have medical conditions that place them at higher risk of negative health outcomes or death from COVID-19, according to the Centers for Disease Control (CDC, 2021). This combination of the pandemic and being forced to advocate for educational supports led to additional stress, pain, and anxiety for disabled youth and their families. After the pandemic subsides, the education system must reevaluate how accommodations and other services are provided to students with disabilities so that they can receive the quality education they are legally and ethically entitled to.

FOSTERING WORTHINESS, DISABILITY PRIDE, AND DISABILITY IDENTITY DEVELOPMENT IN SCHOOLS

The antidote to ableism in schools is promoting an asset-based approach that affirms worthiness, pride, and the development of disability identity in school. Asset-based approaches include curriculum expansion, instructional methods, and demonstrating allyship. First off, disabled students must see themselves represented in the curricula and in the staff that is employed by the school district. Representation matters—it is an important way of signaling the worthiness of disabled lives and helping promote the development of a positive disability identity development. Nario-Redmond and colleagues (2019) emphasize the importance of including disability history and culture in mainstream academic curricula (both higher education and K–12 education). School librarians can do an inventory of library books to ensure that disability-related books with accurate representations are available in their collections. Individuals with influence on state education standards can assess whether disability is an integrated part of the curriculum. Some states have laws requiring that disability history and awareness be a part of the curriculum (e.g., Kansas, *Senate Bill 41, Statute K. S. A. 72-7538*; Washington, *Revised Code of Washington 28A.230.158*; New Jersey, *Chapter 35 of Title 18A of the New Jersey Statutes*), though a comprehensive picture of what laws are enacted and how many states have adopted this requirement is not readily available. Policymakers, administrators, and educators need to ensure the content taught is relevant, accurate, and vetted by disabled people.

Educators can help to normalize conversations about disability in an affirmative atmosphere by being more open about disabilities and/or chronic illnesses they may have, by inviting guest speakers or parents with disabilities into the classroom, or by initiating class-wide conversations about disability. Conversation starters might include:

- What do you think of when you hear the term "disability"?
- Who do you know who has a disability? What types of things do they do?
- What do you remember being taught about disability?
- What do you think other people think about people with disability? What have you heard? Or maybe seen on TV?

There can be more specific questions for one-on-one conversations with disabled students. It may be beneficial to do an activity to help facilitate conversation about disability identity. For example, the Disability Identity Circle (see Figure 1.1) involves participants placing an X to demonstrate where their disability "falls" in relation to themselves. This activity can reveal where individuals place their disability identity in relation to their core: is it internal, is it on the fringes, is it outside of their conscious thought?

Figure 1.1. Disability Identity Circle Activity

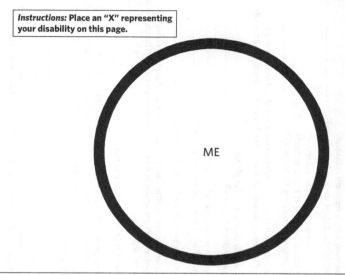

Source: Forber-Pratt et al., 2019.

For older disabled students, the Who Am I? activity (see Figure 1.2; Forber-Pratt et al., 2019) includes a series of reflective questions about the individual's personal sense of self. It asks participants to quickly list their most relevant identities and then reflect on their inclusion of disability and disability identity as part of that list. This activity supports a discussion of the integration of disability in the individual's sense of themselves as a whole, especially in relationship to other intersectional identities that they may also hold and value. These activities can be used by educators in individual or group sessions to facilitate discussion and exploration. It is important to understand there is no right or wrong way to respond.

Further, instead of vocalizing disdain or annoyance with providing accommodations or not providing them at all, educators should provide accommodations in a timely manner, periodically checking in with disabled students to see if the accommodations in place are working well and adjusting them accordingly. Additionally, it is important to empower and teach older students to advocate for their own needs. This can be done by not only allowing but strongly encouraging disabled students to attend and participate in their IEP/504 meetings and inviting them to provide their input on their accommodations and future goals. School psychologists and school counselors can support students who may be struggling with the complex process of disability identity development through educational workshops and counseling if needed. For those in high school settings, school counselors should become well-versed in the available resources to support and promote the college search process for their disabled students

Figure 1.2. "Who Am I?"

Who Am I?

Purpose
To generate a list reflecting categories with which you identify.

Instructions
Complete the statement, "I am _____," rather quickly 20 times in the spaces provided below. Do not think too long about your responses as no answers are right or wrong.

1. I am _____
2. I am _____
3. I am _____
4. I am _____
5. I am _____
6. I am _____
7. I am _____
8. I am _____
9. I am _____
10. I am _____
11. I am _____
12. I am _____
13. I am _____
14. I am _____
15. I am _____
16. I am _____
17. I am _____
18. I am _____
19. I am _____
20. I am _____

When you have finished, divide your responses according to the underlying categories you are able to recognize. This strategy can help you gain a picture of the image you have of yourself.

How many entries represent individual traits (singer, dancer, student, for instance)? _____

How many entries represent collective affiliations (member of a choir or dance company or soccer team, for instance)? _____

Disability identity is often used to describe a sense of **self** that includes one's disability and feelings of **connection** to, or solidarity with, the disability **community**.

How early on your list (if at all) did disability identity appear? _____

If you do not identity as having a disability, is able-bodied or non-disabled on your list? _____

If so, how early on your list did this appear? _____

Racial group identification is often used to describe a sense of group or collective **identity** based on one's perception that he/she/they shares a common heritage with a particular **racial** group.

How early on your list did racial identity appear? _____

What do these placements suggest about you and your identities? If they appeared toward the bottom of the list, to what do you attribute this? If they appeared toward the top of the list, to what do you attribute to this? If they did not appear at all, to what do you attribute to this?

_____

What would you miss if your disability (if applicable) were taken away from you?

_____

What would you miss if your able-bodiedness (if applicable) were taken away from you?

_____

Adapted from: Cushner, K. (2003). *Human diversity in action.* (pp. 41–42) Boston: McGraw Hill.

Source: Activity modified from Cushner (2003).

(for further reading on such resources, see AccessibleCollege.com and ThinkCollege.net).

Being an ally to the disabled community is a critical component when facilitating conversations with students about disability identity. Educators hold immense power in schools, and disabled students are hyperaware of intentional and unintentional ableism. Educators are encouraged to first explore their own potential biases, worldviews, and meaning making around and about disability. Andrews (2019) writes about disability as a form of cultural competence. Hipolito-Delgado (2014) argues that cultural competence alone is the minimum standard, and that the gold standard is that of allyship. To be an ally requires more than basic awareness, knowledge, and skills—rather, allies use their social privilege to support and advocate for the marginalized community (Hipolito-Delgado, 2014).

Specific elements of allyship that signal support for students' disabled identity and worthiness include embracing principles of universal design. Universal design is the premise of intentionally ensuring buildings, products, services and environments are accessible to all. Universal design is one strong way of signaling the rejection of the medical model of disability. With universal design, an individual is not defined by their impairment; rather, the starting point is access for all. In fact, many elements of universal design benefit individuals without disabilities. For example, receiving explicit directions in multiple modalities (verbally, in writing, with pictures and meaningful color coding) benefits many students with disabilities but also students who are English language learners. Disability should not be an afterthought, and universal design serves to ensure that students can access the educational learning environment with ease and with minimal frustration, frustration that might otherwise cause them to want to distance themselves from a label or a disability identity.

Educators have an obligation to act as an ally to their disabled students. An example of allyship might be asking a bus driver or other cars to stop blocking the accessible curb, or interrupting the showing of the video to turn on the captions or reschedule the showing altogether if captions are not available. These are tangible steps to signal that disabled lives are not only worth living, but that they are valued, equal members of the school community and that their identities are worth sustaining.

While this valuing is important at the student, classroom, and school level, there are also ways to demonstrate this allyship at the district and educational policy level. Education policy tends to rely on older, dated language with roots in the medical model of disability and laced with ableism. To flip the narrative to a more asset-based approach, policymakers and education leaders should first and foremost recognize disability as an aspect of diversity. Disability can then be celebrated and should be named alongside other examples of diversity in policies to affirm it and allow disabled students and staff to be seen in such policies. As mentioned earlier, one natural intersection with education policy is the requirement adopted by many states to teach about disability awareness and disability history in school. But such a requirement should also be explored within general teacher preparation programs, school psychology programs, school counseling programs, and educational leadership programs. The responsibility should not be placed only on special educators to have knowledge of disability, because disability is an important aspect of student diversity. Furthermore, districts should analyze their hiring practices and include disability as a metric of diversity to ensure students have role models among the teachers and staff who also identify as disabled.

Currently, all 50 states and Washington, DC have established legislation related to bullying prevention (Maag & Katsiyannis, 2012; Yell et al., 2016). Of these state-specific laws, only 13 have language specific to reducing bullying of youth with disabilities, 12 of which refer directly to federal civil rights laws (Rose & Gage, 2017). Given the data on victimization experienced by students with disabilities, allies in the educational policy space ought to consider this lack of disability-specific anti-bullying legislation when advocating for policy changes to better meet the needs of students with disabilities in a positive and affirming way. There are numerous other ways in which allies can and should engage in the educational policy space, but these examples provide a starting point. Allyship involves showing up for the disabled community in particular ways: through action and modeling certain behaviors, but also through constant learning, shifting mindsets, and challenging dominant ideas about disability (Forber-Pratt et al., 2019).

These are examples of some of the tangible steps educators can take to embrace an asset-based approach to foster disability identity, pride, and worthiness. The importance of this supportive mindset is in stark contrast to education's fraught history with eugenics and ableism by which people with disabilities have been (and continue to be) devalued. The enduring ableism that exists in our schools continues to create barriers to a quality education for disabled students and devalues the worth of disabled students in their school communities. The goal of this chapter is to equip educators with a solid understanding of why disability identity, pride, and worthiness should be fostered among students along with specific steps and suggestions that can be adopted and implemented in schools. Our disabled students deserve this investment. Furthermore, by implementing asset-based approaches to disability identity, educators and other school staff can present disability as a valued aspect of diversity. This asset-based approach can fundamentally alter their nondisabled peers' views on disability and help them unlearn ableist stereotypes. Helping nondisabled students to value disability will empower the next generation to disrupt ableist structures in our society that devalue and oppress disabled people. We must build an asset-based approach that supports the development of a positive and healthy disability identity, honors the lived experiences of disabled students, and affirms their worth as valued members of their school community.

CHAPTER 2

Cultivating Positive Racial-Ethnic-Disability Identity
Opportunities in Education for Culturally Sustaining Practices at the Intersection of Race and Disability

Seena M. Skelton

There is compelling research establishing the connection between identity development and academic performance of minoritized students. Studies have demonstrated that racial centrality is important for youth of color (YOC) and linked with positive academic outcomes (Chavous et al., 2008). Scholars examining the importance of disability identity for people with disabilities (Forber-Pratt et al., 2017) conceptualize disability as a social construct, like race. Much the same as individuals who share racial or ethnic identities, disabled people employ common cultural tools, perspectives, and knowledges to navigate within and around social and political systems not designed with them in mind (Brewer et al., 2012) to pursue their full participation in society; in doing so, they are defining for themselves disability culture and identity. Curriculum and instruction that acknowledges and draws from cultural practices of those with disabled identities have the potential to sustain disabled youth (Banks & Hughes, 2013; Waitoller & Thorius, 2016) just as pedagogies that draw from and seek to sustain cultural tools and knowledges of minoritized racial and ethnic communities have had positive effects on the cultivation of racial identity as well as academic performance and resiliency of YOC (Hanley & Noblit, 2009).

In this chapter, I assert that for disabled YOC, cultivating ethic-racial-disability identity formation is important and can contribute to positive academic and social outcomes. Recalling my own childhood experiences as a Black disabled student and recipient of special education, I examine ways my racial and disability identities were sustained, as well as marginalized in school. I suggest key considerations for educators to support ethnic-racial-disability identity formation through Culturally Sustaining Pedagogy that explicitly accounts for student disability at the intersections of race and ethnicity.

DISABILITY AS CULTURE AT THE INTERSECTION OF RACE

Disability as culture rejects the notion that disability is an individual's problem due to a failure of or injury to the body or mind (Bogart et al., 2018). Body/mind differences are understood to be a part of natural human variation (Wendell, 1996). Problems associated with disability are therefore situated as societal constraints due to the assumption that everyone functions according to a socially constructed idea of normal (Wendell, 1996). This construction of disability frames disabled people as a minoritized group that, while diverse, shares common contemporary and historical experiences, sociopolitical interests, and a distinct social identity apart from their nondisabled peers (Brown, 2002).

The disability community is the largest minoritized group in the country and is the most diverse as well. In terms of racial and ethnic diversity, only one in five adults with disabilities are white (Center for Disease Control and Prevention, 2020) and 86% of students ages 3–21 served under the the Individuals with Disabilities Education Act (IDEA) are children of color (National Center for Educational Statistics, 2020). The proportion of people of color (POC) making up the disability community necessitates a conceptualization of disability culture that centers the lived experiences of disabled people at the intersection of disability and race.

Considering the sociopolitical beginnings of the modern era of disability culture in the United States often associated with the Disability Rights movement in the1970s, one can recognize the connectedness between disabled activists' call for disability consciousness among disabled people and the rise of racial consciousness in the 1960s Black Power and Chicano movements, which emphasized racial and ethnic pride, championed self-determination, and promoted collective interests and enfranchisement through political action for Black people and people of Mexican descent (Mantler, 2013). Using these movements and others as a blueprint, disabled activists defined disability consciousness as embracing disability as one's identity and membership in the disability community, as well as stressing the importance of collective power across disability communities to fight for self-determination and full integration in society (Barnes & Mercer, 2001), further advancing the concept of disability as culture.

Today, disabled cultural leaders of color centering race and with a focus on racial inequities in life outcomes have illuminated divergences between the sociopolitical objectives, and cultural tools/knowledges of disabled communities of color who grapple with interlocking oppressions of ableism and racism and those of white disabled people. Although there are differences in how disability culture is defined in terms of priorities, histories, and practices across disability communities, most agree on the concept of disability identity as a foundational element of disability culture. However, for disabled POC, disability identity formation also is mediated through one's racialized experiences. As a Black disabled woman, learning about my racial-disability heritage has led to my own disability consciousness raising and has been a critical part of my evolving identity development. Since identity formation begins in childhood, I propose that identity development for disabled YOC must be considered as part of, and in relation to, their ethnic-racial identity development.

DISABILITY IDENTITY

The process of identity formation is dynamic, facilitated by social interactions with important people in our lives, usually individuals who share similar traits such as race (Kirk & Okazawa-Rey, 2018). Disability identity can be defined as ways in which disabled individuals perceive themselves, their bodies, and interactions with others and/in their surroundings (Forber-Pratt & Zape, 2017). Unlike developing one's racial or ethnic identity, a person with a disability must make meaning of their impairments in relation to the societal meaning assigned to those impairments while forming an identity around disability often without the benefit of role modeling typically provided by close family members and peers as is usually the case with race (Forber-Pratt & Zape, 2017).

The examination of disability identity can be traced back to 1963, when sociologist Erving Goffman studied the effect of societal views on the self-concept of people with disabilities. Negative societal views about disability and the marginalization of disabled people often led to internalizing shame and feeling stigmatized, causing many disabled individuals to minimize their differences in order to be accepted in society (Darling, 2019). The disability rights movement led to a radical shift from deficit and stigma-based disability identity models to a positive framing of disability (Shakespeare, 2014). Although there have been several theoretical models of disability identity development, Forber-Pratt and colleagues (2017) developed an empirical model of disability identity development that explored internal and external dynamics of disability identity formation: the Psychosocial Disability Identity Development model (PDID). The PDID model (Forber-Pratt et al., 2017) identifies four developmental statuses of disability identity development:

1. Acceptance—assenting to the reality of one's impairment
2. Relationship—seeking out and forming relationships with others with similar impairments to learn the ways of the group

3. Adoption—embracing the core values of disability culture and engaging with the disability community
4. Engagement—becoming a role model who helps those who are still learning the ways of the group

Having a positive disability identity can reduce the internalization of stigma often associated with disability (Shakespeare, 2014).

ETHNIC-RACIAL IDENTITY

Although various race-specific models of identity development have been theorized, researchers have also conceptualized ethnic-racial identity as a meta construct because of the ways the two are often conflated in lived experiences (Aldana, 2015; Rivas-Drake et al., 2014). Accordingly, ethnic-racial identity is described as a multifaceted phenomenon that reflects one's personal beliefs and attitudes about their ethnic-racial group(s) and the social processes through which these beliefs develop over time (Rivas-Drake et al., 2014). Ethnic-racial identity is theorized to include the following dimensions (Aldana et al., 2015):

- Exploration—actively thinking/learning about one's group
- Centrality—the importance of one's racial and ethnic group membership to self
- Private regard—sense of connectedness to and pride in one's group
- Public regard—perceptions of how others view one's group
- Ideology—beliefs about how one's group should function in society

Ethnic-racial identity has been associated with several indices of life outcomes including life satisfaction, self-esteem, and psychological well-being (Settles & Pratt-Hyatt, 2011). Additionally, ethnic-racial identity has been linked to positive academic outcomes: academic achievement, protective factors against the impact of negative school racial climate, high school completion, and college enrollment (Hurd et al., 2012).

For disabled YOC, disability identity development does not occur in isolation or apart from an exploration of their ethnic-racial identity, and in turn the cultivation of their ethnic-racial identity is filtered through perceptions of disability (Alston et al., 1996). Therefore, it stands to reason that positive ethnic-racial-disability identity has life-fortifying benefits of supporting disabled individuals of color to resist the internalization of deficit societal messages related to their multiple marginalized identities, navigate interlocking systems of oppression, and find community. Schools can serve a pivotal role in development of a positive ethnic-racial-disability identity for disabled YOC.

SCHOOLS AS POWERFUL SOCIALIZING AGENTS

Through formal and informal curricula, the school is a powerful socializing agent and influencer of youth identity development. The schooling experience is in part shaped by an informal curriculum, often referred to as the hidden curriculum. How students perceive themselves in academic spaces is affected by how they experience the hidden curriculum and can influence personal choices that impact their educational outcomes (Howard, 2003). While it is inclusive of the formal curriculum, the hidden curriculum goes beyond the goals, methods, materials, and assessment of individual classroom instruction to include broader school elements such as activities, routines, structures, and content through which students are taught values, beliefs, and attitudes (Halstead & Xiao, 2010). For disabled youth, forming a disability identity is an important part of their development (Stolz, 2010); the hidden curriculum can provide opportunities for ethnic-racial-disability identity development of disabled YOC.

In the remainder of this chapter, applying the PDID model's statuses and ethnic-racial identity dimensions, I engage in an autoethnographic analysis of my public K–12 school experiences as a Black disabled student receiving special education, to examine and illustrate how my ethnic-racial-disability identity was sustained and marginalized through formal and hidden curricula. I close by suggesting how culturally sustaining practices could be effective in creating opportunities for ethnic-racial-disability identity development.

HAVING A DISABILITY

I was born with a rare genetic disorder called Escobar syndrome, which causes physical and health impairments. I am short in physical stature and have tightening and shortening of muscles in my elbows and knees, scoliosis, and minor respiratory difficulties. I was significantly smaller than most children my age, and because of the severe muscle constriction in my left leg, it was amputated when I was eight and I began wearing a prosthesis. Other differences in how my body was developing became more evident as I aged. My spine took on the "S" curve indicative of early-onset scoliosis. Throughout my schooling experiences, however, these differences became more than idiosyncrasies of my personhood; they meant something about me that made me an individual apart from children in my neighborhood. Starting school marked the beginning of my identity as a person with a disability, but this was not the case for my racial identity. I always knew I was Black.

MY RACIAL IDENTITY

I was born and raised in Detroit, Michigan. By the 1970s, millions of African Americans migrated from the south to the Midwest and the white flight, redlining, and violence targeting African Americans who sought to move to suburban areas made Detroit one of the most segregated cities in the United States (Darden et al., 2010). Being Black was a part of being a Detroiter; Black music streamed out of car windows and during backyard cookouts, and there were Afro-centric bookstores, barber shops, and beauty salons filled with Black women, girls, men, and boys on neighborhood corners. Being Black meant community.

When I started school, being Black was who I *was*—I recognized the struggles that were part of my racial heritage and appreciated the resiliency of Black people, which contributed to my racial pride. But my disability was something I *had*—something that needed to be fixed with doctors, leg braces, and surgeries. My view of disability, and my disability identity, would evolve (and still is evolving) as I matured into adulthood. Today, I reject that disability is inextricably linked to pathology (Blustein, 2012) and claim disability as one of my many social identities (Skelton, 2019).

RECALLING THE PAST TO LEARN AND IMPROVE THE PRESENT

Memories bring our "changing sense of who we are and who we were coherently into view of one another and enable the role of the past in the present to be explored" (Keightley, 2010, p. 57). I do not presume my personal memories alone should be taken as objective historical facts but rather as "constructed and reconstructed accounts of the past acting in and on the present" (Keightley, 2010, p. 67). To organize memories of school-based opportunities to support my ethnic-racial and disability identity development, I focus on elements of the hidden curriculum including activity, environment, structure, and content (Halstead & Xiao, 2010), in relation to the PDID model's identity developmental statuses and the ethnic-racial identity dimensions.

Cultivating Disability Identity by Centering Disability in the Hidden Curriculum

My first school was Oakman Orthopedic Elementary. The single-story school was built in 1932 specifically for the public education of children with physical, health, and cognitive impairments (Detroiturbex.com, n.d.). Oakman had extra-wide hallways with low handrails, physical and occupational therapy rooms, an infirmary, showers, and a dental clinic. By 1970, Oakman was the elementary school for special education students living on the west side of the city, identified with the state of Michigan's special education category "Physical or Otherwise Health Impaired" (Michigan State Board of Education, 1987). In 1978, the school was opened to nondisabled students in the neighborhood. However, students with disabilities and nondisabled students were taught in segregated classrooms until 1982 (Detroiturbex.com, n.d.).

One of my first school memories was of the day my mother and I visited Oakman. What I recall most was seeing other children with disabilities for the first time outside of the clinic. I saw children with crutches and walkers, children who wore leg braces, and children who were in wheelchairs being pushed by adults or rolling themselves going about their daily routines. Over the years, classrooms and hallways included nondisabled children as well, although 60% of the student population remained students with disabilities (Detroiturbex.com, n.d.).

Using the PDID model development statuses and the informal curriculum domains (Halstead & Xiao, 2010), I will illustrate aspects of my education experiences that supported my disability identity development, and highlight missed opportunities. During elementary school, qualities of the school's physical environment, planned with disabled children, cultivated the PDID status of acceptance (i.e., assenting to the reality of one's impairment). Because of features such as hallway handrails at just the right height for young children and all around the building, supports that a child with ambulatory impairments might need were always there. Activities built into the curricular program also supported acceptance of disability; in accordance with students' individualized education programs (IEP), students received physical, occupational, or speech therapies in spaces specifically designed for these services rather than ad hoc spaces like hallways or stairwells. There was a sense that supports were ordinary parts of educational processes, attending to disabilities not as *special needs*. Moreover, medical services provided by the full-time nurse were also available to nondisabled students. While disabled students accessed these services to assist in management of health-related issues such as chronic asthma, epilepsy, juvenile diabetes, catheter maintenance, and so on, nondisabled students accessed them for cold remedies, injuries from accidents, and the like. Because of these factors in the arrangement of school, including environment, structures, student demographics, and activities, disability was recognized and acknowledged, and there was a sense of community and opportunities to form peer support networks, addressing the PDID status of relationship (i.e., seeking out and forming relationships with others with similar impairments to learn the ways of the group). Disability was centered in school activities in ways that were not stigmatizing. Nondisabled students were acculturated into a school culture where disability was normalized.

My classmates had an assortment of disabilities. These representations along with educators' affirming activities supported the PDID status of adoption (i.e., embracing the core values of disability culture and engaging with the disability community). As my classmates and I moved up in grades, we would help new students with disabilities learn routines and norms and welcomed them into our community. In these ways, we were operationalizing the PDID status of engagement (i.e., becoming role models who help those still learning the ways of the group).

After elementary school, neither my middle nor high school buildings were constructed with disabled students in mind, and the majority of the students enrolled in these schools were nondisabled. In 7th grade I was "mainstreamed," and although most of my elementary schoolmates transitioned with me to the same middle school, once we were placed into general education classes we were no longer in daily contact. School-provided opportunities for disability identity development decreased.

However, in middle school, there were a few instances that supported positive disability identity development. One occurred via an activity planned by a general education teacher. In 7th grade, I enrolled in a film production class where I was the only disabled student. Yet it would become one of my favorite classes in part because the teacher, Mr. K, structured lessons using project-based learning, which created opportunities for me to interact with nondisabled peers and build connections in ways not afforded to me before. This was noteworthy, because there were many structural challenges to making friends in middle school and high school. I always attended schools located outside of my neighborhood; it was district practice to bus disabled students to schools with particular special education services rather than providing those services in neighborhood schools. In contrast, all nondisabled students in my middle school lived near the school and to one another. Nondisabled students formed relationships not only in school but also during travel to and from school, after school, and on weekends. I was an outsider who did not live in the community, and due to my mainstreaming and teachers' almost exclusive use of whole group instruction and independent seatwork, there were few opportunities for me to form relationships with disabled and nondisabled peers, respectively. Moreover, my elementary school friendships with disabled peers were difficult to nurture as well because we had few opportunities to interact with one another throughout the school day.

A film class activity about the concept of movie genres created an opportunity for disability identity development. Each project team was assigned a genre, wrote a script, and staged one scene: our group was the Spaghetti Western. When we selected actors for our scene, I was chosen to play the "sheriff," who was to punch out the bank robber and spoil the heist. This presented a challenge related to my disability because the student who played the bank robber was almost two feet taller than me. For the first time with this group of nondisabled students, my disability had to be overtly acknowledged. I suggested that someone else play the sheriff in anticipation of stigmatizing reactions from my nondisabled peers. Instead, my groupmates decided we would find a solution that accepted my disability and my role as sheriff. For the first time at school, I experienced authentic inclusion: acceptance of my disability in an inclusive context. An opportunity to exhibit the status of adoption in disability identity development also came as part of a film project encouraged by Mr. K.

In 8th grade, Mr. K. encouraged a group of students with disabilities to produce and enter a documentary about our school experiences into the Detroit Student Film Festival. He assigned me as director, and we titled the film *Our Side of the Story* (Skelton, 1984). Making the film would be the first time in almost 2 years since I began middle school that I would spend significant time with other disabled students. We reconnected and reflected on our school experiences together, and by reestablishing community, we re-entered into the disability identity status of adoption.

Opportunities Missed to Support Positive Ethnic-Racial Identity Development

Shifting back to reflect on my elementary school opportunities for positive ethnic-racial identity development, there was no acknowledgement or appreciation of the primarily Black student population's racial or ethnic identities. Our primarily white educators, administrators, and therapists engaged in color-evasiveness (Annamma et al., 2017); they never connected school content or activities to our racial identities or lived experiences and curricular content almost exclusively reflected Euro-American experiences. There were no planned opportunities that supported the ethnic-racial identity dimension of exploration (i.e., actively thinking and learning about one's racial group). The artwork that hung on school walls consisted of impressionist paintings of white children, often playing in flowered fields. Further, even though community-based organizations sometimes led student activities, in 6 years, none supported the cultivation of ethnic-racial identity dimensions and I only recall one activity that was facilitated by a person of color.

The only elementary school activity that acknowledged students' ethnic-racial identity was deeply problematic and occurred during a school assembly. All 5th-grade students were gathered in the school auditorium. The principal introduced the visitor as someone there to discuss a very important topic. A Black man walked onto the stage. This was the first time a Black person was in our school to lead an assembly, and I recall feeling excited and deeply interested in what was about to happen. We were told that we going to watch a movie—*A Hero Ain't Nothin' but a Sandwich* (Nelson, 1977)—and talk about what we learned. The movie was about a Black junior high school student who became addicted to heroin provided by a local drug dealer and started to sell drugs to pay for this addiction. The student was sent to a drug rehabilitation hospital and when he was released, found out that his best friend died from a heroin overdose.

In my innocence, I had never seen anything like what was depicted in that movie. Everything was so alien to my life and lived experiences, including how the actors portrayed how Black people talked, walked, and acted. The experience was awful, and the excitement of having my racial identity affirmed as part of the school curriculum was quickly dashed. In that moment what became evident and contributed to my early development of the ethnic-racial identity dimension of public regard (i.e., perceptions of how others view one's group) was that white educators in my school perceived my racial identity as being susceptible to criminality and dysfunction. They believed Black students would relate to the movie's stereotypic tropes, and that 9- and 10-year-olds needed to learn to "just say no" to doing and selling drugs because of what we might be exposed to in our homes and neighborhoods. Despite statistics at the time indicating that white and Black people used drugs at similar rates and that white people were more likely to sell drugs (Human Rights Watch, n.d.), I doubt a similar movie was shown to 9- and 10-year-old white children in nearby suburban elementary schools. White children's innocence was preserved, while we were made to confront addiction, overdoses, death, and drug dealers in a school movie screening.

Cultivating Ethnic-Racial Identity by Centering Race in the Hidden Curriculum

Whereas, my elementary school experience included little to no acknowledgement of the ethnic-racial identities of the predominantly Black student body, there was an intentionality in my middle and high schools, particularly among educators of color, to instill cultural knowledge and racial pride in their students in line with the ethnic-racial identity dimension centrality (i.e., the importance of one's racial and ethnic group membership to self). I attended Charles R. Drew Middle School, named after the African American surgeon and researcher who organized the first U.S. large-scale blood bank. We learned about our school's namesake and other Black historical figures, which supported students' ethnic-racial identity development of public regard. Representation of Black role models were abundant; my middle and high schools had Black male principals, and many of the educators and staff were also people of color. The representation of Black professionals in both schools promoted the development of my ethnic-racial identity ideology (i.e., beliefs about how one's group should function in society). Black culture was reflected, if not in depth within the formal curriculum, certainly in the informal curriculum. School activities incorporated content and routines such as performing the Black national anthem, "Lift Every Voice and Sing," following the national anthem before school sport events and assemblies. I recall one middle school assembly when an African dance and drum troupe performed, and the performers made connections between the popular radio music and moves we would show off at school dances and traditional rhythms and movements performed in tribal ceremonies in Zimbabwe and Nigeria. Activities such as these supported my and other students' development of private regard (i.e., sense of connectedness to and pride in one's own racial-ethnic groups).

I attended high school from 1984 to 1988: now considered the golden age of hip-hop. Although a far cry from today's hip-hop pedagogy (Morrell & Duncan-Andrade, 2002), educators leveraged youth culture (Paris & Alim, 2014) and used hip-hop culture in cocurricular activities to connect with students and to connect students with cultural knowledge to support positive racial-ethnic identity development. However, despite concerted efforts by my middle and high school educators to interject cultural content in the informal curriculum, formal academic programs centered whiteness at their core, from the texts that made up our school's literary cannon to the presentation of U.S. history and geography. There was little effort to highlight literacies and contributions of people of color in science, technology, literature, or the arts. Doing so would have leveraged curriculum content toward the advancement of my and my classmates' ethnic-racial identity development. Moreover, with regard to disability culture, there was no recognition of disability as an aspect of our social identity.

SUPPORTING POSITIVE ETHNIC-RACIAL-DISABILITY IDENTITY DEVELOPMENT WITH ASSET PEDAGOGIES

Research has demonstrated links between positive academic and social outcomes and ethnic and racial identity formation. Additionally, positive disability identity has life-affirming effects for disabled individuals. I offer that a strong ethnic-racial-disability identity could have life-fortifying benefits for disabled individuals of color. Identity formation is shaped, in part, by school experiences (Lannegrand-Willems & Bosma, 2006); for disabled YOC, asset pedagogies (APs) can mediate learning toward the cultivation of positive ethnic-racial-disability identity.

APs center the experiences, cultural histories, heritage, community languages, and valued practices of minoritized communities (Ladson-Billings, 1994; Paris & Alim, 2014). Culturally Sustaining Pedagogy (CSP), a particular stance of AP, "seeks to perpetuate and foster linguistic, literate, and cultural pluralism as part of the democratic project of schooling" (Paris, 2012, p. 95). Scholars have proposed the extension of CSP to include the cultural histories and practices of disabled people as a means of sustaining disability cultures (Waitoller & Thorius, 2016).

RECOMMENDATIONS FOR CULTURALLY SUSTAINING PEDAGOGY FOR DISABLED YOUTH

CSP (re)positions the goal of teaching and learning for YOC to that of supporting students to "explore, honor, extend, and, at times, problematize their own heritage and community practices" (Paris & Alim, 2014, p. 86). Rather than a set of discrete decontextualized practices, CSP is a theoretical frame in which instructional and curricular practices reflecting the core principles of CSP can be operationalized. These principles include (1) educational outcomes that are not centered on white, middle-class (able-bodied) norms; (2) supporting and sustaining youth cultural and heritage practices; (3) cultural flexibility that acknowledges the shifting and evolving nature of cultures and that recognizes multilingualism and multiculturalism are increasingly linked to access and power; and (4) critical analysis of youth cultural practices that reinscribe marginalizing notions (Paris & Alim, 2014). Next, I describe examples of how CSP could be used to cultivate ethnic-racial-identity formation for disabled YOC across the hidden curriculum domains of content, structure, activity, and environment, with connections back to my own schooling experiences.

Center the Heritage Practices of Disabled POC in the Curriculum to Instill Disability and Racial Pride for Disabled YOC

As a disabled youth, the absence of disabled people in the curriculum reduced school-based opportunities for me to learn about and embrace my disability identity. By incorporating content about the disability rights and justice movements as well as iluminating the presence and contributions of disabled people in our society and throughout history, curriculum can assist in eliminating inaccurate and stigmatizing narratives about disability, decenter whiteness and able-bodiedness, and support the sustaining of heritage practices found in disabled communities of color, such as intersectional political activism (e.g., Brad Lomax and his leadership in the Black Panther Party).

Create Sustaining Structures for Disabled YOC Cultural Practices and Opportunities to Critically Interrogate Practices That Reproduce Marginalization

As an adolescent, I was conflicted between wanting to abandon practices that amplified my disability but that were useful for navigating nondisabled spaces in order to be accepted by nondisabled peers. At the same time, I reveled in those few times and spaces away from the gaze of nondisabled schoolmates where I found respite from the emotional and physical toll of performing able-bodiedness. By acknowledging disabled people as members of minoritized group, educators can recognize the need for disabled students to build community with each other. Similar to student clubs like Black Student Unions or Gay-Straight Alliances that create support networks for Black and LGBTQ+ students, strategies like establishing affinity groups for students with disabilities (like the student documentary crew I directed) could create safe spaces for disabled students and provide opportunities for them to share cultural practices for addressing identity-related challenges and support self-critique of problematic practices that reinforce stigmatizing notions of disability—all important for racial, ethnic and disability identity development.

Engage Activities That Increase the Presence of Disabled Adults of Color to Expand the Conceptualization of Achievement

Indices of achievement in my school experiences reflected dominant cultural norms in terms of race and ability. For example, there was always one goal on my IEP related to demonstrating independence, regardless of my actual academic performance. This hyperfocus on independence rather than *interdependence* centered the dominant cultural value of individualism and did not take into account the notion of collectivism more valued in Black cultures (Carson, 2009) nor the practical necessity of many disabled people across racial groups to rely on the supports of others.

Engaging in activities to increase school presence of disabled adults of color contributes to a society in which disabled people and their cultural practices are recognized and valued. Additionally, the increased presence of disabled adults from diverse backgrounds provides opportunities for students to observe various ways of living race (Paris & Alim, 2014) and disability. Disabled adults of diverse races and genders can impart to students cultural practices useful for navigating overlapping systems of oppression, demonstrating resilience, power, and expanding how achievement is conceptualized.

Practice Radical Accessibility and UDL Principles to Create Environments That Support and Sustain Disabled Youth's Cultural Practices for How They Use Their Bodies and Minds

Not since Oakman Elementary School have I encountered a physical space that provided such freedom in my ability to navigate my surroundings without difficulty. Implementing principles of Radical Accessibility—where accessibility needs for disabled people serve as the foundation upon which everything else is built (Kozyra, 2021)—can support creating environments where disabled youth use their bodies to navigate their surroundings in ways that are most natural for them. Additionally, Universal Design for Learning (CAST, 2018)—the development of flexible learning spaces that address variability in bodies and minds—can normalize disability as well as linguistic and cultural differences within instructional environments.

REFLECTING ON THE PAST TO IMAGINE A FUTURE WHEN BLACK DISABLED YOUTH ARE SUSTAINED AND FORTIFIED

As a Black disabled education scholar-practitioner, reflecting on my own childhood experiences through these analytical frames was both an emotional and instructive endeavor. Excavating the depths of my childhood memories to surface pivotal incidents that contributed to the formation of my self-identity, I recovered and interrogated both painful and joyous memories. I found myself smiling as I recalled the Spaghetti Western class activity and the student film documentary, realizing that it was during these activities that I first felt *seen* in school. I re-experienced my childhood disappointment, related to the school screening of the movie *A Hero Ain't Nothin' but a Sandwich* and the mild shame I felt at realizing the depictions in the movie were how my teachers, for whom I had great affection, viewed me . . . us . . . their Black students, and then with an adult comprehension, resentment toward the racist assumptions of those educators.

As disabled people and specifically disabled people of color, we are constantly contending with deficit attitudes toward disability and race, inaccessible environments, and discrimination impacting our psychosocial well-being. In fact, adults with disabilities report experiencing mental distress almost five times as often as nondisabled adults (Centers for Disease Control and Prevention, 2020), and disabled people of color are more likely to experience financial, housing, and food insecurity than our white disabled counterparts (National Disability Institute, 2019).

These race-linked stressors may cause disabled people of color to internalize oppression, leading to doubts of self-worth and self-confidence (National Disability Institute, 2019). Just as a positive racial identity has been found to be a protective factor against the negative impacts of racism (Austin et al., in press), I assert that cultivating a strong ethnic-racial-disability identity through culturally sustaining pedagogies can have life-fortifying benefits for disabled YOC.

CHAPTER 3

Smooth and Striated Spaces
Autistic (Ill)legibility as a Deterritorializing Force

Sara M. Acevedo and Robin Rosigno

Neurodivergent activists and neurodiversity scholars in the United States and beyond have argued that autistic cultures represent a cornucopia of kinship systems, practices, systems of presentation, and artifacts (Acevedo, 2020, 2021; Acevedo & Nusbaum, 2020; Klar & Wolfond, 2020). Throughout history, various autistic cultures have made significant scientific, literary, technological, political, and philosophical contributions to society (Silberman, 2015). One of those contributions is particularly relevant to the overall framework of this chapter and focuses on the political gains of the neurodiversity movement (Kapp, 2020 Davidson & Orsini, 2013; Robertson, 2009). Expanding on these political gains and leveraging their favorable momentum, this chapter will explore the autistic lived body as a dynamic life force rich with liberatory potential. We draw from Guattari's (1986) *nomadic* philosophy—or a philosophy of movement and flow—and expand on the idea of autistic illegibility (i.e., ways of being that escape clinical labeling systems) to argue that this is a strategy often used by autistic people and is an asset for collective liberation. We employ "feral methods and rogue genres" (Chen & Puar, 2021) to explore our own experiences and the friction between autistic modes of being and the various educational institutions we inhabit. We resist biomedical and identitary orientations and focus on what autism *does instead of what it represents*. In essence, this chapter begs the question: How can we think about autism as an asset without availing ourselves to be consumed by the neoliberal institution?

A combined exploration of feral (autistic-designed) grassroots education methods and rogue (i.e., not affixed to a single theoretical lens) APs support our idea that autism is a dynamic site of resistance. To translate these ideas into applicable pedagogical methods and practices, we offer two examples of community-based education projects designed and implemented by autistic grassroots educators as well as some of the strategies we use in our pedagogy to disrupt hegemonic schooling practices, particularly those aimed at neutralizing "neurodiver-agency" (Acevedo, 2020). To present this information, we employ a combination of auto-ethnographic vignettes and discourse analysis, and ultimately demonstrate the subversive potential of this work and its role in temporarily stalling the proliferation of neoliberal agendas in education. The stakes here are both intellectual and material. Autistic students are subject to extreme forms of school-based violence, and our intervention here allows for lines of flight, subversive acts of resistance, and demonstrates the role AP can take in dismantling intersecting systems of oppression experienced by autistic students.

HISTORICAL, POLITICAL, AND PHILOSOPHICAL *ORIENTATIONS*: THE AUTISTIC *LIVED BODY*

Over the past 2 decades, the neurodiversity movement has made great strides in gaining recognition as an integral part of disability activism in the United States and more recently in some parts of Europe and Latin America (Autistic Self Advocacy Network, 2021; Vidal Gutiérrez & Acevedo, 2017). In the United States, where the movement originated in the early 2000s, leading organizations such as Autistic Self Advocacy Network, Autistic Women and Non-Binary Network, and Autistic Hoya have documented a political trajectory of online organizing, demonstrations, and campaigns leading to policy changes as well as writings, and artistic and cultural developments spearheaded by grassroots neurodivergent communities (ASAN, n.d.; Giwa Onaiwu, 2020). Although traditionally the stories of neurodivergent people (including people with neurodevelopmental disabilities and psychiatric disabilities) have been marked by silence and neglect, as a concept and as a movement, neurodiversity has received significant attention in more recent years (ASAN, n.d.; Dind, 2021; Simpson, 2019). Critical disability studies scholars,[1] for instance, utilize neurodiversity as an emancipatory analytic through which to examine and interpret the causes and effects of systemic ableism on multiply marginalized "neurodiver-agents" (Acevedo, 2020).

In addition to utilizing a neurodiversity framework as an emancipatory analytic, neurodivergent scholars (Acevedo & Nusbaum, 2020; Roscigno, 2020; Williams, 2018) conceptualize and deploy it as an ontological orientation toward the world—as both a matter of how we experience our own (*lived*) body (Husserl, 1912; Merleau-Ponty, 1945/2002) and how we inhabit space and orient ourselves about other beings, objects, and the environment (Ahmed, 2006). Husserl's (1912) *lived body* (a body experienced and experiencing) and Merleau-Ponty's expansion of the concept to include an understanding of "being bodies" as opposed to "having bodies" (Carman, 1999) acquires particular significance for critical disability studies insofar as disability's lived space is theorized as a site of cultural and political struggle and liberation (Erevelles, 2014; Mitchell & Snyder, 2015;

Paterson & Hughes, 1999; Titchkosky, 2011). Merleau-Ponty's conceptual shift is significant here, considering that "knowledge is the product of a specific position [or orientation] that reflects particular places and spaces" (Sanchez, 2010, p. 2258) and the fact that disability's neurocorporeal history highlights the tension between visible and invisible bodies (of knowledge) as they appear (or disappear) in specific places and spaces; spatially, temporally, and epistemologically speaking.

We are two autistic early career scholars who conduct action-oriented research across various disciplines, including critical disability studies, critical autism studies, activist anthropology, spatial analysis, teacher education, and disability studies in education. Our research agendas are intimately linked with our activist work. Our scholarly interests are expansive and span various systems of social injustice—our primary focus is the interlocking systems of oppression that sustain capitalism: settler colonialism, racism, ableism, xenophobia, among others. We come to this work both as critical autism studies scholars and as autistic activists. In this chapter, we explore how multiply-neurodivergent people living at the intersection of other marginalized identities reimagine themselves at the edge of institutional illegibility (Deleuze &Guattari, 1987). Sara M. Acevedo is a trained historical linguist and an activist anthropologist who specializes in critical disability studies and grassroots struggle. Her contributions to critical disability scholarship are informed by her engagement with disability justice activism and her own lived experiences as a multiply neurodivergent Mestiza woman living with chronic illness, and an immigrant born and raised in Colombia. Robin Roscigno is an autistic scholar/educator/activist trained using critical disability studies to enact school reform and policy changes that reduce harm done to disabled students within schools. She is a white, U.S.-born, cis woman, and a parent to an autistic child who currently attends public school.

We agree with Haraway (1988) that there is situatedness to our "embodied accounts of the truth" (p. 578) and further argue that if bodies (of knowledge) are indeed situated, then they too function as orienting vehicles of perception. Differently put, we are as we know, and we orient in relation to what we know to be carnally "true." For instance, neurodivergent scholars orient in relation to what we know to be "true" of our *lived bodies* in sensory hostile environments—how we experience them and how we are experienced in them; this tension accounts for "the intercorporeal aspect of bodily dwelling" (Ahmed, 2006, p. 544). While we don't pursue a critique of environmental hostility here, we contextualize it to then focus on what that hostility produces (or what it incites) beyond deterministic biosocial approaches to "atypical" neurology. More specifically, we highlight the ways in which neurodiver-agents reorient toward emancipated environments where we may creatively dwell otherwise. We begin by describing the intellectual landscape that is the subject of this book: the tensions and possibilities between AP and critical disability studies. We then turn to map our theoretical approach to defining this relationship—by way of Deleuze and some notable interventions to Deleuze's work. We plot out a framework that inverts both "asset" and "pedagogy" and is resistant to commodification and tokenization. What follows are autoethnographic vignettes detailing our experiences navigating educational institutions as autistic scholar-activists and educators. These vignettes are meant to orient and disorient—to position the reader alongside the authors within spaces not built for us. We challenge readers to experience—rather than consume—and to find moments of resistance, levity, and liberation within and against the institution.

CRITICAL DISABILITY STUDIES AND AUTISM SCHOLARSHIP

Emerging out of the disability rights movement, disability studies sought to describe and theorize the political, social, and economic relationships that contributed to the continued marginalization of disabled people (Albrecht, 1992; Barnes et al., 2002; Corker & Shakespeare, 2002; Erevelles, 2016). As it has grown and matured over several decades, the discipline has seen a progressive, reflexive shift in its focus of study and research. Informed by the revolutionary work of intersectional grassroots disability activism, both nationally and transnationally, critical disability theory draws attention to disability and disablement as it intersects with other marginalized experiences/identities—including race and ethnicity, class, age, gender identity, sexual orientation, citizenship status, and so on (Meekosha et al., 2013; Minear, 2011).

The field of disability studies has impacted thought and practice in DSE, most notably the distinction between the medical model of disability and the social model of disability. Scholars in DSE have contested medicalized notions of disability through reframing disability as a failure of environments—schools—to accommodate disabled people, rather than a medicalized deficit within an individual's bodymind. The social model's reframing of deficit to be environmentally located rather than individually located is an appealing way to discuss the problems of schooling for disabled children, as it succinctly reframes issues of access and student success. However, the social model was never intended to account for one's *experience* of disability, a point we will return to in our analysis.

Disability studies in education also has been impacted by CDS and produced a body of scholarship that has most notably contributed to more inclusive education for students with disabilities living at the intersection of multiple oppressions. Scholars of disability studies in education argue that schooling for multiply marginalized students is historically exclusionary and rooted in ableist beliefs, attitudes, and practices. Inclusive education, as a challenge to special education, seeks to improve schooling for all students, as opposed to the model of "special" education for students with disabilities. Inclusive education scholars have contributed improved pedagogical practices and more accepting, accommodating environments for disabled students.

Critical autism studies (CAS)—an emergent, vibrant subfield of critical disability studies—has contributed an exciting body of work that examines the autistic experience through a pro-neurodiversity lens. Coined by Joyce Davidson and Michael Orsini (2013), CAS is a broad, interdisciplinary field that thinks about autism as a range of diverse experiences, cultures, identities, and theoretical and methodological possibilities. CAS scholarship has addressed schooling for autistic children through a range of different lenses including queer theory, post-structuralist theory, political economy, and new materialism (Bumiller, 2009; Douglas et al., 2019; Nadesan, 2013). More importantly, CAS scholarship diverges from inclusive education scholarship to think about autism and autistic ways of being as (re)orienting onto epistemologies. We contend that autistic ways of being are fundamentally disruptive to hegemonic notions of education, and thus neuroqueer the very notions of both "asset" and "pedagogy."

ASSET PEDAGOGY

Asset pedagogy (AP) is a term for a body of scholarship emphasizing the need for educators to see students' differing cultural backgrounds and neurocorporealities as a strength, rather than the white-supremacist belief that the disparities in outcomes between white students and POC students are representative of deficit within the child or their culture (Ladson-Billings & Tate, 1995; Yosso, 2005). While rooted in the legacy of slavery, Jim Crow, and institutional racism, the rhetorical of "cultural poverty" was codified into American schooling through Lyndon Johnson's War on Poverty (Erevelles, 2014). This initiative provided special funding for compensatory programs aimed at addressing disparities in outcomes between affluent (white) students and economically disenfranchised BIPOC students.

AP scholarship implores educators to develop a set of skills and competencies that are essential to successfully teach students from historically marginalized backgrounds. Among these is the need for educators to see children's cultures as strengths, validate student experiences, and build on prior knowledge. AP is inclusive of several critical responses to cultural poverty discourses, including equity pedagogy, culturally relevant pedagogy, culturally sustaining pedagogies, and critically culturally sustaining revitalizing pedagogy. And while the finer points of difference between these approaches are beyond the scope of this chapter, as a body of scholarship AP calls for a fundamental rethinking of schooling that attends to the ways schools reproduce white, hegemonic norms and values, including compulsory able-bodiedness (McRuer, 2016) and able-mindedness (Kafer, 2013).

AP calls for educators to critically examine their own biases, in belief, practice, and principle, and the way schools reproduce white supremacy through the erasure of forms of knowledge and expression that are outside of "norms" of language, behavior, and learning valued by white, able-bodied, cis-heteropatriarchal society. It calls for incorporating and centering multiple cultural knowledges and practices in the classroom. AP scholars have consistently warned, however, about the potential for AP to be relegated to "special celebrations," and other tokens of "inclusion" without a redistribution of material resources and a focus on justice for students from marginalized communities.

In keeping with the focus of this edited collection, we draw on AP in conjunction with Critical Disability Studies to complicate relationships between autistics, autism, education, and schooling. We argue that autistic embodiment is a nonlinear, or "sliding" (Yergeau, 2018), ontological and epistemological orientation to the world and often manages to escape the stifling grip of the current U.S. disciplinary systems of schooling, thus offering a challenge to what it means to *know* and *learn*. Through our analysis, we demonstrate how the asset/deficit binary continuum can be transformative through autists' own resistance to binarism and legibility. We draw on Deleuze and Guattari's work, which is by and large a philosophy that escapes institutional legibility, and a critical expansion to Deleuze and Guattari's work (Bogard, 2000) for the purposes of articulating the productive friction between deficit and asset—to make space for multiple iterations of autistic identity that do not easily or voluntarily submit to discursive discipline. Along these lines, rather than understanding autistic identity and autism as stable signifiers, we argue that the illegibility of autistic subjects within educational systems that gravitate toward centers of power is the greatest "asset" to revolutionary change.

THEORETICAL FRAMEWORK

Nomadology

To articulate the generative tension among AP, critical autism studies, and disability studies, we turn to Deleuze and Guattari (1987). We draw on two specific concepts: text-as-practice and nomadology. We are familiar with and share the validity of feminist critiques that characterize Deleuze and Guattari's philosophy as "obscure" and often removed from the materiality of the social-political struggles their philosophy explores (Spivak, 1999). We nevertheless agree with Schult (2019, para 3) and the idea that "'nomad thought' in *Mille Plateaux* . . . formed a sub-commentary on the authors' own endeavor of text-as-practice." In other words, we share an interest in the interplay between form, content, and action and believe that the notion of illegibility is of political utility to our current line of inquiry. In the same vein, we find the notion of *nomadology*, to be understood as antistatist human geography, useful in framing a socio-spatial (material) reading of autistic illegibility as a form of resistance to institutional control and punishment. To be more specific, in the case of autistic students and at a most basic and instinctual level, resistance to institutional control and punishment entails immediate survival through a rejection of felt neurocorporeal discomfort/pain/distress. For example, in encamped educational spaces, such as residential schools like Judge Rotenberg Center, students are subjected to restrictive and coercive behavioral programming. Rather than theorize resistance as a legible, cohesive activist agenda, we theorize it starting with a concrete instance of resistance as immediate survival. One such example is found in the temporary reshuffling of the teacher–student power dynamic (and affect) as the autistic student bites the teacher to communicate discomfort, pain, or any other painful/distressing sensation or feeling (Acevedo, 2021; Roscigno, 2020). Although temporary, the rupture of an illusion of full control over another's neurocorporeality activates a line of flight[2] that punctures through the system of meaning that legitimizes the teacher's authority over that of the student.

Beyond immediate survival, however, nomadology entails an expansion away from confining or "sedentary" (Deleuze & Guattari, 1987) spaces and reclamation of fluid and heterogeneous forms of *beingknowing* outside of state enclosures such as the special education classroom or the therapy room. Overall, the insight we draw from Deleuze and Guattari's philosophy helps us to shed light on the creative lines that cut through everyday forms of exclusion. This perspective is useful to us in outlining an argument that positions APs beyond education systems operating on differential inclusion through selection and sorting processes; these are processes that routinely target students whose racialized subjectivities become legible within education sorting systems. Our argument here is that the most revolutionary effects of APs occur in-against-beyond what is understood as "legitimate" education—structurally, materially, and in terms of curriculum. This is especially the case with schooling in the neoliberal age, which enables and emboldens corporate-style administrators to conceptualize and practice education as a transactional process, rather than a critical and creative one (De Lissovoy, 2014; Freire, 1993; McLaren, 2002).

As we conceptualize and practice education as a critical endeavor, we are reminded of its humanizing approach to education. AP embodies the same approach insofar as practitioners focus on students as agents and producers of knowledge, rather than passive recipients and consumers of knowledge. This approach to teaching and learning foregrounds students' lives experiences and multiple cultural backgrounds as the basis for the design and implementation of a curriculum that is conscious of and responsive to their material realities. This approach not only disrupts the modern certainties overseeing so-called legible forms of education—what they should focus on, measure, and accomplish—but also cultivates a generative common where students' cultural and material realities are fully integrated into their educational experience. As a result, what they learn and what they themselves contribute to their learning community represents what they themselves experience beyond formal schooling settings—in their communities, with their friends and families.

Smoothness and Striation

Bogard (2000) uses Deleuze and Guattari's concepts of smoothness and striation to discuss social relations of power and bodily inscription. He describes Deleuze and Guattari's six models—technological, musical, maritime, mathematical, physical, and aesthetic—according to the distinction between smooth and striated space and advances a seventh machine, a societalizing machine. He argues that societalizing smoothing machines both generate "blockages and exclusions," and zones of "inclusion, vitality and freedom" (Bogard, 2000, p. 271). Bogard (2000) argues that smoothing machines

> cut or tear bodies from their surroundings, produce streams of waste, and deposit new surfaces. Like a hurricane, they leave a line of destruction, but also a leveled plane. Like a fine polish, they cover over an imperfection. (p. 270)

The school and the therapy clinic function as societalizing smoothing machines by mediating the social development of children and youth. They are created to "dovetail other bodies" (Bogard, 2000, p. 288). However, through the process of smoothing, a by-product appears—striation. Smoothing is created in the wreckage of striation through heat and friction. Put another way, the process of smoothing contains within it lines of flight.

Bogard's addition of a societalizing smoothing machine to Deleuze and Guattari's work undergirds our approach to AP critical disability studies. Like scholars working within AP, we also see schools as places of onto-epistemic violence. But we also agree with Bogard that this friction and process of striation is productive of smoothing or practices of resistance. Bogard's addition to Deleuze and Guattari's text is a useful analytic for thinking through bodily inscription as a form of institutional control and punishment and the production of noncompliant subjectivities at the interstices of smooth and striated spaces—outside of identity politics. Ultimately, our use of this political-philosophical framework seeks to further complicate postmodern narratives of subjugation through the lens of Bogard's notion of *incorporation*, which he describes as the act of polishing and severing.

To exemplify and ground these processes in everyday life, we describe various sites of attempted striation within education: "therapeutic" schooling (Deacon, 2006) and the special education machine. Our purpose here is to describe the encounter between autism and these "striating machines" as productive of smooth geographies, lines of flight, and potential liberation. That is to say—autistic illegibility *is* in and of itself a *nomadic* force.

THE VIGNETTES

Sara

I posit that neurodivergent ways of *beingknowing* operate as feral methodologies insofar as they generate nomadic lines of perception-sensation that cut through dominant epistemes creating other modes of existence. These nomadic orientations enable strategic uses of identity and thus challenge dehumanizing discourses of neurodivergence—including in the realm of schooling. Notably, the same itinerant lines that activate strategic uses of identity escape a system of capture embedded into identity markers of *Otherness*. The auto-ethnographic vignette below provides concrete examples of the theories outlined above.

I am an autistic, Mestiza, immigrant, early-career scholar in a tenure-track position at a well-regarded public university. I teach disability studies (DS) and instruct undergraduates pursuing majors in the applied professions (among them speech pathology and audiology, psychology, and social work). I teach disability theory, methods, and praxis from within a critical pedagogy tradition (Freire, 1993). This means, among other things, that my teaching style prioritizes cooperative learning over competition while encouraging autonomy, agency, curiosity, and critical inquiry as antidotes to passive knowledge consumption. The use of critical consciousness *as a strategy* seems to be a well-kept secret in contemporary critical education literature, but it is a common practice within liberatory education circles. All of this is to say that I have used *strategy* to redirect students from a tendency toward knowledge consumption to the much less comfortable task of developing a critical consciousness. Case in point, I am painfully aware that a great majority of information about autism in online archives and databases is dangerously (if not deathly) partial to the biomedical and charity models of disability (McGuire, 2018).

It is also the case that these sources of information about autism are framed through racializing systems calling for *civilizing* interventions. *Civilizing* projects are the pillars of white supremacy and call for the social and biological cleansing of *deviancy*. In the industrialized societies of the Global North, these projects are emboldened by the medicalization of everyday life and the monetization of disability service and care systems, among others. With that knowledge, I encourage students to use external resources and textual evidence to sustain their claims when working with content *about* or *on* disability *without* disabled people online. I do not initially alert them to the gross misrepresentation of autism and autistic people, both in the scholarly literature and in online archives and databases. This is because one of my strategies entails allowing unmediated exposure to epistemic injustice (Fricker, 2007) to then observe growth through exposure to course materials, class discussions, group work, self-directed inquiry, self-reflection, and finally integration. Indeed, after conducting this experiment several times, I now know that it yields a fertile ground for several engaging discussions about disability in/visibility, mis/representation, and epistemic and material injustice.

An example of an exercise conducted in class is described in the following. After students have had several opportunities to seek out resources to support their claims about a certain topic—let's say, for instance, autism and identity—I gather us as a whole class and project my computer screen. Together, we search for entries *about* autism online. When typing "autism" into a Google search, the first three results on screen in order of appearance are "What Is Autism?" "Autism Speaks Home," and "Autism Society: Home." The first organization, Autism Speaks, has long been flagged by autistic activists and labeled as a "hate group" that funnels funds for research intended to eliminate the autism "gene" and to find a "cure" for autism, which they depict with pseudoscientific "certainty" as "a devastating disease, as something so undesirable, autistics are said to be better off dead" (Sequenzia, 2014, para. 32). The second, Autism Society of America, is an autism charity organization that has "advocated for policies that have harmed autistic people, such as the . . . Autism CARES Act, which has invested billions of dollars into research, treatment, and cure and very little funding for education and services for autistic people" (Crossman, 2019, para. 31). At this point students begin to visibly show signs of discomfort, shock, surprise, some even verbally express guilt saying they "should have known," or question themselves out loud, "How could I not know this?" My response to these questions is always rooted in a historical-materialist approach to the erasure of select epistemic experiences. I make sure to validate their sense of frustration, guilt, and often embarrassment, and then redirect their thoughts to the fact that disability has been purposely erased (whether by omission, neglect, or misrepresentation) from all historical annals. I also explain that this is not an accident or an oversight and that its consequences aren't met with passivity. We face similar issues in contemporary society, and the same is true of our community's collective response to erasure today—we draw from material, cultural, and care networks we share in a reclaimed commons that allows us some degree autonomy from state control (Piepzna-Samarasinha, 2018; Sins Invalid, 2015; Wong, 2020).

Discussing Sara's Vignette

I echo Michael Bérubé's (in Linton, 1998) conceptualization of disability as the most "labile and pliable of categories" to describe education in terms akin to his. As an organizing (sorting) system, education is "unstable . . . and subject to all manner of social and historical vicissitudes" (p. xi). A historical-materialist approach to education yields a temporally and spatially situated analysis of education systems along a legitimate/illegitimate continuum. Education "experts," often tasked with gatekeeping, determine what counts as *legitimate* education, simultaneously situating *illegitimate* education as its opposite. In other words, dominant epistemes foreclose other forms of knowing. As historical analyses (always partial and biased) demonstrate, struggles over meaning occur between those who argue the *legitimacy* of a value system according to a set of arbitrary parameters and those who push against the validity of said system. What is also at play and rarely visible in this power relation (Foucault, 1982) are forms of resistance that remain illegible against "a set of a priory rules that allow the condition of possibility of discourse in a given period" (MacNay, 1994, p. 52). Differently put, antagonistic epistemic forces (i.e., deficit-based versus AP) are always at play. Notably, what emerges at the intersection of this push and pull of forces goes unnoticed amid more visible forms of struggle. This is precisely what is revolutionary and liberatory about *illegible* and *rogue* forms of meaning-making—the more they are discredited and ignored, the more room and freedom they have to expand away from the centers of power and toward the periphery materially impacting positive social transformation. I offer one concrete example of this phenomenon below.

Community-centered organizations such as the Autistic Self Advocacy Network (ASAN) and the Autistic Women and Nonbinary Network (AWN), whose leadership is primarily autistic, have been in operation for over a decade now (15 and 11 years, respectively). Both organizations have been largely influential in supporting educational, cultural, and political literacy within various autistic communities and in launching life-sustaining initiatives such as the Autistic People of Color Fund. Despite ASAN and AWN's contributions to reproduction and survival of autistic culture and political activism under hostile socioeconomic and political conditions, their presence remains largely illegible amid the vast amount of pseudoscientific information that circulates about autism as an object of interest (of research and/or intervention) rather than a wholesome human experience.

Critical pedagogy emphasizes the importance of building intentional learning communities that are politically generous and culturally spacious enough to support students intellectually and affectually as they process and integrate new perspectives. Exposure to shifting paradigms evoke "real-time" emotions and reactions that emerge when students' received knowledge is challenged and, in some instances, even shattered. For many, this realization is a ripe opportunity for a shift in perspective, insofar as they recognize the importance of dismantling interlocking forms of oppression and actively working toward sustainable social change in their own communities or practice. To support and encourage this transition, as illustrated in the vignette, I hold a structured discussion about the cycle of inaction that comes with guilt and the guilt that comes with inaction, so that students might move beyond an initial sense of helplessness and into acceptance and conscientious action. This is especially important for future professionals in the applied fields, as their power of intervention and influence in disabled peoples' lives remains largely unchanged despite decades of struggle actively subverting oppressive power dynamics—that is, a battle over meaning between those who hold socially sanctioned (legible) authority and those whose subjectivities are formed around arbitrary constructs resulting in nefarious material consequences (state-sanction restraint and seclusion practices, for instance).

Building generous and spacious learning environments that enable students to gradually process exposure to altering paradigms also entails exposure to other ways of being and knowing as well as the foreseeable possibility of building more-just futures. I have indeed observed that simultaneously calling attention to processes of resistance and resilience as well as creative adaptation generates a new sense of hope and responsibility—not only to amplify alternative ways of beingknowing, but more importantly to honor and embolden them in their profession.

I kickstart this process with the second part of the activity, which introduces students to autistic literacy through the work of autistic activists, grassroots educators, and scholars. Because this work remains invisible amid a vast amount of misinformation about autism, especially if one does not know what exactly to look for and how to look for it, we conduct another search as a group. I navigate to a resource that I have known to encourage students to continue to seek information directly from sources rooted in personal lived experience, so that they may be more equipped to actively challenge and subvert the material implications of totalizing narratives with their affinity groups (in this case, other applied professionals). The specific resource I discuss here is an infographic titled "Before You Donate to Autism Speaks, Consider the Facts" authored by ASAN (2020). I argue that it is equally important, if not more so, to introduce students to instances in which those most impacted by dominant narratives succeed in challenging and even temporarily upsetting them. To summarize, my overall goal with the class activity presented in the vignette is to get students to think about how social groups who endure and survive the material consequences of epistemic injustice in late-stage capitalism produce knowledge that in many instances effectively manages to preserve a community's integrity—physically, emotionally, and psychologically.

I call attention to the transformative quality of feral and rogue and illegible forms of knowledge production, as they demonstrate that education is as "labile and pliable" as the "historical vicissitudes" (Linton, 1998, p. xi) that shape the lived experiences of groups routinely disenfranchised by capitalism. Last, I echo Bogard's argument and language to argue that APs such as those mobilized by ASAN, and AWN operate as smoothing societalizing machines. In other words, because they reject forms of education that polish and sever neurodivergent bodyminds and ultimately result in striation, community practitioners mobilize a nomadic (or, heterogeneous and fluid) approach to knowing and learning that is humanizing, sustainable, and ultimately transformative.

Robin

Scene 1: I apply to a "leadership fellowship" at my institution. "It's prestigious and will look great on your CV," I am told. The call for the fellowship is specifically asking for students from marginalized groups. I write my letter of application about being an autistic graduate student. I describe how I want to increase accessibility on campus and broaden access beyond physical access and ADA compliance. I am accepted. I begin the fellowship. It looks like a model United Nations. We were all hand-chosen, but we look around and know why. All the faculty mentors are white, cis-gender, neurotypical, and able-bodied. We meet once a week to learn about leadership. There are unironic discussions of grit, social skills, and "leadership qualities" that read like a list of things I/we will never be. I exchange knowing glances with others.

We begin to meet afterward to "vent." Everyone feels tokenized. The faculty want to take a lot of pictures. Always pictures. With them in the center. "Tag us on Facebook," they chirp. Weeks go by and the epistemological violence becomes heavy in the air. We are there, with all our diversity, to make slick advertising material for the university, but none of our perspectives are wanted. One day, we are learning about "good social skills" and the faculty mentor tells us an anecdote about a "very unusual" former president of the university that "just stood in the corner at parties." This anti-example is me. I raise my hand. Gently, I push, "I think we need to expand our notion of social skills and think about the different ways people can form relationships. Maybe this specific event was inaccessible to this person. Maybe he would do better in a smaller setting." She snaps, "Well this is the job. This is what's expected." My heart rate rises, and I am near a meltdown. "So, are you saying someone like me can never be a university president? I am confused why I was accepted then." She deflects: "Let's talk about something more . . . positive." I sit in silence—my face is hot. I am stimming now; the wheels are coming off. I start rhythmically tapping my fingers together—thumb to index finger, then middle finger, then ring finger, then pinky, over and over. I am going to have a meltdown, so I walk out and never go back. How do I learn to be a leader from someone who believes people like me can never be one?

Scene 2: I am teaching a masters-level course. I am coteaching the course, and each week one of us leads. The topic for the week is "disability studies." I do not disclose my identity to the class—too risky, I think to myself. However, periodically, I slip in a "we." "We reject ABA on ideological grounds." I make sure I slip in a few asides—"blue pumpkins, Autism Speaks, Good Doctor." My hands are not my "rehearsed" hands; they move and play with my hair and tap, but I am also not naming what this is. A student approaches me after class and asks me if I am autistic, because she is and "game recognizes game."

Scene 3: I am hired to write an educational evaluation for an autistic student. This child is being repeatedly restrained by school staff. I write the report. "X is a ten-year-old student with autism. Due to X's severe deficits in social skills, X needs to be moved to an inclusive classroom where he can benefit from peer models and novel social interaction." I cringe. But I know how this must be legible to a team of psychologists, specialists, and lawyers. This is life or death. This child is being prone restrained multiple times a day. I do not disclose my own identity, as tempting as it is. I want to yell, "She's in overload all day, you monsters!" But I calmly invoke all the "right" language and propose a behaviorist strategy (my favorite one): "Non-contingent reinforcement," AKA stop taking her shit away from her, AKA let her go to the sensory room without an arbitrary amount of "tokens." She is moved to a less-restrictive placement.

Discussing Robin's Vignette

As an autistic scholar-educator, I shift in and out of stable identification as I occupy multiple spaces and identities. In the classic queer theory text *Epistemology of the Closet*, Eve Kosofsky Sedgwick coined the term "nonce taxonomy," which she defines as "the making and unmaking and remaking and redissolution of hundreds of old and new categorical imaginings concerning all the kinds it may take to make up a world" (Sedgwick, 1990, p. 23). In envisioning my own nomadology, I think of the concept of *nonce taxonomy* to describe how disabled scholars create and re-create social categories for the purposes of survival and political gain and use contingent self-identification as a political tool. In the vignettes, I grapple with my own illegibility—the uses and misuses of my identity and the way my bodymind is interpolated. In the vignettes, I demonstrate how an uncontested and celebratory narrative of diversity has the capacity to be subsumed into the project of "diversity management" and how the political utility of leveraging the institutional rhetoric of diversity in certain political contexts is a by-product (striation) formed by the friction of institutional surveillance and discipline.

I assert, in the spirit of Sedgewick's commentary on gay identity, that there is simultaneously a political utility to moving between different understandings of disability (outside and within deficit/asset binaries) as well as "rhetorical and political grounds for underwriting continuously the legitimacy of both" (Sedgwick, 1990, p. 23). This work is essential for moving beyond disciplinary orthodoxy, toward a praxis that recognizes how identity categories are fluidly enacted and performed for the purposes of social change.

Like Sara, I also employ "feral and rogue" approaches to my own identity, shifting between a more cohesively identitary understanding of autism to relishing in the slips and dodges I make as part of my own survival. Because of my investment in critical disability studies, it might be predictable that I have a particular understanding of my own identity, perhaps one rooted in pride or acceptance. However, the true asset here is the way in which I can occupy multiple and contradictory understandings of identity to liberate myself from oppressive structures that intend to control, own, harm, or tokenize me and those with whom I am in community.

CLOSING

Throughout this chapter, we have argued that autistic ways of being are an asset by virtue of our own illegibility. We meander, pause, and play not because we are incapable of legibility but because we ourselves are at risk for consumption by a predominantly neurotypical audience. Our ability to shape-shift and rhetorically dodge easy consumption within this piece is not an accident. We have in many ways offered you an autistic experience of your own, rather than allowing ours to become a neatly packaged plea for our own humanity. We instead have offered a way to think about autism as a potentiality to produce a more expansive understanding of what "assets" autistic people (and autism as an ontological process) may bring forth. We resist the idea of legible subjectivities and practices in favor of multiplicity, ferality, and nomadology. We see autistic liberation located and forged in the fire within the processes of striation and—ultimately—we assert that autistic illegibility confounds the neatness of the metaphor of "asset" contains within it the "stuff" of liberation.

CHAPTER 4

Luring the Vygotskyan Imagination
Notes for a New Bridge Between Disability Studies in Education and Asset Pedagogies

Federico R. Waitoller

This chapter aims to create a new bridge between two fields that, for most of their histories, developed in parallel form: asset pedagogies (APs) and disability studies in education (DSE). While other chapters in this volume focus on the implications of disability culture, history, identity, politics, and teacher training for APs, this chapter focuses on learning science and human development. After all, understanding youth development is a critical component of developing and implementing pedagogies that value and sustain the identities of all minoritized students.

In particular, the bridge I propose to build is based on Vygotsky's (1993) work with disabled youth. There are multiple names for Vygotsky and his colleagues' (e.g., Luria and Leontiev) work, such as sociocultural theory, cultural historical, and activity theory. In this chapter, I draw from Cole's (2005) recommendation and utilize the term cultural-historical activity theory (CHAT) as an umbrella for the work that has developed from Vygotsky and colleagues.

Vygotsky's insights on disability and learning can extend and create a fertile boundary zone for the extensions of APs and DSE. I neither dismiss nor minimize the importance of other ways to bring APs and DSE together. Rather, I hope to extend and strengthen already established connections with a bridge with the potential for increasing the fluidity and frequency of ideas and people crossing between these intellectual communities.

The bridge I propose to build already has established foundations on both banks. On the APs bank, there is a solid Vygotskian foundation as evidenced, for instance, in the work of Funds of Knowledge (FofK; Gonzalez et al., 2005), Third Space (Gutiérrez et al, 1999), and cultural modeling (Lee, 2007). I propose to extend these foundations with Vygotsky's work with disabled youth, which was translated to English in 1993. On the other bank, DSE has a solid foundation in social model(s) of disability. I propose to extend such foundations with Vygotsky's conceptualization of disability, which was a precursor of social models and that overcomes the biology–culture binary. By extending the walkthroughs of the bridge from each side, I aim to join both fields in the middle to generate an asset-based model of learning science for youth with disabilities that can inform practice and research.

I must warn the reader that this chapter does not offer a fleshed-out theory of learning for disabled youth. Rather, the chapter reviews Vygotsky's work on disability and offers some ideas, which, like seeds, I hope can sprout in the form of an AP that accounts for the learning and development of disabled youth. Thus, if the reader is expecting concrete recommendations for research and educational practice to implement the next day, I recommend they move to another chapter of the book. They are outstanding. But if the reader hopes to stimulate their imagination and creativity to imagine how to research and develop more just approaches of teaching and sustaining disabled youth, I invite them to continue and turn until the last page of the chapter.

The chapter is organized in the following way. The first section examines Vygotsky's groundbreaking work on disability and learning. The second section identifies the CHAT principles that provide the foundation for asset pedagogies and offers some ideas to extend them using Vygotsky's work on disability. Then I move to discuss ideas for how to expand social model(s) of disability so that they are useful to understand youth learning and development. I end with some concluding thoughts.

VYGOTSKY AND DISABLED YOUTH

Vygotsky and his circle of colleagues (e.g., Luria, Leontev, Varshaba) challenged the pervasive behavioral approaches to explain human learning. Rather than focusing on individuals' behavior, they centered "artifact-mediated and object-oriented action" (Vygotsky, 1978, p. 40). Accordingly, humans' acts are mediated by cultural historical products (i.e., artifacts) that shape and are shaped by human activity (Vygotsky, 1978). Individuals are equipped with neurobiologically based cognitive functions, including perception, attention, and memory. By working in shared activity, both concrete tools (e.g., a knife or a smart phone) and symbolic (e.g., language and writing) mediate people's interactions, cognition, and cultural patterns (Vygotsky, 1978). Thus, one cannot understand learning and behavior without understanding individuals situated in historically developing cultural activities (Engeström, 1987). Human cognition develops through participating in shared activity in historically and culturally developed practices.

Of interest to this edited volume is the fact that Vygotsky worked with and studied disabled youth while developing his theory of human cognition.

This work was published in *The Fundamentals of Defectology*, which was not translated to English until 1993 (Vygotsky, 1993). This volume compiles the work of Vygotsky with disabled youth from 1924 to 1931. The name of Vygotsky's volume merits a pause and an explanation. Asset pedagogies and DSE scholars and practitioners may feel uncomfortable with the title of his volume. In part, their reaction is justified, and I had the same gut feeling when I first learn the title. The term *defectology*, translated from Russian, means the study of defect. At the time of Vygotsky writings, this was the term that had been used for more than a century in Russia to study the evaluation and teaching of disabled youth (Gindis, 2003). More precisely, at that time the term covered the study of students who were hard of hearing or deaf, visually impaired or blind, or had cognitive disabilities or language and speech impairments.

Vygotsky was responding to and challenging this century-long approach that focused on defects to studying the learning of disabled youth. Vygotsky, instead, focused on their strengths. In fact, Vygotsky was a pioneer of the social model of disability. The predominant view of his time considered disability as a developmental delay or underdevelopment, defining differences between disabled youth and their peers as merely quantitative. Vygotsky rejected this view. He opposed (1) the use of assessments to rank human learning, (2) assuming that disabled youth's abilities are predetermined, and (3) using charitable models to serve disabled youth. Thus, though he used the term *defectology* to reach those interested in this topic, he debunked the term with his research and writing.

Vygotsky understood disability as a sociocultural phenomenon rather than an individual one. He conceptualized dis/ability as learning difference rather than cognitive deficit. He wrote, "[A] child whose development is impeded by a defect is not simply a child less developed than his peers but is a child who has developed differently" (Vygotsky, 1993, p. 30). Giving the example of blind youth, Vygotsky stated, "Blindness is not a disease but the normal condition for a blind child; he senses his uniqueness only indirectly and secondarily as a result of his social experience" (p. 81). According to Vygotsky, "[B]lindness by itself does not make a child handicapped.... This is a sign of the difference between his behavior and the behavior of others" (Vygotsky, 1993, pp. 83–84).

To account for human variation, Vygotsky posited two aspects of development: a biological (lower mental functions) and a sociocultural (higher mental functions). The biological provides the "raw materials" that are shaped through sociocultural interactions (Werstch, 1985). In other words, lower functions allude to the biological predisposition for development, while the higher functions refer to cultural functions that are acquired as individuals participate in cultural activities. Higher mental functions do not substitute lower mental functions. Higher mental functions serve as a superstructure that enables better use of natural functions, allowing in practice for new thinking and acting (Vygotsky, 1978). The child develops higher mental functions only through participating in cultural activities, and it is through this process that the child acquires knowledge and learns how to use cultural tools. The intertwining of lower and higher functions creates a cultural-historical dialectical process that is shaped by individual participation in daily joint activity (Vygotsky, 1978).

To Vygotsky, the principles of human development such as the internalization of external cultural tools and practices were also applicable to disabled youth. According to Vygotsky, in the case of individuals with disabilities there is a tension between lower and higher functions (Vygotsky, 1993). Youth with biological characteristics of disability do not align with the sociocultural tools and signs available to them, which have been developed and optimized for people considered as "normal" or "typically developing." Biological and cultural development diverge, which makes difficult the nurturing of higher mental functions. Consequentially, the child with a disability may find it difficult to participate in a school's social arrangements without supports. This mismatch between biological and sociocultural aspects of the development of disabled youth leads to qualitatively different learning trajectories (Vygotsky, 1993). Thus, Vygotsky did not understand disability as a defect but rather as a human difference that requires different tools to navigate life in a society geared toward those who are "typical" (Bøttcher, 2012; Smagorinsky, 2012).

This understanding of disability led Vygotsky (1993) to identify primary and secondary disability. The former refers to the organic impairment due to biological factors, and the latter refers to difficulties with higher mental functions due to cultural factors. It is this latter cultural context that modifies a child's development and leads to learning struggles. It is the youth's sociocultural context that shapes development and deviation from the "typical" ways of developing. For instance, the learning struggles of a student identified with an intellectual disability are due to the cultural and social arrangements of a classroom rather than the biological differences of the student. These arrangements, over time, shape negatively the learning development of the student, affecting their capacity for higher mental functions.

Further, Vygotsky's conceptualization of disability extends that of disability as part of human difference and diversity. He argued for an asset-based understanding of disability, identifying and building from the strengths and capacities of disabled youth. Vygotsky studied how children with disabilities actively modified their environment and resolved situations using auxiliary means or the help of peers (Vygodskaya, 1999). For instance, Vygotsky (1993, p. 97) argued that the absence of sight "is not merely a defect, a minus, a weakness, but in some sense is also the source of manifestations of abilities, a plus, a strength." Vygotsky (1993, p. 168) wrote, "The cultural forms of behavior serve as the only path of education for an abnormal child. This path means the creation of roundabout ways of development at that point where it proves to be impossible to proceed by direct paths."

Vygotsky named such roundabouts *compensation* and viewed children's psychological differences as a two-sided phenomenon: the absence of an ability is compensated by the extension of other higher mental functions. Vygotsky found that disabled youth circumvented their limitations, developing compensatory strategies to acquire cultural knowledge and forms of behavior (Gindis, 2003). In this way, they traveled a different path to the same goal since "[c]ultural development is the main area for compensation of deficiency when further organic development is impossible; in this respect, the path of cultural development is unlimited" (p. 169). However, compensation processes do not consistently happen spontaneously or in isolation in schools. They require "a concerted volitional effort that is socially reinforced" (Smagorinsky, 2012, p. 12). In Vygotsky's words: "Different symbolic systems correspond to one and the same content of education . . . . Meaning is more important than the sign. Let us change signs but retain meaning" (Vygotsky, 1983, p. 54).

Vygotsky's approach to disabled youth, thus, was asset based, goal oriented, and focused on developing new capacities. According to Vygotsky, disabled youth are active learners who participate in goal-oriented activities to appropriate and modify their environments; they are active agents who control and modify their behaviors and their immediate environment (Vygotsky, 1978). Consequentially, Vygotsky never called children "defective" or "handicapped" but referred to them as "anomalous" (Smagorinsky, 2012). Vygotsky noted the dynamic nature of disability. There is a constant change in the structures and content of development for disabled youth through the internalization of external cultural activities into internal psychological processes. Development includes qualitative and dialectic transformations, in where learning gains and losses occur.

Finally, Vygotsky took a materialist view of disability and referred to prejudice and discrimination to explain secondary disabilities (Gindis, 1995, 2003). Social and cultural arrangements lead to lack of access to cultural tools and knowledge, deprivation, prejudice, and discrimination, which negatively affects development (Vygotsky, 1993). Vygotsky passionately argued for reverting negative societal attitudes toward individuals with disabilities. Vygotsky (1993, p. 66) wrote that people with disabilities "must cope not *so much with these biological factors as with their social consequences*" (emphasis in original). Thus, "the task is not so much the education of blind children as it is the reeducation of the sighted. The latter must change their attitude toward blindness and toward the blind. The reeducation of the sighted poses a social pedagogical task of enormous importance" (p. 86). According to Vygotsky, people need to accept and value, nonjudgmentally, disabled youths' alternative means for learning and being.

BRIDGING ASSET PEDAGOGIES AND DSE THROUGH CHAT

Both DSE and APs can be extended with Vygotsky's insights on disability. On the one hand, APs can incorporate Vygotsky's understanding of disability to include disabled youth's dynamic bio-cultural repertoires. On the other hand, DSE's social model of disability can be expanded with Vygotsky's work, allowing for a more nuanced understanding of the teaching and learning of disabled youth.

Extending Asset Pedagogies: Disability as Dynamic Bio-Cultural Repertoires

For approximately 3 decades, APs have provided teachers, teacher educators, curriculum scholars, and administrators with the foundational and practical tools to design and enact instruction that values and sustains the cultural repertoires and identities of children and youth from minoritized racial and linguistic backgrounds. Though there are different approaches to APs, an important common tenet is that students' cultural repertoires are valuable and useful tools for learning and development in schools and beyond. Humans learn through cultural artifacts (tools and signs) to live in and control their surroundings (Cole, 1996). Different cultural communities, thus, develop cultural tools and practices according to their physical and social surroundings. Individuals learn to use such tools through participating in their communities' activities with other community members (Rogoff, 2003). From this standpoint, students' cultural and linguistic repertoires are valuable and legitimate assets for learning and participation in school activities. The mediational role of cultural artifacts is key for learning and overall development as they regulate and shape interactions between people and the world (Cole, 1996). Yet, as many of the chapters from this edited volume point out, APs have, all too often, ignored or overlooked the cultural aspects of disability (for exception, see Gutiérrez & Stone, 1997), leaving the teaching and learning of disabled youth to the realm of special educators.

One possible explanation for this avoidance is that disability-related education research and practice in the United States have been dominated by behavioral and cognitive paradigms, while APs are based on cultural historical ones. Such rationale is outdated. First, there has been a growing number of CHAT studies examining the teaching and learning of disabled youth; a recent review of the literature found 50 studies using CHAT approaches (Bal et al., 2020). Thus, there is an emerging and growing base to build a CHAT agenda to study the teaching and learning of disabled youth. Further, as reviewed in the prior section, Vygotsky provided useful insights about disabled youth learning that have been largely overlooked and can inform how APs are designed and implemented. It is worth noting, however, that this line of work of Vygotsky was not translated to English until 1993, which may explain the paucity of inclusion of disability-related issues in AP. Thus, the time is ripe for extending APs with CHAT work on disability.

AP scholars and teachers will benefit from extending their utilization of cultural repertoires or practices to incorporate Vygotsky's work with disabled youth. Despite their differences, AP approaches are built upon the principle that students bring to schools a set of valuable cultural repertoires that can enrich and guide pedagogy. Students' *funds of knowledge* (FofK) by Gonzalez, Moll, and colleagues (González & Moll, 2002; Moll, 1992), for instance, are characterized by the practices, tools, and knowledge that communities and families produce "through the social and labor history of families and communicated to others through the activities that constitute household life" (González & Moll, 2002, p. 634). Cultural Modeling (Lee, 2007; CM) is a framework for designing learning environments that connect youths' everyday knowledge, that is, cultural data sets, with learning academic subject matter (Lee, 2007), and in the notion of Third Space, Gutierrez and colleagues call for a more expansive notion of expertise that is based on students' repertoires of practice (Gutiérrez & Rogoff, 2003), which includes what students learn in and outside school.

Vygotsky also developed an asset-based approach to the teaching and learning of disabled youth that can extend the notions of FofK, cultural data sets, or repertoire of practice. Insights on compensation, biological differences, and cultural interactions can expand what asset pedagogies account as students' repertoires. For instance, disabled youth bring with them cultural tools that they develop as they circumvent typically expected ways to carry out academic and out-of-school tasks. AP scholars and teachers could identify and incorporate explicitly such compensatory approaches by drawing on FofK, repertoires of practice, or cultural data sets. Further, APs could attend to how student-developed cognitive tools (e.g., ways to resolve a math problem) and material tools (e.g., use of assistive technologies) mediate and promote the participation of disabled youth in goal-oriented activities and, thus, how such compensatory strategies may shape the evolution of the classroom activity system. For instance, a student identified with a specific mathematics disability may struggle with common ways to learn computation but can compensate by developing alternate strategies drawn from everyday practice to resolve the math problem (see Lewis, 2016; Lewis & Lynn, 2018). Thus, an important question that could guide new APs research and practice is, how can we incorporate, extend, and sustain disabled youths' cultural tools and practices in and through classroom activity?

Further, AP scholars conceptualize culture as dynamic and evolving, challenging monolithic and static views of student culture (Gutiérrez et al., 1999). In FofK, Moll, González, and colleagues work with teachers conducting mini-ethnographies of families to move away from essentializing views of Latinx families. Families' funds of knowledge are not static but evolve as part of the household economy and related repertoires of practice. Lee (2017) also warns teachers and researchers to not fall on static and monolithic views of culture and race. She compels us to understand communities as repositories of historically evolving practices of resilience that are worth sustaining. Gutiérrez and Rogoff (2003, p. 19) propose a cultural historical approach that attends to variations in the "proclivities of people with certain histories of engagement with specific cultural activities. Thus, individuals' and groups' experience in activities—not their traits—becomes the focus." In the latest iteration of APs, Paris and Alim (2017) focus on youth culture as dynamic and evolving, rather than static and fixed.

AP could incorporate Vygotsky's notions of disability as dynamic and evolving. Vygotsky (1978, p. 208) asserted that a "communist pedagogy is the pedagogy of the collective." That is, learning and cognitive development requires a future-oriented perspective that focuses on how disabled youth do and can participate in a culture's teleological direction. Disabled youth, who develop in such collective activities, are active learners who modify cognitive and material tools to participate in classroom activity (e.g., Lewis & Lynn, 2018). In Vygotsky's words (1993, p. 205) "In developing collective thinking . . . *we are eliminating the very reason for the underdevelopment of psychological functions in a blind child*, opening up before him uncharted and unlimited possibilities" (emphasis in original). Such insights can extend current work of FofK, repertoires of practice, or cultural data sets. Learning activities based on AP could account for how disabled youth participate in collective thinking, modifying the tools available to them with the use of auxiliary tools and their cultural repertoires, which are a product of their active modification of their environments outside school. Thus, the goals of APs could include nurturing the potential of disabled youth to develop and learn inside and outside school as they participate in collective goal-oriented activities. Such participation in collective thinking needs to account for compensatory strategies as innovative roads to cultural development and learning. Accordingly, the notion of defect is replaced by one of capacity and value, which can lead to an expanded engagement with cultural activities. Two interesting questions to guide APs: (1) How can we study, value, and sustain disabled youth participation in collective thinking using innovative means? (2) How does disabled youth participation shape the hybrid formation of classroom activity?

Further, APs could account for how disabled youths' innovative means and cultural practices intersect with historically developing cultural tools based on race or language. The interactions of disabled youths' cultural repertoires with their racial and ethnic and language background merits careful consideration. Such interactions generate alternative ways to engage with classroom activity. The chapter by Leroy Moore and Keith Jones entitled "Krip-Hop Nation" in this volume provides a clear example of these intersectional repertoires of practices. In other words, AP teachers and researchers need to recognize cultural adaptation, improvisation, and change in youth with disabilities (Paradise, 2002). Questions worth pursuing for future AP research and practice include (1) How do new forms of being, participating, and learning emerge as the result of disabled youth intersecting group memberships, and (2) how are the innovative means of disabled youth shaped by their racial, ethnic, gender, and linguistic cultural tools and practices?

Extending Social Model(s) of Disability: Toward a DSE Understanding of Human Learning and Development

DSE has emerged as an alternative to traditional medical and behavioral approaches to disability in special education research and teaching. One of the foundational bases of DSE is a social, cultural, and political understanding of disability. Since the civil rights movement, disability activists and scholars have fought against the historical oppression and exclusion of disabled people through the barring of access to social benefits such as education, through the institutionalization and inhumane treatment of disabled people, and through pervasive prejudice against and deficit views of disabled people. A family of disability conceptualizations based on a social understanding of disability, rather than an individualistic and medicalized one, were born out of those social movements. This family of models to understand disability includes the social model of disability (Oliver & Barnes, 2012), minority model (Hahn, 1988), relational/interactional model (Gustavsson, 2004), and cultural model (Garland-Thomson, 2002). Despite some differences among these models, they share commonalities. These models position disability outside of problematic charitable approaches to and deficit models of disability. They conceptualize disability as produced by exclusionary cultural and social practices and as an identity to be reaffirmed. Further, according to social model(s), disability is a core aspect of human experience and diversity. Disability is the norm rather than the outlier. These views of disability do not deny individual differences but attend to how socially produced normative arrangements position some differences as problematic, resulting in negative and long-lasting consequences (e.g., educational segregation).

Yet the development of DSE pedagogies and approaches to teaching based on social model(s) of disability has been limited. In general, DSE scholars (including myself) have not moved beyond proposing Universal Design for Learning (UDL) and broad pedagogies that affirm disabled youths' ways of being (Mitchell, et al., 2014) and attending to issues of intersectionality (Liasidou, 2014; Waitoller & Thorius, 2016). A possible explanation for this limitation is that social model(s) of disability were never conceptualized to inform research on learning or youth development. DSE scholars and teachers, thus, need to expand current cultural, social, and political understandings of disability as they offer useful but limited potential for improving teaching and learning for disabled youth.

Vygotsky's work with disabled youth is a promising starting point to expand DSE work with insights about human learning and development. Vygotsky, as noted earlier, promoted an early version of the social model(s) of disability. His work can serve to deepen current understanding of learning for disabled youth in formal and informal environments and develop pedagogies that are just and inclusive.

As a first step, we need to extend social model(s) of disability toward an understanding of disability as biocultural. Recent developments in neuropsychology have expanded some of Vygotsky's earlier findings providing evidence for a bio-cultural perspective of disability (Artiles et al., 2020; Cole & Packer, 2016). By bio-culture I refer to the following:

> The effects of a series of interconnected feed-downward (culture- and context-driven) and feed-upward (neurobiology-driven) interactive processes and developmental plasticity at different levels (hence, cross-level) are continuously accumulated via the individual's moment-to-moment experiences (hence, dynamic) so that, together, they implement concerted biological and cultural influences (hence, biocultural co constructivism) in tuning cognitive and behavioral development throughout the life span. (Li, 2003, p. 171)

A bio-cultural view of disability conceptualizes learning as a social enterprise; youth with disabilities internalize social and cultural patterns to form higher psychological functions (Artiles et al., 2020; John-Steiner & Mahn, 1996). From this view, there is a continuous spectrum of abilities with a large range of students' differences (Artiles et al., 2020; Protopapas & Parrilla, 2018). Research on neuroscience documented the impact of cultural contexts in the development and ontogeny of the brain, which results in wide variation in the way humans perceive and understand the world around them, the emotional responses they have to it, and the way they act upon it (Artiles et al., 2020). Thus, based on Vygotskyan principles, a bio-cultural perspective overcomes the binary that polarizes disability as either a biological and genetic trait or a cultural identity.

In DSE, a bio-cultural understanding of disability can generate new lines of research and practice that account for how biological factors and cultural historical practices interact in shaping disabled youths' development, learning, and participation in classroom activities. A critical outcome of this research should be developing guidelines and frameworks to create a new generation of APs that account for disability. DSE researchers could examine, for instance, how students' neurodiversity interacts with a classroom's cultural tools, shaping students' participation and learning. Importantly, such understanding can inform the design of learning activities in and outside of schools so we can best support disabled youth to develop higher mental functions that allow them to participate meaningfully in schools and society at large, thus beginning to dismantle structural forms of oppression they experienced every day in and outside school. In other words, learning activities need to be designed to ensure that students can access, challenge, modify, and internalize the sociocultural tools of their communities, always with a critical reflexivity questioning what we are asking students to internalize and for what purposes.

Further, the DSE scholars could expand new lines of research examining how youth with disabilities create compensatory mechanisms or roundabouts extending other mental functions and developing new capacities. Such an approach needs to account for the dynamic and dialectic between students' developments and changes in the activity system in which they participate. There is some recent promising work with students identified with math disabilities (Lewis, 2016; Lewis & Lynn, 2018), students identified with cognitive disabilities (Bøttcher, 2012; Bøttcher & Dammeyer, 2012), and bilingual students (Martínez-Alvarez, 2020) that may lead the way in this effort. DSE researchers could examine what kinds of concerted volitional efforts are needed to support disabled youth in generating new learning mechanisms as well as how disabled youth actively change their environments as they create new tools for learning and participation. Such research could expand ongoing efforts to place students with disability as holders of knowledge and active participants in the research process (see Bertrand et al., 2017; González et al., 2017).

CONCLUSION

Gindis (2003, p. 202) warns the reader that "by no means *The Fundamentals of Defectology* contains a complete theoretical system, ready for application and free from contradictions or limitations. It is an approach rather than a paradigm, a blueprint for further elaboration rather than a tested model." Thus, in this chapter, I did not aim to prescribe as set of guidelines for research and practice. Rather, I aimed to stimulate a Vygotskian imagination to build a new bridge between APs and DSE that will increase the flow of ideas and movement among scholars, teachers, and teacher educators.

To stimulate such imagination, I summarized some of the main tenets of Vygotsky's work with disabled youth and proposed some insights and questions for new lines of research and practice that value and sustain youth with disabilities bio-cultural repertoires. On the one hand, APs could extend their CHAT foundations, incorporating Vygotsky's work with disabled youth. On the other hand, DSE could begin to expand social model(s) of disability toward a bio-cultural model that will provide better analytical and practice tools to design, research, and implement more inclusive learning activities. A Vygotskian bridge offers exciting possibilities for a new generation of APs that accounts for and sustains disabled youth learning and identity development.

Part II

SUSTAINING DISABILITY IDENTITIES WITHIN PEDAGOGICAL APPROACHES

CHAPTER 5

Black Deaf Gain
A Guide to Revisioning K–12 Deaf Education

Onudeah D. Nicolarakis, Akilah English, and Gloshanda Lawyer

The Deaf, DeafBlind, DeafDisabled, Hard of Hearing, and Late-Deafened (DDBDDHHLD) community is a unique, vibrant community with its own cultures and languages. As our community becomes increasingly diverse and interconnected, understanding different cultures becomes crucial. In the DDBDDHHLD community, it is common to perceive hearing as a binary distinction—hearing vs. nonhearing. Woodward (1975) identifies the DDBDDHHLD community based on pathological and sociocultural aspects. The term *deaf*, with a lowercase letter, refers to all people who have hearing losses, regardless of cultural identity. The term *Deaf* with an uppercase D, refers to Deaf people who identify with the culture and primarily use signed language, such as American Sign Language (ASL).

However, the terms *deaf* and *Deaf* are centered on sighted and abled privileges and incorporate Eurocentrism values and ideals. This deaf-hearing binary also places a deaf individual with intersectional identities strictly within one of these categories, without considering any other identity. To address this disparity, the term of *Deaf, DeafBlind, DeafDisabled, Hard of Hearing* (DDBDDHH) was coined by collective members within the deaf community. In some groups within the deaf community, the acronym DDBDDHHCI is used to include cochlear implant users, and DDBDDHHLD to include late-deafened individuals. Using the singular, essentialist, and universalist term "deaf" excludes the physical, cultural, and linguistic experiences of deaf people; the new acronym is a beginning step in recognizing intersectional identities and different experiences (Ruiz-Williams et al., 2015).

Intersectionality is a theoretical framework to help us understand the interactions of various social identities and how these interactions are tied and defined by societal power hierarchies (Crenshaw, 1989, 1991). Intersectionality promotes an understanding of human beings as shaped by the interaction of different social locations, and these interactions occur within a context of connected systems and structural power (Crenshaw, 1989, 1991). The framework of intersectionality helps us to understand that DDBDDHHLD individuals do not experience a single oppression but experience multiple oppressions. Without a basic understanding of the experiences of individuals, we can unintentionally contribute to oppression and discrimination toward individuals within our community. In this chapter, we are intentionally using the acronym DDBDDHHLD (again, Deaf, DeafBlind, DeafDisabled, Hard of Hearing, and Late Deafened) to describe the deaf population and the acronym DDBDDHHCI (Deaf, DeafBlind, DeafDisabled, Hard of Hearing, and Cochlear Implant Users) to describe the K–12 student population. Using these acronyms is a critical step toward intersectional inclusivity to name different oppressive experiences within the community (Ruiz-Williams et al., 2015), as related to race, ability, language, among other characteristics. As indicated, the DDBDDHHLD community is quite diverse and intersectional—and even more so in relation to language.

Language is a central aspect of the DDBDDHHLD community and is a critical and basic tenet of humanity. Approximately 90 percent of DDBDDHHCI children are born to hearing parents (NIH, 2020), and families often face challenges in deciding the most appropriate language, communication mode, and educational plan for their DDBDDHHCI children. Bat-Chava (2000) states that DDBDDHHCI children whose parents are hearing or who grew up in homes where spoken language was the primary mode of communication will likely adopt a view of being deaf as a dis/ability and be encouraged to develop a culturally hearing identity. Many families are convinced, largely in part because of so-called medical professionals' "advice," that the only linguistic option for their DDBDDHHCI child is to acquire spoken language (Lane et al., 1996), as the most efficient means of communication (Nicholas & Geers, 2006). Consequently, many DDBDDHHCI children are language deprived, particularly because they miss the critical period to acquire their natural language: typically, ASL and/or other sign languages.

With ASL, parents and educators can directly and freely ensure full exposure to language and avoid the pitfalls inherent in early language deprivation. However, as we recognize the importance of using ASL to ensure an essential language foundation, we must also recognize that our DDBDDHHCI children increasingly come from diverse ethnicities, cultures, and backgrounds. Despite a plethora of research focused on DDBDDHHCI students, studies that reflect intersectionality and racialized experiences in theoretical frameworks, designs, analyses, or interpretations are scarce (García-Fernández, 2020; Lawyer, 2018; Paranis, 2012; Stapleton, 2015). Deaf education is dominated by white, hearing, female educators even though DDBDDHHCI students of color represent almost 50 percent of the school-age population (Simms et al., 2008). While DDBDDHHCI students are a linguistic and cultural minority that is often multiply marginalized, this marginalization is heightened for nonwhite DDBDDHHCI students because "structures, racism, audism, and oppressive language and academic policies often work against

[DDBDDHHCI] children's early struggle to acquire language, an academic foundation, and a healthy cultural identity" (Simms et al., 2008, p. 394). This is also true for curriculum; Black DDBDDHHCI students are marginalized from the curriculum (Stapleton, 2015) because educators typically do not modify the content appropriately nor provide a pedagogical framework, particularly for Black DDBDDHHCI students who are language deprived, because the pedagogical framework does not make sense to these students, or educators are not able to apply an intersectional lens to their teaching. We need to examine the critical aspect of humanizing pedagogy specifically for Black DDBDDHHCI students and explore how educators teach and adapt pedagogical techniques to address equity, all the while building a strong language foundation. It is time for the classroom to be accessible and equitable for all, so another Black DDBDDHHCI student will not have to experience injustice as a result of a lack of accountability in deaf education.

We offer this chapter on Black Deaf Gain toward this purpose. Inspired by the theoretical framework on Deaf LatCrit (García-Fernández, 2014), we seek to address the need for humanizing pedagogy specifically for Black DDBDDHHCI students and to help teachers examine their own pedagogical practices, shed deficit-based lenses, and sustain equitable pathways for access and inclusion. We aim to explain how Black Deaf Gain allows educators to identify and respond to antiblackness, racism, ableism, and linguicism in deaf education and in the formation and implementation of asset- and strength-based pedagogies. As a result, educators and administrators can affirm the importance of culturally sustaining pedagogies (Paris & Alim, 2017) in classrooms to promote inclusion and belonging.

We begin with a brief description of the DDBDDHHLD community, discussion of tensions and resistance in the DDBDDHHLD community, and re-visioning deaf education using asset- and strength-based pedagogies as guided by the theoretical frameworks of Black Deaf Gain (Moges, 2020), Deaf LatCrit (García-Fernández, 2014), Post Modern Audism (Wright et al., 2021), and Culturally Sustaining Pedagogy (Paris, 2012). We then provide practical examples of asset- and strengths-based pedagogies for DDBDDHHCI students, focusing on Black Deaf Gain to disrupt pervasive assumptions about Black DDBDDHHCI students and conclude with a brief discussion of future courses of action to include research focusing on asset- and strength-based pedagogies for other marginalized identities and the perception of other intersectional DDBDDHHLD identities as advantageous and a "gain."

THE DDBDDHHLD COMMUNITY

The DDBDDHHLD community in the United States has its own unique culture and identity. Stapleton (2015, p. 571) states that the "[DDBDDHHLD] community is dynamic, and members of this community are very diverse in their range of hearing loss, cultural connections, and the methods they use to interact with the dominant hearing world." However, not everyone in the DDBDDHHLD community identifies with Deaf culture; some may fully embrace all aspects, while others may embrace only some aspects of Deaf culture. Others may reject the culture outright.

Each person in the DDBDDHHLD community experiences different forms of oppression. They experience audism (Humphries, 1975), described as when DDBDDHHLD people experience discrimination, prejudice, or negative attitude from hearing people based on their hearing threshold or status. They experience linguicism, which Skutnabb-Kangas (1988) described as an unequal division of power and resources between groups that are defined on the basis of language (in this case, ASL). They experience ableism (Lewis, 2021), a form of oppression that leads people to determine who is valuable based on a person's language, appearance, and/or ability to excel in society. Black DDBDDHHLD experience anti-Black racism, which Dumas and ross (2016) described as prejudice and/or discrimination toward Black individuals. DeafBlind individuals experience vidism and distantism. Vidism is defined as a visual barrier to access, while distantism is defined as a refusal to provide tactile access such as ProTactile, or tactile sign language (Morrison & Johnson, 2020). That is, the DDBDDHHLD community is a multiply marginalized community, and the intersectional identities of its individuals are being ignored; this results in tensions and resistance within the DDBDDHHLD community as DDBDDHHLD people internalize oppression rather than focus on dismantling systems of oppression. Examples of internalized oppression include when sighted Deaf people perpetuate vidism and distantism against DeafBlind people for using ProTactile to communicate or when "non-Disabled" Deaf people reject DeafDisabled individuals because their bodies/minds function differently.

These examples demonstrate how Deaf culture, history, and language are traditionally centered on the experience of Eurocentric, sighted, able-bodied, white Deaf people. Parasnis (2012, p. 64) states, "The experiences of white American Deaf ASL users have created a perception of Deaf culture as a monolithic overarching trait of all deaf people and has suppressed recognition of the demographic diversity of individuals within the [DDBDDHHLD] community itself." There is a significant need for understanding the impact of intersectionality on the identity formation of individuals negotiating multiple marginalized social identities in the deaf community.

TENSIONS AND RESISTANCE IN THE DDBDDHHLD COMMUNITY

Earlier, we briefly explained tensions and resistance in the DDBDDHHLD community related to the use of the term *deaf*. In this section, we discuss the stigma of dis/ability in the DDBDDHHLD community. Individuals with disabilities have been subject to discrimination and mistreatment throughout history. In society, disability is most often defined as a limitation of function because of an impairment. This medical, or pathological, model of dis/ability frames being deaf as a dis/ability that needs to be remedied in order for DDBDDHHLD peoples to assimilate into a normative hearing society. Haegele and Hodge (2016) state that this view is strongly normative and likens deafness to ill health. That is, dis/ability is viewed as a problem that needs to be medically cured so DDBDDHHLD individuals can function in society. Medical and educational advice are frequently rooted in a framework of viewing DDBDDHHLD peoples as defective (Hall, 2017), as in need of being "fixed" by receiving amplification devices, such as hearing aids or cochlear implants, and acquiring spoken language *only*. There have been historical oppressive practices treating and perceiving DDBDDHHLD individuals as intellectually disabled or mute (i.e., unable to speak). For instance, oralism was a method of educating DDBDDHHCI students. The method did not allow students to use ASL, and the focus was solely on teaching students to speak and learn to hear with their hearing devices. To date, it is very common for schools to prioritize speech therapy over content-based classes like sciences and math (Chapple, 2019). In addition, the technological advancement of the cochlear implant, a surgically implanted device to create electronic stimulation of hearing nerve fibers, has had a central role in pedagogy for DDBDDHHCI students. Yet Deaf individuals (noted with capital *D*) have been adamantly opposed to oralism and cochlear implants both as seriously invasive treatment with limited efficacy and as a threat to Deaf culture (Tucker, 1998).

In contrast, the social model of dis/ability suggests that it is not one's bodily function that limits abilities; rather, it is society. DDBDDHHLD peoples do not view being deaf as a deficit or a problem, but rather as being part of a cultural group with its own language, customs, and beliefs (Lane et al., 1996). Rejecting "dis/ability" has been a strategy used within DDBDDHHLD communities to challenge this normative ideology and hegemony (Burke, 2014). Embracing Deaf culture is an act of resistance to the idea of "dis/ability," of views of oneself as a deficiency or disabled (Gertz, 2003). We approach this work from a disability justice framework (Sins Invalid, 2019, 2020). We acknowledge that bodies/minds can function differently, and contexts matter for how these differences manifest. In other words, we recognize the social construction of dis/ability that results in power differentials and subordination.

There are two issues we must highlight associated with the rejection of the dis/ability label and identity. First, Deaf individuals fall within the definition of disability that entitles those individuals to the protections of the U.S. dis/ability rights laws, regardless of whether those individuals consider themselves as having a disability. Because of the U.S. dis/ability right laws, Deaf individuals are forced to accept being labeled as disabled in order to receive access to their fundamental rights as a human being (Lane et al., 1996). Second, rejection of the "dis/ability" label in the DDBDDHHLD community denies the very existence of DDBDDHHLD individuals who embrace dis/ability as their identity and particularly, those who are DeafDisabled or DeafBlind. Oftentimes, "nondisabled" Deaf individuals define what is "normal" to them, which is deeply rooted in white supremacy, ableism, and audism and often excludes what does not fit in the normalcy of Deaf culture, which may include the DDBDDHHLD. For instance, Deaf epistemology relies heavily on personal testimonies and personal experiences of Deafsighted individuals. "Nondisabled" Deaf individuals have internalized the power of the hearing culture in the United States, as a dominant culture that marginalizes them as a disabled group such as DeafBlind and DeafDisabled individuals (Burke, 2014), and they internalize ableist views and values toward DDBDDHHLD as a strategy of empowerment (Robinson, 2010). These are views and values that we, the authors, do not share. To resist the label and identity of dis/ability, we are ignoring the key roles on the intersections of race, gender, sexuality, and dis/ability in our lives—affecting our experiences with discrimination in different ways. In the DDBDDHHLD community, dis/ability is often erased from conversations on an individual's identity. We recognize that the tensions and resistance are deeply rooted in white patriarchal supremacist ideals. If we intend to fight oppression, we need to take into account how intersecting identities impact DDBDDHHLD individuals, and dis/ability needs to be part of the conversation. More so, we should be collaboratively joining in the larger conversation with Black and Brown disabled theorists on how whiteness has pervasively colored what it means to be disabled (Miles et al., 2017; Thompson, 2016). It is our responsibility to work together collectively to deconstruct any system that suggests any form of exclusion on individuals with disabilities.

REVISIONING DEAF EDUCATION

The field of educating DDBDDHHCI children in the United States has existed for over 2 centuries. Students in Deaf studies and deaf education are familiar with stories about how deaf education in the United States came to be, regarding Reverend Thomas Hopkins Gallaudet (white/hearing) and Laurent Clerc (white/deaf) as being the fathers of deaf education in the United States (Van Cleve & Crouch 1989). However, history documents deaf children (a disabled group) as educated by deaf adults (a disabled group as well), which was an act that in itself resisted audist, ableist, and white supremacist ideals of normative hearing bodies knowing what was best for educating DDBDDHHCI children.

However, uncritical analyses of these acts of resistance also came to be complicit in causing further harm toward marginalized communities within the DDBDDHHLD community. For example, much of the literature on deaf education has homed in on DDBDDHHLD deficits, such as the inability to be literate, a lack of academic readiness, and deprived of language, among many others (see Hall, 2017; Mayer, 2010; Paul, 1998; Traxler, 2000). The intentions behind such scholarship were to remediate, rehabilitate, and repair DDBDDHHLD children.

As mentioned earlier, a small but growing literature base has resisted deficit perspectives on what it means to be DDBDDHHLD and how one should be educated (see Bauman & Murray, 2014; Gertz, 2003; Ladd, 2008). An even smaller base (García-Fernández, 2014; Moges, 2020; Wright et al., 2021) has proposed that the definitions of DDBDDHHLD be expanded even more and that the multiple cultures within the community be considered assets and positioned as a critical foundation for pedagogies in deaf education. In the following section, we provide examples of and elaborate on the aforementioned authors' asset-based perspectives on the DDBDDHHLD populations in the United States.

ASSET PEDAGOGIES AND THE U.S. DDBDDHHLD/CI EXPERIENCE

Black Deaf culture provides the first and longest documented (though hidden) history of sustaining dis/ability culture within schools. This community also can be examined as a source for interrogating dis/ability because race and dis/ability are always being scrutinized since both are marginalized identities in the United States. We want to connect the journey of Black DDBDDHHCI individuals in the United States to asset pedagogies by connecting to Waitoller and Thorius's (2016) expansion of Culturally Sustaining Pedagogy and also broadening what we have come to define as asset pedagogies (APs) by proposing the inclusion of Black Deaf Gain (2020) and Post Modern Audism (Wright et al., 2021).

Culturally Sustaining Pedagogy

Culturally Sustaining Pedagogy (CSP) was first proposed by Paris (2012) and expanded by Paris and Alim (2014) with three shifts that distinguished CSP from previous iterations and traditions of APs: (1) to foster and sustain linguistic, literate, and cultural pluralism in educational practices; (2) to value practices not just for access to dominant culture and language practices; and (3) to interrogate and critique traditional and evolving ways that youth participate in progressive and oppressive practices. Adding to these shifts, Waitoller and Thorius (2016) clarified how dis/ability could and should be considered within CSP with the following explicit additions: (1) ability in addition to language, literacy, and culture must also be included in considerations of pluralism; (2) dis/ability as an essential part of cultural identity fluidity; and (3) the necessity of interrogating what cultural aspects of dis/ability should be sustained.

Together, these are much needed shifts in existing APs, as the U.S. school context has been since desegregation times a colonial space of anti-Blackness: forcing negatively racialized peoples to disappear into whiteness. These contexts also have been disablist: forcing dis/abled individuals to disappear into ableness. CSP seems like an appropriate response for uplifting negatively racialized and dis/abled students by valuing the many identities they embody while simultaneously addressing problematic and harmful behaviors within the cultural/linguistic groups in which these students find themselves.

Post Modern Audism

Another AP we lean toward is the recently proposed Post Modern Audism (Wright et al., 2021). Post Modern Audism (PMA) challenges the Eurocentric, ableist, single-lens approach of Deaf Critical Theory (DeafCrit) (Gertz, 2003). PMA also rejects the essentializing of the U.S. DDBDDHHCI communities as one deaf community. Wright et al. (2021) propose the following tenets for PMA:

- Becoming Deaf, DeafBlind, DeafDisabled, and Hard of Hearing is different for all, and highly individualized.
- Rejects audism, AND racism, AND ableism by both deaf and hearing people.
- Embraces Signed Languages as part of the DDBDDHH communities—including ProTactile ASL.
- Defines Deaf Culture as a culture of communities (DDBDDHH).
- Rejects and dismantles normative and proximate practices within our communities.
- Rejects the able/disabled duality as is pursuant to the U.S. legal framework.

The tenets advanced by PMA are especially important in naming the systems of oppression that were ignored within DeafCrit, for rejecting practices both within the DDBDDHHLD communities and in hearing communities that perpetuate these oppressive systems, for recognizing that the journey of becoming DDBDDHHLD is unique to every individual, and for advancing ProTactile as the innate right of U.S. DeafBlind communities. Naming ProTactile as a sign language to be embraced is timely as more schools that serve DeafBlind students are beginning to make ProTactile accessible to students at younger ages as part of their access to language and curriculum, which may mean earlier identity development/acceptance for DeafBlind children and more equitable access to the curriculum.

PMA lays a strong foundation for Black Deaf Gain. And together, CSP and PMA show the importance of highlighting the unique experiences and oppressions that groups of individuals may face externally as well as within their own dis/ability communities. This is particularly important for Black DDBDDHHCI students who may experience anti-Blackness, racism, and linguicism within the essentialized white Deaf community, as well as audism, ableism, antiblackness and systemic racism, and linguicism within the larger hearing society. This is why it is essential to this discussion that we recognize Black Deaf Gain as an AP to be employed within DDBDDHHCI communities and uplifted within U.S. society as a whole.

Black Deaf Gain

Black Deaf Gain draws from a legacy of Black and Brown folks who have used critical race theory to challenge the silenced and ahistoric approach applied to Black, Indigenous, and People of Color (BIPOC) Disabled and Deaf people (see Chapple, 2019; García-Fernández, 2014, 2020; Lawyer, 2018; Stapleton, 2015). Moges (2020) leverages Deaf Latinx Critical Theory (Deaf LatCrit; García-Fernández, 2014). Deaf LatCrit is a newer iteration in the legacy of CRT and the first truly CRT-based intersectional analysis of the deaf experience. It "overwrites" the lack of acknowledgement of intersectionality in DeafCrit and provides a historical review of Black DDBDDHHCI individuals in the United States. Moges (2020) uses historic documents to define Black Deaf Gain using the four tenets of the Deaf LatCrit framework; Black Deaf Gain:

- Defines the multiple identities and oppressions (antiblackness, systemic racism, linguicism, audism [and ableism]) Black Deaf folks experience in the United States (intersectionality).
- Names the educational and communicative dichotomy and the implementation of white Deaf educational policy (ideologies).
- Explores the linguistic research into Black ASL (consciousness).
- Invokes counternarratives to help others understand from the lens of the Black Deaf perspective (storytelling).

History and culture within the DDBDDHHLD community are rooted in white supremacy and the "repetitive master-narrative from a white perspective, which lacks a Black Deaf centralized history" (Moges, 2020, p. 70). The Black DDBDDHHLD community has a deeply rich history that continues to be marginalized by various components of the DDBDDHHLD community. During the segregation era, Black DDBDDHH students attended segregated residential schools; this contributed to the development of Black ASL (BASL; McCaskill et al., 2011) used by large Black Deaf communities in the southern United States and that has historically been ignored in favor of uplifting ASL as the only U.S. sign language (Moges, 2020). Although BASL has long been unrecognized and accepted in the DDBDDHHLD community, it is gaining mobility with increased education, research, and awareness. Black Deaf Gain demonstrates how despite the oppression of white oral education and societal discrimination and deprivations, BASL still flourished and manualism (i.e., sign language) was preserved because of Black Deaf students and educators. Black Deaf Gain offers both racial and linguistic capital; for these reasons, we believe Black Deaf Gain is an AP worthy of naming and advancing.

CSP, PMA, and Black Deaf Gain are examples of three theories that can serve as APs that center dis/ability and DDBDDHHLD/CI communities in the United States while also interrogating systems that seek to erase Deaf and Disabled populations or push them into onto-epistemic conditions of negation. In this way, these three APs can serve not only to develop but to sustain dis/ability and recognize dis/ability as an identity and cultural tool. The authors of both Black Deaf Gain and PMA openly state the importance of DDBDDHHCI communities' input, challenges, and expansions of the applications of these theories in order to better reflect the realities of these diverse communities. In the next section, we provide examples of how Black Deaf Gain can be applied as an AP in the K–12 context.

BLACK DEAF GAIN FROM THEORY TO APPLICATION

Intersectionality

Throughout this chapter, we have demonstrated how the DDBDDHHLD community is diverse as well as intersectional. However, the K–12 educators and administrators of DDBDDHHLD students often do not reflect such demographics (Simms et al., 2008) and lack an insider advantage for being able to connect with their students. As history has indicated, the idea of having a deaf educator teach deaf students was a radical one that resisted normativity and paternalization. Even more so, having DDBDDHHLD educators and administrators with multiple intersectional identities would address Wright and colleagues' (2021) PMA tenets regarding the importance of individualizing the DDBDDHHLD experience and embracing the many varied sign languages, including ProTactile, from U.S. regions and other countries. Therefore, applying a Black Deaf Gain lens to deaf education could involve addressing the barriers that have excluded Black Deaf and other Deaf teachers of color from the field.

Since the era of desegregation, there has been a drastic decline in Black Deaf teachers within Deaf education, which has been due to linguicism (the suppression of BASL to privilege ASL and the suppression of ASL for English); ableism (not wanting to normalize being DDBDDHHLD by allowing teacher role models in the field); anti-blackness (restricting the intellectual movement and propagation of ideas by Black people); and audism (manifested as the "hearing knows best" and "hearing helper"; Lawyer, 2022). Removing systemic barriers such as standardized English test requirements that supersede all other teacher candidate traits and disrupting the 90/90/90 (percent of hearing, white, and female-identified dominant professionals in deaf education) field would be one way to address the intersections of anti-Blackness, audism, and linguicism. In this way, BIPOC DDBDDHHLD students would have increased access to language and cultural models beyond their DDBDDHHLD identities. In turn, instead of delayed identity formation (Lawyer, 2018), Black DDBDDHHLD youth might have opportunities to develop and embrace their cultural, linguistic, dis/abled, and other identities at younger ages.

Ideologies and Consciousness

In order to promote an asset- and strengths-based pedagogy practice, Wright et al. (2021) state that one needs to reject all -isms and perceive the deaf culture as a culture of communities. The ideology of what it means to be DDBDDHHLD needs to be redefined and restructured. According to Holcomb (2012), the value and ideology of the deaf community was centered around communication access because it allowed one to engage and connect with one another—which was the definition of being whole. With that definition, the Black DDBDDHHLD community was able to embody the true meaning of being whole as they did not have obstructions, such as the oralism movement, impede their communication access throughout their schooling: an experience that the white DDBDDHHLD community experienced. In retrospect, it was a Black Deaf Gain to have not experienced feeling less than whole due to lack of communication access. The narrative framing of how Black DDBDDHHLD persisted through multiple barriers of oppression and remained engaged and connected with communication access was the very definition of the deaf community's ideology of itself and a rejection of all -isms, affirming the assets and strengths of a culture of communities within the deaf culture (Wright et al., 2021).

To establish the ideology of self and the community, one must have true consciousness. The definition of consciousness is to be in a state of awareness, aware of one's presence in the world and in their communities. In the spirit of asset- and strength-based pedagogies, guided by Black Deaf Gain, a curriculum on Black Deaf studies within the K–12 schools would raise consciousness about what it means to be a Black DDBDDHHLD person. This educational approach would dismantle the construct that the deaf experience is a monolith and distinguish the Black DDBDDHHLD experience as rich, varied, and a culture worth studying. Resources for this approach include the growing scholarship on BASL and publications of the Black

Deaf experience by Black Deaf scholars themselves shared by Moges (2020; see Dunn, 2005; Hill, 2012; McCaskill, 2005; Moges, 2017). In addition, Gallaudet University recently developed the Center for Black Deaf Studies as an outreach and resource center on the teaching and learning of the Black Deaf experience (Gallaudet University, n.d.) and in the implementation of asset- and strength-based pedagogies that teach Black Deaf history, Black ASL linguistics, Black Deaf sociology, as well as Black Deaf education. Access to these resources would reframe and solidify the consciousness of the Black DDBDDHHLD presence.

There are several approaches we feel could address ideologies and consciousness using a Black Deaf Gain lens. First, foregrounding erased and marginalized histories within DDBDDHHLD populations is valued in Black Deaf Gain. By understanding the importance of multiple communities within the deaf community, one will know the historical value and contributions of such communities. For example, Moges (2020) shared the impact of *Miller et al. v. Board of Education of District of Columbia et al.* on how segregation ended in the United States for DDBDDHHLD students. In addition, Mr. Andrew Foster, the first Black deaf graduate of Gallaudet College, dedicated his entire short life to establishing over 30 schools for the deaf in Africa from 1956 to 1987 (Dunn, 2005; Hairston & Smith, 1983). Many more documented and undocumented narratives highlight the significant contributions or gains of the multiple communities within the deaf community. However, educators should be cognizant in outsourcing multiple funds of knowledge (Yosso, 2005) in order to gain insight into communities that have been ignored for so long.

Second, intersectionality would be central to instructional and curricular instruction. For instance, Moges (2020) discussed Black Deaf Gain as instrumental toward the preservation of manualism in schools for the deaf during U.S. segregation. Manualism was at risk of being endangered due to the rise of oralism: an instructional philosophy geared toward rehabilitating DDBDDHHLD people into inhabiting hearing-normative bodies. white DDBDDHHLD students were considered worthy investments in such rehabilitation approaches, while Black DDBDDHHLD people managed to maintain their use of BASL because they were deemed unworthy of rehabilitation due to their Blackness. Moges (2020) posited that such a situation allowed for continual access to education and communication for the Black DDBDDHHLD community. Therefore, the idea of being Black DDBDDHHLD in the United States was advantageous in resisting audism and linguicism. This example of intersectional fund of knowledge would promote an asset- and strengths-based pedagogical opportunity for teaching DDBDDHHLD students.

Third, there are very few resources available in BASL, and as older users of BASL pass away, funds of linguistic knowledge are also in danger of leaving with them. Schools would be ideal places for tying in linguistic and cultural funds of knowledge through community and school collaborations to develop BASL corpus. It would be essential to develop BASL corpus without imposing white ideologies of "standardization." We recognize that there is wide variance in BASL across the United States, with both regional and generational differences. Those differences should be embraced as part of the diversity and variation of language. These varieties of BASL should be uplifted within schools. Time and resource investments should be made in BASL curriculum development just as those investments have been committed over the years in ASL curriculum development.

Storytelling

Storytelling is a central tenet in CRT because it "shifts the frame" (Crenshaw, 1989) and "looks to the bottom" (Matsuda, 1987). In indigenous communities, stories are told by the elders and are considered connections between the past, the present, and the people themselves (Iseke, 2013). Dixson and Rousseau (2006) describe storytelling as centering the experiences of marginalized groups as sources of knowledge. The power of holding and sharing stories were considered forms of resistance against the master narrative and the sustenance of the counternarratives were instrumental toward the survival of marginalized communities. Coles (2019) justified the power of storytelling by positioning its use as a form of literacy and as a tool for reclaiming the narrative from dominant discourses. Being armed with the knowledge of language and literacy would be the antithesis to the anti-Blackness pervasive in today's literature. Educators of DDBDDHHLD students, using an asset- and strengths-based pedagogy, should teach the role of storytelling and how it could be an act of defying racism, ableism, audism, and linguicism (Cannon, 2018; Cannon & Hernández-Saca, 2021; Moges, 2020; Stapleton, 2016; Sutton, 2020). Students' counternnarratives would promote a sense of pride and ownership of their presence in this world.

To share stories is to pass them on to a receptive and attentive audience. Stories can be ephemeral, disappearing the minute a story ends. Or they can be documented through multimodal ways as a way of leaving evidence. Mia Mingus' (2009, 2012) blog, Leaving Evidence, stated that leaving evidence is a way to ensure our voices, our traumas, our healings, and our experiences never get concealed. In the DDBDDHHLD community, our stories are documented through art, videos, and print (Moges, 2020), and we add social media. Until recently, much of the stories erased the intersectionality of the DDBDDHHLD experience. For example, Deaf View/Image Art (De'VIA) was a political movement through art that centered around the white Deaf and DeafBlind resistance, liberation, and experience of the world (Durr, 1999). As a counter, a recent art exhibit, "Black is Black: Blackity AF" (2021), at the National Technical Institute of the Deaf's Dyer

Arts Center, displayed Black DDBDDHHLD art—sharing counternarratives via art. Documentations of ASL with videos were privileged to those who had access to a camcorder and film. One of the earliest recordings of ASL was of George Veditz in 1913, a white male-presenting deaf person, making the argument of why ASL was a gift from God to the deaf people (Veditz, 1997). To the authors' knowledge, there have yet to be uncovered videos about the Black DDBDDHHLD experience in 1913. For decades the documentation and/or evidence of Black DDBDDHHLD stories remained small but growing. It was not until the social media boom, where everything started to change. McClain (2016) shared the power of social media in documentation, promoting activism, and the sharing of stories. Social media provided a platform and a greater reach in ensuring story longevity. More and more Black DDBDDHHLD people felt empowered to create counternarratives, and now these stories are being seen by people outside of their communities, more so than in the past through other mediums. The social media boom was a case of the phoenix rising for the Black DDBDDHHLD community. As a result, these narratives can be used in the classroom to promote an asset- and strengths-based practice. There is an indigenous saying, "Every time an elder dies, a library dies with them" (Fairchild, 2015), and with social media in our lives—we might be able to save these libraries.

CONCLUSION

We now understand that the system of deaf education was originally never designed for Black DDBDDHHCI students and has continued to be a space for anti-Blackness. Drawing on the strengths of Black DDBDDHHCI students is of utmost importance in promoting racial equity considerations. Using the Black Deaf Gain framework as an asset- and strengths-based pedagogical approach will promote academic success and well-being for Black DDBDDHHCI students, who may have already faced systemic barriers in education due to the anti-Blackness, audism, ableism, and linguicism that is prevalent in the deaf education classroom today. A radical pedagogical approach like Black Deaf Gain will validate and affirm racialized experiences inside and out of the classroom with incorporation of counternarratives by uplifting the stories and voices of other Black DDBDDHHCI students. In order to prioritize and promote student agency, deaf education can maximize opportunities for Black DDBDDHHCI students to create initiatives that center their lived experiences and their perspectives. However, it would be remiss of us to pursue our revisioning of deaf education with the Black Deaf Gain framework as the sole guide and the solution to all. This is especially true without the mention of the contributions and "Gains" of other non-Black DDBDDHHCI students of color and those with multiply marginalized identities, who have contributed (without recognition) to the pillars of deaf education and to the community itself. Sadly, these omissions reflect the limitations of the current literature and scholarship in a field that aims to disrupt the white, hearing, able-bodied, patriarchal status quo in deaf education. We recognize the critical role research has on leaving evidence and call upon non-Black DDBDDHHLD of color and with multiply marginalized identities to join us in our pursuit in creating new and expanded asset- and strength-based pedagogies for all DDBDDHHCI students. It is time for us to identify, study, and enhance the existing efforts in reforming systems toward equity for all.

Ultimately, it is imperative for us to be laser-focused on understanding and addressing educational inequalities and build systems that embrace equity. In order to do this, we must dismantle and redesign the deaf education systems currently at play that have reinforced anti-Blackness, racism, audism, ableism, and linguicism. We must move toward the revisioning of deaf education, which views opportunity and education as a human right for all DDBDDHHCI students of color and with multiply marginalized identities. Most of all, the revisioning of K–12 education will guide DDBDDHHCI students of color and with multiply marginalized identities toward honoring the full range of ways of knowing, developing, exploring, and valuing their racialized intersectional identities.

CHAPTER 6

Disability Critical Race Theory as Asset Pedagogy

Subini Annamma, David Connor, and Beth Ferri

In this chapter, we explore how educators can foster liberatory classroom ecologies and cultivate resistance against oppressive practices in schools that oftentimes pass for "normal"—remedial curricula, reductive pedagogy, and retributive relationships. First, we describe disability critical race theory (DisCrit). Next, we illustrate how a DisCrit disposition is informed by a dual asset-based understanding of disabled students of color. Subsequently, we feature a framework for developing a pre-school–college DisCrit classroom ecology first suggested by Annamma and Morrison (2018), focusing upon three interrelated elements: (1) curriculum, (2) pedagogy, and (3) solidarity with students. Finally, we provide examples of how DisCrit is being enacted in teacher education across these same three elements.

Disability critical race theory (DisCrit) was developed to interrogate the intersection of *racism and ableism* in all aspects of education (Annamma et al., 2013). DisCrit is best understood as theory-in-progress, with its seven tenets designed to illuminate longstanding and emerging issues of educational inequities with a view to providing alternative framings, explanations, and solutions. In brief, DisCrit focuses on ways that the forces of racism and ableism circulate to uphold notions of normalcy, oftentimes in neutralized and invisible ways. DisCrit therefore focuses on how legal and historical aspects of disability and race have been used separately and simultaneously to deny rights and maintain inequities. DisCrit also foregrounds the social constructions of race and ability, and how these constructions have traditionally placed groups outside of societal norms. In addition, DisCrit recognizes whiteness and ability as forms of property, while acknowledging that gains made for disabled people and people of color have largely been achieved due to interest convergence of white, middle-class, able-bodied citizens. Ultimately, by centering the voices of multiply marginalized populations, DisCrit seeks to address current inequities within educational research and, by extension, society at large, requiring activism to resist unjust systems and reimagine equitable ones. It is important to note that DisCrit's intellectual lineage of resistance stretches back to the work of Cooper (1892/1988) and DuBois (1920), to the litany of Black feminists and scholars such as Lorde (1984), Crenshaw (1989), and Collins (1990), as well as to more recent theorizing connecting racism and ableism in education by scholars such as Artiles and Trent (1994), Blanchett (2006), and Erevelles (2011), all of whom influenced our thinking in profound ways.[1]

Asset-based pedagogies (APs) actively seek to challenge deficit perceptions of students of color, offering a more a culturally relevant and hopeful learning experiences by redefining student's abilities, acknowledging their contributions, and providing support through socially just pedagogies (Cammarota, 2011). Critical special educators (Artiles, 1998) and disability studies scholars (Baglieri et al., 2010) have likewise rejected detrimental depictions of students with disabilities, reframing deficit-based conceptions in favor of more holistic understandings. In her groundbreaking book, Linton (1998) "claimed" disability as a minoritized identity, advocating that it be recognized as a source of strength, pride, and knowledge. The politicization of disability is both a call to activism (Heumann, 2020) and a rejection of longstanding associations of shame and stigma (Brown, 2003).

It is only recently, however, that race and disability have been considered *simultaneously* as multiplicative identities in advocating for new classroom ecologies (Annamma & Morrison, 2018). As Waitoller and Thorius (2018) note, "intertwined scientific, political, and economic purposes have historically solidified the relationship between racism an ableism" into a relational system (p. 371). Tangible consequences of this collusive relationship include exclusions from all aspects of society and the reproduction of these patterns across generations. To counter this phenomenon, we assert that APs, including those evolved from a DisCrit framework, possess the power to challenge and dismantle unjust practices within education.

Before discussing curriculum, pedagogy, and solidarity, we first emphasize the need for educators to critically reflect upon their own perceptions, policies, and practices to consider how they challenge and perpetuate the systemic oppression of marginalized students. We also encourage educators to adopt a stance of cultural humility (Nomikoudis & Star, 2016), as this helps in the work of becoming and remaining a reflective practitioner—someone who seeks to connect with and support all students within a healthy, functional classroom ecology.

GOING AGAINST THE GRAIN: CREATING A DISCRIT CLASSROOM ECOLOGY

Ecologies are made up of relationships among organisms and their physical surroundings. A DisCrit classroom ecology, according to Annamma & Morrison (2018), means moving beyond traditional practices of teaching and toward engaging critical curricula, embracing diverse forms of pedagogy, expanding notions of relationships. In such a classroom ecology, students are positioned as valued resources—important to the functioning of the whole, rather than being considered liabilities or "at risk" for failure.

As we have written elsewhere, the perturbing nexus between race and disability—historically and presently—is premised upon the idea that each construct is dependent upon the other to establish racial hierarchies, which are further defended by scientific racism and deficit thinking (Connor & Ferri, 2013). As consequence of the interdependence of racism and ableism, schools and classrooms in the United States have largely evolved into dysfunctional ecologies in which race and disability are treated as dysfunctional outflows and funneled through existing educational structures and practices. Students of color are, for instance

- Underrepresented in gifted programs and advanced placement classes (Ford, 2013), yet overrepresented in special education placements, particularly those with intellectual and learning disabilities (Skiba et al., 2006);[2]
- Underrepresented among those awarded with the highest test scores and GPAs (Ford, 2010), yet overrepresented in disciplinary incidents, emotional disabilities, and those pushed out of schools (Losen, 2015); and
- Underrepresented in post-secondary education, yet overrepresented in carceral settings (Okilwa, 2017).

The grim legacy of historical and structural racism and ableism can paint a hopeless picture of diminished possibilities for disabled students of color—a picture that needs to be countered with hope and refocused on assets. For example, in their initial exploration of DisCrit classroom ecologies, Annamma and Morrison (2018) called upon DuBois's, "gift theory." As Rabaka (2010) explains, DuBois's articulation of the double consciousness of Black people includes both the oppressor's view of Blackness, one imbued with white supremacy that assumes universality and associates Blackness with less than, and one informed by the distinctiveness of the Black experience, one rooted in reality that recognizes oppressions and possible disruptions. DuBois recognized this "second sight" as a gift, enabling a more honest analysis of a society that oppressed people of color possess and deploy. As DuBois asserts, the inter-workings of racism are most visible to those who experience it. Multiply marginalized people of color, therefore, have a clearer understanding based on first-hand knowledge of how social processes of oppression are mutually constitutive and the possibilities for individual and community resistance. In the following sections on curriculum, teaching, and solidarity, we explore how "going against the grain" is imperative in creating substantive change.

Element 1: DisCrit Curriculum

The word *curriculum* has multiple interpretations but generally describes a course of study consisting of learning goals, methods, materials, and assessments guided by local, state, or national standards. It also includes the "hidden" curriculum of unstated social rules and undergirding values (Margolis, 2001). The "absent curriculum" is composed of concepts and histories not featured in the official course of study, which negatively impact those who are actively erased (Wilkinson, 2014). These three versions of curricula raise important questions, including: Who gets to decide what is/isn't in the curriculum? Who/what is reflected in the content and in what ways? What is purposefully included and excluded? Whose histories are taught and whose are omitted? For the purpose of this chapter, we move between all three interpretations of the curriculum.

Generally speaking, the teaching of race in American classrooms has been critiqued as superficial—featuring a handful of major events and historical figures that are relegated to a concern of the past and presented without explicitly addressing structural racism (Noguera & Alicia, 2020). Most recently, a national concern about teaching *anything* to do with race has led to a rush to ban any reference (real or imagined) to critical race theory (CRT), an academic discipline designed to illustrate how racial inequities are ingrained via systems and structures and embedded within law and other cultural institutions, such as education and health care (Crenshaw et al., 1996). Banning the discussion of race in classrooms across the United States speaks to a desire to control and limit the national conversation. Interestingly, disability is also rarely addressed in the curriculum (Valle & Connor, 2019). Even when it is discussed—for example, in depictions of disability in contemporary literature—racially minoritized groups are still underrepresented (Koss & Paciga, 2020). Moreover, disability may still be cast within deficit-based perspectives, medical understandings, and stereotypic tropes such as overcoming adversity (Baglieri & Lalvani, 2019).

To provide a more robust picture, curriculum must explicitly name intersectional injustices faced by people of color (POC) and help students explore ways multiply marginalized individuals and groups have *always* fought, and continue to fight, intersecting oppressions (Barclay, 2021). By doing this, all students witness how multiply marginalized POC have been central to the history of America. Furthermore, linking the past to the present can help multiply marginalized students of color better understand their own lives and the connections between current and past injustices.

To counter partial and incomplete histories that reduce individuals to fragments of their full humanity, the *full* representation of multiply marginalized people, featuring the full complexity of their identities, histories, and cultures, is long overdue. Students may not learn, for instance, that Harriet Tubman, Civil War hero and conductor of the underground railroad, also had epilepsy. Images of Sojourner Truth, abolitionist and women's rights activist, often conceal her injured hand. Other erasures include Fannie Lou Hammer, a civil rights activist, who had polio, was forcibly sterilized by the state, and suffered permanent injuries from police; Brad Lomax, the Black Panther who helped lead the historic 504 disability rights protest in San Francisco, had multiple sclerosis; and Dennis Billups, fellow Black Panther who was visually impaired, urged disabled Black people to join the disability rights movement.

Many disabled Black artists have also been presented without mention of their disabilities or minimizing its impact, such as Maya Angelou (selective mutism as a child) and Harry Belafonte and Octavia Butler (dyslexia), with few exceptions, such as 19th-century musical prodigy "Blind Tom Wiggins." There have also been examples of POC with disabilities who create art, literature, and music from the complexity of their lived experiences, such as writer and poet Audre Lorde (legally blind, cancer), singer/songwriters Ray Charles and Stevie Wonder (blindness), abstract expressionist Beauford Delaney (chronic depression), musician Nina Simone (mental health), Mexican artist Frida Kahlo (physical disabilities), and musician Michael Fuller and artist Stephen Wiltshire (neurodiversity). Sharing these examples speaks to ways in which lived experience provides unique, nuanced ways of interpreting the world (Hadley & McDonald, 2018).

The virtual absence of multiply marginalized POC from the curriculum and their contributions to history and culture is an important gap waiting to be filled—as their underrepresentation reinscribes a white supremacist curriculum that centers whiteness and ability norms. Take, for example, the well-intended but inadequate idea of Black History month, which, as many scholars note, allows the rest of the year to remain white without naming it as such (Lee et al., 1997). Indeed, white students must also be accountable to critical perspectives about ways in which power circulates and is (re)inscribed, promoting greater understanding, and collective responsibility for resisting the status quo. As Sleeter (2011, p. 18) notes, a more balanced curriculum produces critical and political consciousness as well as "higher levels of thinking" for all students.

In addition to the examples above, race and dis/ability can be incorporated in many ways throughout the curriculum—for example, in science (critiques of eugenics and racialized pseudoscience), in math (word problems and statistics about rebellions by the enslaved), in literacy (first person narratives), and in history (civil rights and disability rights). Students can then connect these histories to robust forms of resistance to present day injustices, such as Black Lives Matter protests of systemic racism and police brutality, Colin Kaepernick's "taking a knee" protests for POC killed by police, and vigils for disabled children and youth killed by family members and caregivers.

To counter the trauma of systemic violence and erasure, teachers must also provide access to the creativity, joy, innovation, and contributions of disabled people of color. These might include a graphic novel about Krip-Hop Nation (Moore, 2019), Audre Lorde's poetry (2000), Alice Shepperd's dancing (Sheppard, 2019), or Solange Knowles's music (Munguia, 2018), to name just a few. Fortunately, there is a wealth of disabled activists and artists of color (accessible via blogs, books, YouTube, and TicToc videos) whose experiences and observations offer valuable insights, while celebrating multiply marginalized people of color (Wong, 2020).

Element 2: A DisCrit Pedagogy

By pedagogy, we refer to the general practice of teaching, including teachers' decisions about how they connect to students, select and/or create instructional materials, engage in discussions, collectively generate knowledge, unite a classroom community, and assess learning. We adhere to Freire's (1970) notion of the pedagogy of the oppressed, viewing education as dynamic and interactive, where each participant brings a world of knowledge that must be tapped into to work collectively against injustices in society. In other words, when teachers value the knowledge(s) that students bring to the curriculum (including historical, cultural, social, and personal contributions), there are greater opportunities for authentic connections, meaningful learning, and social justice.

In addition to DisCrit, we also cull from frameworks of culturally responsive, relevant, and sustaining pedagogy (CRRSP). As both CRRSP and DisCrit are grounded in asset-pedagogical approaches, each merits a brief explanation to highlight their specific contributions. Culturally responsive teaching (Gay, 2002) centers the lived experiences of historically marginalized students of color, acknowledging the legitimacy of their cultural heritages, nurturing connections between home and school, recognizing the value of students' own cultural resources, and integrating culturally representative materials into the curriculum. Culturally relevant pedagogy (Ladson-Billings, 1995) focuses on particular teaching methods that foster academic success by recognizing students' cultural competence and expanding their critical consciousness. Culturally Sustaining Pedagogy builds upon culturally relevant approaches by "support[ing] young people in sustaining the cultural and linguistic competence of their communities while simultaneously offering access to dominant cultural competence" (Paris, 2012, p. 95). All three of these interconnected pedagogical approaches recognize the value of focusing on multiply marginalized students, illuminating ways in which students are systematically enabled or disabled, and creating innovative solutions through praxis. What DisCrit adds to these approaches is its insistence on thinking about ways in which students are—through the nexus of racism and ableism—positioned as uniquely vulnerable to receive an inferior education, experience segregation and exclusion, and face potential banishment from society (Ben Moshe, 2020), and simultaneously how multiply marginalized students participate in individual and community resistance.

Implementing DisCrit pedagogy requires that we teach higher-order thinking skills, rather than remedial-centric approaches that are frequently offered to multiply marginalized students. Of concern is that CRRSP are all but nonexistent in many traditional special education programs, or misleadingly appropriated (Thorius et al., 2018). Additionally, teacher education programs and calls for CRRSP rarely feature critical notions of disability, such as those found in disability studies in education (Friedman et al. 2019). Thus, a DisCrit classroom ecology informed by CRRSP integrates universal design for learning (Waitoller & Thorius, 2016) and explicitly situates learning within an anti-ableist and antiracist context.

Drawing from rich historical and cultural practices in POC communities, methods for culturally sustaining planning, pedagogy, and assessment have been foregrounded by scholars such as Paris and Alim (2017) and Muhammed (2020). In contemplating assessment, Annamma and Morrison (2018, p. 383) argue that the evaluation of student abilities must be informed by their "cultural repertoires, identities, and out of school practices to widen what is assessed."

Relatedly, students should be supported to access content and demonstrate their learning in the way that is most efficient for them. This might require teachers to have more expansive notions of assessment, including what constitutes reading or writing, as students make use of tools and resources that support their literacy development. Students might access content and provide evidence of their learning in multiple ways (e.g., oral, written, visual, performance, PowerPoints, media aps, webinars, podcasts, or a combination of these and other means). Assessments within a DisCrit classroom ecology must be conceptualized broadly, rather than only toward standardized examinations and student comparisons to justify exclusionary placements or tracking. Helping students track their individual growth and progress over time through portfolios and rubrics values each student and serves as motivation.

DisCrit values a sociocultural perspective of learning (Gipps, 1999) in which a teacher's role is to mediate knowledge, creating dynamic interactions in which students learn from each other. Furthermore, when learning is viewed as an ongoing process, with opportunities to "check in" with other students and teachers for understanding, students have evidence of their own learning and progress. As part of classroom culture, interdependency is valued in the process of learning, rather than independent performance being seen as the highest form of knowledge demonstration. This type of classroom ecology encourages an open discourse in which understanding and respecting perspectives of others is the norm (Gipps, 1999).

Some recent studies have shown the value of a DisCrit approach to pedagogy. Whitney (2018), for instance, re-envisions both pedagogy and learning disabilities through a Black girl's literacy framework. In her study of a 7th-grade Black girl named Raquel, Whitney illustrates the importance of sociocultural lenses and culturally responsive pedagogy, which helped her to see how Raquel's "agentive identity offered a counternarrative to the institutional identity ascribed to her as a student with a learning disability" (p. 205). Similarly, in examining the poetry writing practices of Raquel and her classmate, Sapphire, through a pedagogical approach that centered youth experiences and identities, Stornaiuolo and Whitney (2018) explain their pedagogical choices as re-storying. By working toward "racial justice through a young person's eyes" they helped to foster a figured world in which the student "was positioned as a maker, artist, and writer" (p. 211).

In another study, three white DisCrit-grounded researchers paired up with self-identified activist teachers of color and worked in dyads to further develop what could be done when enacting a DisCrit classroom ecology (Locke et al., 2022). All six researcher-participants identified and named master narratives, surfaced tensions and barriers encountered by teachers in navigating oppressive systems, and developed tools to assist teachers in disrupting the status quo to promote equity and access. The authors noted that, for the teachers, "DisCrit affirmed [their] actions rooted in solidarity and resistance . . . and empowered them to apply the lens to more aspects of their practice." Locke et al. also call for "education scholars . . . to reposition their research to not just include but actively learn from teachers, especially teachers of color whose lived experiences more often mirror the lived experiences of students with multiply-marginalized identities." In each of these studies we see examples of DisCrit solidarity.

Element 3: A DisCrit Solidarity

Solidarity with students is essential to creating and maintaining a DisCrit grounded classroom. We define our use of solidarity in the context of a DisCrit classroom ecology as teachers being in substantive relationship with their students and recognizing that their students face racism and ableism (and other forms of oppression) in schools and communities. Teachers must understand that students enter their classrooms with critical insights and a host of emotions about lived inequities. To work together, there must be an emphasis on building and nurturing authentic relationships. Teachers who are outraged by systemic inequities must use their outrage in constructive ways to foster meaningful relationships built on care, respect, and love, rather than hyperfocusing on behavior and management.

If student behaviors in class are unacceptable, teachers should primarily self-manage by diffusing situations, giving space to students, and facilitating conversations aimed at problem solving when students are ready. These actions run counter to the impulse to remove and refer students that often results in a slippery slope of special education labels and risks for suspension that become the gateway for students entering the juvenile justice system (Annamma, 2018a). Such actions, once initiated, also breed mistrust, severing relationships. Conversely, when students trust teachers, they feel more comfortable engaging in class dynamics and taking pride in their work. Solidarity requires that we are respectful of students' culture, provide opportunities for them to be heard and grow as learners, and understand that they have not internalized "badness" but rather are often struggling to navigate a bad system. In sum, for the purpose of solidarity, it is necessary to reject many commonplace practices such as "zero tolerance," exclusionary punishments, and hypersurveillance, replacing them with student-centered and restorative approaches (Sellman et al., 2013).

DisCrit solidarity reorganizes our classrooms into "spaces that center Students of Color" and views them as valuable and integral to the classroom and with "lived experiences and everyday knowledge" that contribute to a shared learning context (Annamma & Morrison, 2018, p. 71). Teachers who create these classrooms find ways to strengthen the identities and skills of multiply marginalized students of color. They are aware that their students navigate a world outside that is suffused in daily racist and ableist macro-, meso-, and microaggressions that remain unseen by most dominant groups, including many white educators. Teachers subsequently aim to ensure that their classrooms do not replicate these negative experiences and, instead, offer spaces where students have a deep sense of belonging.

As Waitoller and Thorius (2016) have acknowledged, disability is a marginalized ontology, and yet, it is a way of being. Disability, therefore, is a cultural and political identity to assert with pride, generating specific knowledge(s) that counter damaging narratives (Wong, 2020). Cultivating a DisCrit disposition ensures that each educator "presumes competence" (Biklen & Burke, 2006) and provides supports that allow students to demonstrate it (Ashby & Kasa, 2013). In sum, the concept of disability is firmly rooted solidarity, pedagogy, and curriculum in DisCrit Classroom Ecology.

CULTIVATING DISCRIT WITHIN TEACHER EDUCATION

Having discussed DisCrit curriculum, pedagogy, and solidarity in preK–20 contexts, we also want to document ways in which DisCrit has recently been taken up in teacher education contexts. Kulkarni et al. (2021), for instance, asserts that while DisCrit is "at the margins of teacher education" (p. 654), it has the ability to inform curriculum, including disciplinary teacher education—such as science, math, ELA, and social studies—with "radical possibilities" (p. 664). For teacher educators, DisCrit can help illuminate systemic inequities, including current cultural norms, that must

Disability Critical Race Theory as Asset Pedagogy

be recognized and resisted (Love & Beneke, 2021). Additionally, DisCrit contributes to multicultural and inclusive education by positioning race and disability in the center of curricular reform, including embracing pluralism and diversity as curricular practice (Baglieri, 2016). DisCrit has also been taken up by Fornauf and Mascio (2021), who integrate DisCrit and universal design for learning (UDL) within a rural teacher residency program, stating that the "gradual incorporation of the tenets of DisCrit improved our ability to support preservice teachers' examination of structural inequities in school practices" (p. 671). Likewise, Migliarini et al. (2022) utilized DisCrit within teacher education to explore the limits of inclusive education in centering the perspectives and needs of immigrant students labeled with disabilities in the United States and Italy.

DisCrit also challenges the whiteness and ability-oriented nature of teacher education (Annamma, 2015), as well as white "innocence" that permeates the curriculum. Shallish et al. (in press), for example, examined ways that whiteness operates within pre-service teacher experiences, and how privilege can be invoked to leverage disability accommodations and avoid "undesirable" student-teacher placements. In another example, Beneke and Baustein-Siuty (in press) illustrated ways in which pre-service teachers' life experiences allowed them to sidestep deeper analyses of socio-economic and racial inequities.

In terms of pedagogy, Ellis-Robinson (2021) used a DisCrit framework in an action research project with a network of "educators, community providers, and community stakeholders" (p. 703) who worked together to create professional development that would foster cultural competence in pre-service and special education teachers. Based on this work, the author developed a series of "passion projects," including an equity lab that asked all participants to examine their identity and experiences and consider how they impact teaching practices; a collective focus on culturally responsive practices and equity literacy; and developing standards for equity. In another example, Banks et al. (in press) called attention to DisCrit's potential as "a theoretical framework and pedagogical instrument to empower those living at the intersection of disability and race/ethnicity to apply tools of resistance." They described how they implemented DisCrit in the classroom to empower intersectional identities via participatory action research, examining multiply situated historical figures, building solidarity-based alliances, and supporting bi-directional activism for teachers and students. Banks et al. assert that "teachers should begin to share with students how the construction of a self-defined identity, which is created independent of whiteness and ableism, can be liberating and emancipatory for those who are truly marginalized."

One of the radical possibilities of DisCrit is its emphasis on asset-based perspectives, such as Clark et al.'s (2022) portrayal of teaching young women with complex support needs and chronicling ways in which they resisted teacher moves. In their study, Clark et al. highlight the race evasiveness of segregated practices for multiply marginalized disabled students. In comparing the pedagogical practices of teachers and support staff toward a Black student named Freedom and white student named Missy, the authors chronicle a series of different responses. They conclude, "Missy and Freedom are treated quite differently despite their similar learning profiles and disability labels. The teaching staff attend to Missy in ways that attribute meaning to her interactions, while Freedom is controlled and redirected," calling attention to how teacher beliefs and expectations are manifested in their actions.

In another example, Dávila (2015) observed Latinx students in special education classrooms, exploring the concept of microaggressions. Using a social justice framework informed by CRT and DisCrit, Davila documents microaggressions in the form of a general disregard for students by teachers, low expectations (often internalized by students), and instances of bullying. Davila describes the "collective impact" (p. 461) on students who witness humiliating microaggressions, where one is targeted but the negativity is actually absorbed by all those present. In another study, Banks (2017) explicitly employs DisCrit as a theoretical framework to examine ableism and racism in school settings in order to "better understand the educational experiences of African American male students labeled with learning disabilities as described in their own words" (p. 97). One participant shared, "In my education career [because I was] an African American male and had ADHD, teachers put me in two boxes—disabled and African American" (p. 105). He continues, "Then with me above six-feet tall, they expected me to be aggressive. [Teachers] have had to check themselves, but after I talk to them about my learning style, they would see me in a whole different light" (p. 105). Here, the student reveals how he actively works against stereotypes and proactively explains his learning needs in order to gain teacher cooperation.

In terms of solidarity, many DisCrit scholars self-identify as people of color with disabilities (Banks et al., in press; Padilla, in press). Their positionality, coupled with their scholarly commitments, inform their suggestions for practices to foster a more equitable education and society at large. Other researchers use DisCrit to call attention to practices that maintain and exacerbate inequities, and to call for change. For example, in Morgan's (2022) analysis of legal practices, she unpacks "public disorder" as the criminalization of poverty and the absence of understanding by law enforcement of race and disability. In another example, Annamma (2018) confronts the criminalization of difference in public schools that results in incarceration as a withholding of a meaningful education. In keeping with this topic, Cabral et al. (in press) interpret solidarity as a form of relational work in conjunction with critical pedagogy and curriculum when working with an incarcerated disabled girl of color. In addition, Payne-Tsoupros and Johnson (2022) call for the abolition of school police, documenting their negative effects.

The authors note how, in its focus on the interplay of racism and ableism, "DisCrit shows why particular groups of children are especially vulnerable to school police." Similarly, moving from a pedagogy of pathologization to one of empathy and care, Migliarini and Annamma (2019) offer practical ways for teachers to resist norms of hypersurveillance, hyperlabeling, and hyperpunishment, and work against the reproduction of societal inequities in classrooms.

CONCLUSION

In closing, we acknowledge that creating a DisCrit classroom ecology requires both novice and seasoned educators to foster deep antiracist and anti-ableist commitments to transformation, equity, and solidarity. We also realize that undoing racism and ableism is not sufficiently centered in many teacher education programs and in-service professional development. Cultivating a DisCrit classroom ecology is imperative, and yet there are many ways to approach this work through curriculum, pedagogy, and solidarity with students. Furthermore, we agree with Locke at al. (2022) when they write, "Educational research must embrace actual classroom practice to illuminate and refine theory. This conscious shift transforms theory from vision-based to action-based." In this way, even more radical possibilities can be actualized.

CHAPTER 7

Krip-Hop Nation Puts Back the Fourth Element of Hip-Hop
Knowledge with a Political Limp

Leroy F. Moore Jr. and Keith Jones

As Black disabled hip-hop artists and community activists, we recognize the importance of bringing the creative elements of hip-hop into teaching and learning to connect with Black and Brown students' lives and realities (Emdin, 2010). Hip-hop culture has impacted youth across the world, particularly Black and Brown youth, and has been used as a bridge into school subjects that leave behind African American, Latino/a, and Indigenous youth, like science (e.g. Adjapong & Emdin, 2015). The power of bringing hip-hop into the classroom is that it connects youth culture to their learning activities and goals, and uses complicated communication elements of hip-hop to explore issues that matter to them and their communities (Stovall, 2006). It also gives teachers a way to connect curriculum and teaching to students' identities and attention to social movements impacting Black and Brown communities.

But, even as teachers use the elements of hip-hop to connect and learn with their students, there are some issues with mainstream hip-hop that need to be called out. As Paris and Alim (2014) tell us, hip-hop can reproduce ideas and practices based on homophobia, misogyny, and racism, and must be interrogated. But it's more than that. Just like we've discussed about the hip-hop movement outside of schools, hip-hop as it has been used in schools has been absent of a disability framework and has erased and ignored the existence of Black, Brown, and Indigenous disabled people, artists, and communities. Also, hip-hop has reproduced the same ableism that exists in society and schools more broadly, such as using language like "crazy" and making fun of disabled people or even making them out to be the devil (Moore, 2017).

Because we love hip-hop, but also because of these issues, between 2004 and by 2007 we created with our friend Rob Da' Noize Temple a new movement in hip-hop called Krip-Hop Nation, a collective of hip-hop musicians with disabilities from all over the world that today has over 300 members. As people with disabilities, we knew about disabled people and what's important to us, but we didn't see that in mainstream media, including hip-hop. Leroy first spotlighted disabled hip-hop artists in the early 2000s, co-producing and co-hosting a three-part series on what he called *Krip-Hop* for a Berkeley, California, radio station. The series appeared on KPFA's *Pushing Limits*, a program focused on news, arts, and culture for the disabled community. The series' popularity inspired Leroy to collaborate with Keith and Rob to create Krip-Hop Nation for disabled musicians, since little cultural work or music by people with disabilities had been recognized. Krip-Hop Nation was born, toward the mission of advocacy, education, access, music, art, and justice issues that impact Black and Brown disabled communities, but also everyone.

Since this is a book about sustaining disabled youth at other identity intersections like race and sexual identity, we discuss Krip-Hop Nation to critique and extend hip-hop and other asset pedagogies (APs) so that Black disabled youth are sustained: that their talents, histories, and rights are understood and taught about in schools, and they are valued for the whole of who they are, including being disabled. In this chapter, as founders of Krip-Hop Nation, we talk a little bit about the beginning of how and why we formed Krip-Hop Nation and why and how we use Krip-Hop Nation's music, history, politics, new language, and theory to not only uplift our Black disabled community but to correct hip-hop and AP scholars, media creators, and the whole industry/culture about the absence of a disability framework. Then, we discuss how teachers and students can bring Krip-Hop Nation politics into schools and classrooms alongside and intersecting with other kinds of APs discussed in other chapters of this book.

LAYING THE FOUNDATIONS OF KRIP-HOP NATION: LEARNING AND MAKING BLACK DISABLED HISTORY

The origins of Krip-Hop Nation started with the first author of this chapter, founder Leroy F. Moore Jr. I am an African American writer, poet, and community activist with cerebral palsy. I was born in New York in 1967 to an activist father loosely connected to the Black Panthers. My father's record collection back in the late 1970s was my early education about being Black and disabled because I saw Black disabled male blues, jazz, and soul singers—from blind Willie Johnson to Walter Jackson with his crutches—on their album covers. I saw the album cover of the Black opera, *Porgy and Bess* (Gershwin et al., 1935), with a Black physically disabled man on it and it changed my life. I was empowered. But then I brought what I saw into my school and felt the first in a long line of oppressions I've experienced in education to hush hush that history, my full Black disabled identity. And continued to experience it, like the erasure in being taught about Harriet Tubman but not her disability and how she used her full identity to lead other Black people to freedom.

My upbringing sensitized me to the challenges faced by African Americans and the disabled. As a youth, I discovered that most people had little knowledge of the historical treatment and experiences of disabled African Americans, including Black disabled resistance. Black disabled resistance was not taught in schools, but it goes all the way back to the creation of the United States and every era from the capture of Africans to slavery to Jim Crow to the blues to the Black Civil Rights Movement to hip-hop.

As Black disabled man living in the 21st century who grew up in the disabled and Black community back on the East Coast in the 1970s and 1980s, I have seen how the Black community has been left behind in the disability movements, from civil rights that have led to disability pride, models of disability, disability arts/culture, and disability studies, and that also lead to publications like newsletters to magazines to news articles to books to movies. However, throughout history, Black disabled people have lived and resisted not only mainstream white nondisabled society and white disabled society, but also Black nondisabled society. I learned about the dozens, blues, Jim Crow, minstrel shows, medicine shows, freak shows, circus, the Black Arts Movement (BAM), the Black Power Movement, hip-hop, and beyond. Across all of these, Black disabled individuals not only resisted but also contributed to laying the foundations of hip-hop and other forms of cultural expression, like blind and disabled blues artists contributed to all kinds of music and arts today.

I also learned about the connection between *the dozens*, disability, and hip-hop. The dozens is a complicated verbal rhyming game that tests emotional strength and creativity. It is usually played by Black boys who take 12 turns insulting each other's families, especially their mothers (Majors & Billson, 1993). But the game also uses a lot of ableist comments about intelligence and bodies. Lewis (2017) raises this issue when talking to Black communities about our "humor, wit, rhyming, & signifyin'" as part of "Black Joy, Black Culture, Black Resistance and Black Love," but also teaches us, "Disability Ain't for Ya Dozens (or Demons)." TL tells us:

> The Black community is well known for our jovial nature, our tendency to use words that we think are less demeaning for family members and relatives with disabilities, and for invoking religion in response to revelations. Turns out that none of this uplifts our people's humanity. Not only does it contribute to stigma and discrimination against Black/Disabled people, but these make it that much more difficult for Black people to be loved, cherished and at peace within our own communities. Moreover, it perpetuates the violent oppression visited upon us by white people. (n.p.)

The ableism that shows up in hip-hop led Leroy to begin research, initially in the music industry, and connect how ableism in hip-hop is internalized and reproduced from the roots of how anti-Blackness and ableism has harmed and killed Black and Black disabled people.

GETTING TO KRIP-HOP NATION'S POLITICS

Krip-Hop Nation's tagline is *Krip-Hop is more than just music*. Krip-Hop Nation is a social movement that uses Black and youth culture toward liberation and recognition of the contributions and struggles of Black disabled communities. Krip-Hop Nation is a collective of musicians, artists, and activists who create and perform hip-hop music and apply hip-hop elements toward disability justice (Sins Invalid, 2015). But also, like we say in the title of this chapter, Krip-Hop extends the OG (original) elements of hip-hop to include the central element of Krip-Hop: *knowledge with a political limp*. Knowledge with a political limp means that Krip-Hop Nation is more than music and "bling bling"; it is about Black disabled political advocacy and education and taking back what has been taken from us to oppress us.

Even our first face-to-face meeting was political. It was at the 2004 Democratic National Convention in Boston, where we almost got kicked out because of all the questions we were asking about Black Disabled representation and access. After the DNC, we were in a music studio for Keith's latest CD at that time. Between songs Leroy asked Keith if he ever saw another physically disabled artist in hip-hop. We both laughed, then wrote out the framework of Krip-Hop Nation from this starting point: that disabled artists are erased in hip-hop, and that even though hip-hop is led mostly by Black artists, Black disabled artists are ignored and pushed out. Krip-Hop makes sure Black disabled artists are "seen" and perceived in hip-hop, and accounts for how they have been "unseen" and pushed out, and on the flip side, how ableist language has been used in hip-hop to oppress disabled, and especially Black disabled people. Leroy is now in his fifties and is still learning, creating, and trying to educate his communities and institutions about people with disabilities, especially Black disabled people, by using art, music and political activism throughout time and hoping to build a foundation for future little Leroy. However, before we get there fully, we must not only recognize the oppression but also set a way to unlearn so we can we can see the ways we oppress others in our own community.

Even though, in general, the Black nondisabled community in the 21st century uses a mixture of religious/charity models of disability, it's not all of their fault! Because of the oppression of early Africans in the United States and the violence and death inflicted on their bodies by enslavers and the state, the common practice of hiding disability meant life or death on top of the force of a new religion that taught about the "miracles" of healing disabled bodies. All this killing of bodies that couldn't work in a slavery/capitalist state shaped early African American's understanding of disability in their communities. We concur with Leary's (2005) proposition that African Americans experience what she has termed Post Traumatic Slave Syndrome (PTSS). Her thesis holds that the exploitation, pain, and trauma that endure in "slavery's afterlife" (Hartman, 2006) were produced from the pervasive dehumanization and indifference to the harms caused by slavery to Black people. Black people have never received acknowledgement, apology, compensation, or therapeutic treatment that would enable them to both cope with and make sense of the abuses, teachings of slavery, and the white supremacy that replaced it. How the Black nondisabled community's understandings of disability are connected with experiences of enslavement, therefore, have not been addressed either.

Reframing Hip-Hop Pedagogy with a Political Limp

In this section, we provide guidance to reframe hip-hop pedagogy around four areas: claiming space, reclaiming language, reframing disability, and education toward liberation.

Claiming Space

Krip-Hop Nation points out that Black disabled people are here, have been here, and are in the hip-hop, music, and art communities more broadly. It is important to point this out because Black disabled artists have been and continue to be erased in hip-hop. This is also what we find when we read and learn about what is out there about hip-hop pedagogy. Not only are Black and Brown disabled artists left out of the classroom, and need to be "seen," but cultural ways of communicating in Black disabled communities are also important as a way of reclaiming our space as knowers and knowledge producers. For example, in call and response (Smitherman, 1977) or co-MCing in the classroom, which are two hip-hop pedagogy approaches (Adjapong & Emdin, 2015), it is important for Black disabled communication styles to be acknowledged and embraced. This means pacing, volume, position in classroom, technologies, and timing need to be accessible and affirming.

Next, since 2004, Krip-Hop Nation has become an international collective and has put out many music projects, but where are they in the classroom and in schools? Krip-Hop MCs and musicians have performed internationally at festivals like DADAFest in Liverpool, UK, and have created new terminology, theory, books, films, and college lectures; Krip-Hop today is a subculture of hip-hop and our movement belongs in teaching and learning. Some examples include Leroy's book *Black Disabled Art History*

101 and Black Disabled Ancestors, as well as poetry and spoken word, lectures, and performances.

Keith's music is also important for classrooms, but he also shares his own educational experiences through lectures, films, and interviews. Many other creative, artistic, and historical resources by Black/Brown artists/activists with disabilities in organizations like Sins Invalid, National Black Disability Coalition, and Harriet Tubman Collective are also relevant to classrooms where Black/Brown disabled youth have been erased and excluded. These are resources for claiming space for Black disabled youth in schools.

Next, in many of his talks, Keith teaches about the low expectations he experienced in school, where many disabled students are expected to stay in high school for more than 4 years, and the shock of nondisabled people when disabled students go to college. And then as adults, nondisabled people have "no expectations of us doing anything besides collecting a check every month" (Jones, 2018). So, another way Krip-Hop can inform hip-hop pedagogy, and really any asset-based teaching and learning in schools, is by making sure Black youth with disabilities belong and that there are high expectations of them from teachers and other students. This can only happen if Black/Brown disabled youth claim space for themselves and what they know and want in their lives, but it also means educators have to make space where Black disabled youth are considered valuable and full members of school and classroom communities.

Overall, Krip-Hop Nation can offer educators, students, and community members more inclusive, open, and welcoming learning communities locally, nationally, and on an international level by reclaiming space for Black and Brown disabled people.

Reclaiming Language and Reframing Disability

Like for other oppressed groups, the power to define the language of who we are was taken from people with disabilities and language was turned on us to oppress us. Before people with disabilities had civil rights, a movement, and arts, many placed labels on us like "crazy," "lame," "cripple," and "retarded." Of course, now with our civil rights and disability studies and culture, we have named ourselves and used the negative terms to our own benefit, not only to shock people but to respect that these words are our history and we must reclaim them and flip them into a cultural and political lens that shapes a process of unlearning and relearning. This is at the heart of Krip-Hop Nation's politics.

Connected to Krip-Hop Nation's politics is its own lingo. Leroy has explained that Krip-Hop" is a play on "Hip-Hop." Although the "Krip" part of the name refers to "crippled," it is spelled with a "K" to avoid association with the Crips. But more importantly, this spelling uses Black culture wordplay to change standard English spelling; Krip is our Black disabled reclaiming of the term "Crip" that had been reclaimed by white disability communities from ableist language and individuals.

Next, as we know, terminology and the power to define language about your identity is important. Most often new terminology originates in the streets, as it started in games like the dozens for hip-hop. Related to disability, often academia adopts new disability language, giving legitimacy to the work of disabled folks, but without acknowledging their work and therefore delegitimizing and erasing them. Most of the language of disability has been taken from us, including by those in medical industry and school educators and special education professionals. Krip-Hop Nation politics can inform APs to make sure students with disabilities/disabled students get to define themselves as they interact with more resources and materials from people who look, sound, talk, communicate, and move like them. Until we take back our identities through language, redefine them, politicize them, and sometimes change them altogether, our work and who we are will continue to be defined by others.

We also have to do the same when communicating about the way oppression impacts Black disabled people and communities. Here's an example: although the term *ableism* has been defined by disability advocates from dominant culture, if you put Black in front of anything coming out of disability it must first be stripped down, then reshaped and reinterpreted through the experiences, histories, and words of Black disabled people. By now, we must know that the Black disabled experience in America has different roots than our white disabled counterparts; the same is true about the forms and impacts of exclusion from education for white versus Black disabled youth. Because of the need of Black disabled people to heal our wounds inflicted by our Black community, one by one or collectively, it is imperative that we tell our stories and define new terminology, definitions, art, music, and political views and provide education and resources for our Black community. That is why Leroy has coined the term *Black Ableism*, while knowing there are many Black disabled people who have thought about and experienced this phenomenon. We know that the definition of ableism is generally about discrimination and social prejudice against people with disabilities or who are perceived to have disabilities. Ableism characterizes persons as defined by their disabilities and as inferior to the nondisabled. On this basis, people are assigned or denied certain perceived abilities, rights, skills, or character orientations. But if we take this definition and apply it at the intersection of the Black experience reaching back from the capture and shipping of slaves to the teaching of disability and the harming and killing of our bodies, almost everything we have done helped shaped Black Ableism toward Black disabled people.

Black Ableism is discrimination and social prejudice against Black people with disabilities or those who are perceived to have disabilities from nondisabled people as far back as slavery. For example, enslavers used disability as a reason to devalue an enslaved person because of what he/she could/could not contribute to the plantation. And we, a new people who emerged out of slavery, also saw by the enslaver's example that disability meant devalued. Therefore, Black people internalized that disability was a sin, something that needed to be healed using the outdated religious model of disability mixed with the tragedy/charity model of disability that says that disability is essentially a test of faith in order to be saved from one's disability. That means that if the person does not experience the physical healing of their disability, he or she is regarded as having a lack of faith in God, is a victim of circumstance, and is deserving of pity.

This means that how disability is defined for Black and Brown youth has to be reframed too, especially in other APs where disability has remained an object of pity in otherwise critical approaches to teaching and learning like hip-hop pedagogy (Paris & Alim, 2017). Teaching and learning activities have to surface and root out Black (and of course all) ableism, because it can cause many deep-rooted problems in a Black disabled youth and adult—ranging from low self-esteem to trying to overcome or hide one's disability to, most importantly, not having a community.

When it comes to reframing disability, we have to start by recognizing the ableism in most communities and schools and how this works together with racism, and then reframe Black disability as political, historical, and cultural. So, Krip-Hop Nation's politics can also teach APs that focus on race and disabilities, that Black Ableism can only be eradicated by stripping what the Black community has been taught about disability through the lens of oppression and then rebuilding. This rebuilding process must be conducted by coordinated teams and resources created by Black disabled people, family members, and yes, educators, who have had a presence in both the disability and Black communities. For Black disabled students and their families, the rebuilding will lead to a path of Black disabled youth empowerment and a commonality with our Black community. The Black community will be all the richer by embracing our disabled sisters and brothers from a historical, political, participatory, and cultural way of life.

Education Toward Liberation

Racial justice activists, including those in education, have been working toward liberation through and outside schooling for a long time. But school treatment of disabled students is dominated by a special education framework that still considers disability something that needs to be fixed or cured in a student. Krip-Hop Nation politics, all of them, are toward empowerment and deep education. This is desperately needed in the Black community, the Black disabled community, and in the hip-hop arena whether it is in or out of schools.

To bring Krip-Hop Nation's politics in line with goals of other APs like hip-hop and Culturally Sustaining Pedagogy and even UDL, we must approach the goal of Black disabled empowerment and liberation as a building process that might take a while to go through, as youth may have to go through stages to question mainstream special education and to unlearn what has been forced on them about disability. Black disabled empowerment as a goal of a curriculum informed by Krip-Hop politics intentionally examines and overturns students' erasure, exploitation, pity, and "overcoming" disability. Krip-Hop politics also examine identity politics that pressure youth to hide or downplay aspects of their identities that aren't seen as having as much importance (usually disability), alongside intersectional community empowerment that accounts for disability as much as anything also that makes someone who they are. As they are exposed to knowledge from Black/disabled artists and activists from around the world, through songs, poetry, visual arts, and writing, students can step up and help to correct how society views us as persons and artists with disabilities.

Altogether, the beliefs and commitments of Krip-Hop Nation have led us to new and exciting possibilities to continue to grow and build our communities, our tools for resistance, and our solidarity across oppressed groups. Krip-Hop Nation politics can inform teaching and learning to do the same and create schools and classrooms where Black/Brown and other disabled youth use their talents to advocate and teach not only about themslves but about the system we live under as it pertains to being a person of color in conjunction with having a disability, and challenging mainstream and even asset-based curriculum on ways they frame disability. Curricula and teaching that center Black disabled people, experiences, and resources also recognize our Black disabled ancestors, knowing that we are building on what they left us, and that nothing is new, just borrowed. Krip-Hop Nation politics also teaches our youth in schools about and toward disability solidarity and collaboration around the world.

Krip-Hop Nation's politics requires building processes that move us from erasure, exploitation, and pity to identity politics of self-empowerment, to seeing ourselves politically and culturally through speaking, singing/rapping, and writing. Krip-Hop Nation means living with an activist lens on what affects us and our allies in our communities and organizations. Through song, poetry, visual arts, and writing, we realize that we are stepping up and correcting how society views us as Black men with a disability/artists with disabilities, and at the same time we know we wear many hats: those we wear when want to advocate and those we wear when we just want to celebrate.

CHAPTER 8

Breaking Down Barriers
Hearing from Children to Learn to Teach Inclusively in Bilingual Education

Patricia Martínez-Álvarez and Minhye Son

When teaching bilingual children with a disability, the unique intersection of language, culture, race, and dis/ability[1] differences often becomes an amalgamation of labels (i.e., English language learners or ELLs and disability labels), which does not accurately define them. For children carrying multiple labels in our school systems, it is important that their multilayered identities are considered and fostered simultaneously in balanced ways (Crenshaw, 1991).

Even though many children experience intersecting forms of differences, asset pedagogies (APs) in bilingual and bicultural education have not traditionally accounted for disability. As a result, APs have failed to recognize and address the multilayered forms of exclusion bilingual children with a disability experience in schools. For instance, children learning at the intersection of language and dis/ability differences in schools might be relegated to taking on an identity of needing "help" and "care," rather than being empowered to enact agency (Tronto, 1993). This contradicts the germaneness of learning from children and their families and communities reported in bilingual and bicultural education funds of knowledge (FoK) research (Moll, 2014). That is, complex urban systems might, at times even inadvertently, aim to assimilate bilingual children with a disability into "culturally normative ways," keeping the rich knowledge and practices of minoritized children outside of our classrooms (Greenstein, 2014, p. 382).

Integrating children's practices and knowledge (e.g., FoK) into the school curriculum requires the nurturing of the volitional actions diverse children take as they enact agency (Martínez-Álvarez, 2020). Originating from the Latin verb meaning "to will" or "to wish," a volitional act is a human psychological function defined as the "act of making a choice or decision," which, however, involves a socially cultivated "power to choose" (Merriam-Webster, n.d.). This chapter aims to remediate the limited attention given to disability by APs focusing on bilingual and bicultural education. To achieve this purpose, we explore the agentive dynamics that took place as bilingual children with and without a disability were invited to participate in reflective conversations after student teachers taught lessons.

In this chapter, we chose to use "person-first" language (as in "children with a disability"), instead of "identity-first" language (Hypoxi-Ischemic Encephalopathy [HIE] Help Center, 2017), such as "disabled children." With this choice, we aim to center the bilingual children who, while being identified with a disability, might not refer to themselves as disabled individuals. The reasons for this might connect to the historical deficit perspectives on the learning of bilingual children (Greenfield, 2013), to the negative consequences that disability labels often have for minoritized children, or to aspects of the well-documented misdiagnosis of disabilities with bilingual children (Ortiz et al., 2011). Nonetheless, we recognize that identity changes fluidly (Gee, 2000), and the ways through which children and their families integrate disability identity could evolve along the child's life (Gill, 1997).

In the sections that follow, the chapter first defines the key terms used to explore surfacing agentive dynamics, including examples and explanations about how these concepts contribute to expanding APs to account for disability. It then provides an overview of the project used to explore these dynamics. Employing vignettes from this project, the chapter consequently illustrates an intersectional analysis centered on the volitional actions that participants took and the circumstances and reactions surrounding these agentive efforts. The chapter concludes by synthesizing the main arguments and contributions and providing recommendations for classroom practice.

DEFINITION OF THEORETICAL CONSTRUCTS

Building on cultural-historical activity theory (CHAT), this chapter employs the concept of hybrid space and the Vygotskian process of double stimulation. The constructs of agency as manifested in the volitional actions that children take, and the consequent collective responses that these actions ensue, are used to explain the process of double stimulation. These constructs, defined in the following subsections, are tools to expand APs through a radical inclusive pedagogical approach that attends to intersecting forms of exclusion by accounting for disability as culture.

Radical Inclusive Pedagogy and Asset Pedagogies

Radical inclusive pedagogy centers the need "to promote an understanding of learning as contextualized and relational" (Greenstein, 2016, p. 80). However, current neoliberal ideologies have led to a view of education as an "end product that needs to be effectively manufactured" (Greenstein, 2016,

p. 81). Contrary to this view of learning as a product, this chapter asserts a view of education as a process that assists children in constructing their multiple ways of being in relation with others, without being forced onto fixed identities (Greenstein, 2016).

Traditionally disability is relegated to a separate space within research efforts embracing critical pedagogy (Freire, 1972), funds of knowledge (Moll, 2014), or any of the theories requiring direct attention to culture in education such as culturally relevant pedagogy (Ladson-Billings, 1994), among others. Scholars in the critical disability studies have consequently denounced the absence of disability as a cultural trait (Greenstein, 2016). Employing CHAT can help in remediating historical monolithic views of difference.

Cultural Historical Activity Theory

CHAT builds on the legacy of Lev Semyonovich Vygotsky (1896–1934), and his main contribution of learning as being always mediated by humans during active participation in endeavors (Vygotsky, 1978). CHAT hence centers the role of the educational context as children engage in learning activity, and the role that agency and the resulting volitional actions children take have in learning processes (Vygotsky, 1978). From a CHAT perspective, it is essential that critical forms of agency are recognized as socially produced and culturally mediated (Vygotsky, 1978). With its emphasis in cultural-historical mediated action, CHAT can promote radical inclusive pedagogies that simultaneously account for both bilingualism and biculturalism and disability. The concept of hybrid space can help in theorizing such accounts and recognizing the multiplicity of cultural traits, including disability.

Hybrid Space

There is a need to foster hybrid learning spaces where disability is situated as a cultural asset as much as bilingualism and biculturalism (Martínez-Álvarez, 2020). For that, it is important to realize that a hybrid space is a contested space where different and at times contrasting cultures and knowledge enter contact with potential mutual qualitative transformation (Bhabha, 1994). This is directly connected to the relevance of validating and integrating minoritized children's resources in education, both bilingual and bicultural as well as disability-related resources. For instance, bilingualism and biculturalism and disability differences can be recognized as cultural traits and be more equally embraced when teachers validate children's ways of speaking (i.e., translanguaging), their home and communities' knowledge and practices (i.e., community cultural wealth), and their multiple ways of multimodal meaning making (e.g., reading printed texts but also using visuals or audio-recorded resources, allowing various ways to expressing knowledge like drawing or speaking rather than always writing, or situating children with a disability as knowledgeable experts across topics). Opportunities for bilingual children with a disability to enact agency through individual volitional actions that are considered at the collective level are essential in generating hybrid learning spaces.

The Construct of Agency

Attending to different layers of difference simultaneously involves ensuring that bilingual children with a disability have certain control over their learning. However, bilingual children with a disability might enact agency in ways that are not fully recognized or fostered in educational processes. For instance, they might take action to deviate a potentially difficult activity by avoiding the classroom or resisting to engage in a proposed task.

Erevelles (2000, p. 32) has called for a reconfiguration of "human agency" in the context of disability. The author explained that "[d]isabled scholars and activists . . . have sought to define a disability culture that is based on the recognition of their *different* bodies—not in spite of their disabilities but because of them" (p. 32). This idea supports a view of disability as central to the experience of the person with a disability. Our understandings of agency must expand from the traditionally accepted psychological and *individualistic* perspective. Rather, agency must be understood as part of a cycle of *collective* recognition of the volitional actions that individuals take and as situated in the cultural historical contexts where agency is enacted.

Volitional Actions as Manifestations of Agency

As bilingual children with a disability enact agency, they take volitional actions (i.e., willingly act upon things to alter their circumstances). While individuals themselves might originate the volitional actions, children's actions can only expand and become transformative through "collaboration and collective agency" (Haapasaari et al., 2014, p. 258). That is, when a child expects not to succeed in a reading activity and proposes a different direction for the activity, such volitional action will not assist the child in exploring different identities, unless the teacher and peers attend and respond to the child's proposal (Martínez-Álvarez et al., 2020). In this sense, volitional actions become meaningful when they are embraced collectively through transformative agency, which is explained by the process of double stimulation (Sannino, 2020).

The Process of Double Stimulation

Agency has historically been interpreted as being enacted through self-regulatory systems from a psychological standpoint (Bandura, 1989). Advanced from this view, CHAT builds on a renewed perspective about agency focused on individual's volitional actions enacted while working with others in a shared learning effort. As human beings work together, they bring artifacts to mediate their activity (i.e., beliefs, knowledge, language), as well as other cultural historical aspects such as their ways of dividing labor (i.e., who does what in a classroom), or rules to guide their efforts (i.e., children must raise their hands before sharing and respond when asked a question) that are different for the different individuals within the groups involved. For instance, a Latinx child might not want to directly respond to a teacher's question when in the whole-group setting because of cultural differences in the ways children communicate with adults.

As these different cultural historical elements collide, it is typical for the participants to experience "conflict of motives" (Sannino, 2015, p. 2). In this example, the child might want to remain silent but feels the pressure to respond to the teacher. To address this arising conflict, the child will take volitional actions using artifacts. For instance, the child in this scenario could point to the answer, or turn to a peer, rather than speak. In Vygotsky's (1978) terms, such process is conceptualized as the principle of double stimulation, with the first stimulus being the conflict of motives (e.g., the child's desire to remain silence conflicting with the social pressure to answer) and the second stimulus being the volitional action that draws on artifacts intended to mediate a collective pathway out of the conflict (e.g., pointing or turning to a peer instead of speaking). In this sense, from a CHAT perspective, efforts to promote the volitional actions of bilingual children with a disability, and the recognition of their agentive enactments, can be promoted through this Vygotskian (1978) proposed process of "double stimulation." Through the process of double stimulation, children "can intentionally break out of conflicting motives and change their circumstances" (Sannino, 2020, p. 7).

The CHAT-based theoretical constructs defined above can help expand APs as they are tools to analyze and understand children's volitional actions and the collective negotiation that takes place with bilingual children with a disability. This chapter provides examples from a teacher learning project that show how bilingual children with and without a disability enacted agency and the potential conflicts of motives they were trying to address.

The project employed to illustrate the ideas in this chapter took place across three dual language bilingual programs. A dual language bilingual program (DLBP) is a form of bilingual education where teachers and children use two languages to learn content and language and which has multiple positive learning outcomes for all children (Lindholm-Leary, 2001). Given the benefits children gain from learning bilingually, ensuring that these programs attend to and serve children with a disability is essential, and expanding APs can help in achieving more inclusive DLBPs.

When learning in DLBPs, opportunities to enact agency are important to allow multiply diverse children to learn within "in-between" spaces, where they can more safely take risks and experiment with different identities.

Such spaces required careful planning and dedicated attention to cultivate the efforts of bilingual children with a disability (Martínez-Álvarez, 2020). A summary description of the project employed to illustrate the ideas in this chapter follows.

OVERVIEW OF THE PROJECT

As mentioned, the study from which this chapter drew illustrative examples took place in three highly diverse public elementary schools with DLBPs (two Spanish and one Mandarin) in a large northeastern city in the United States. Twenty-three children, several of whom were simultaneously labeled as ELLs and as having a disability, participated in the first few minutes of the reflective conversations following lesson observations. Children's disability labels typically included specific learning disability (SLD), speech and language impairment (SLI), and/or autism spectrum disorder (ASD). Ten bilingual and racially diverse educators (i.e., four student teachers, four mentor teachers, and two university supervisors) took part in these post-lesson reflective conversations.

There were 11 post-lesson conversations in this project where the student teacher, their mentor teacher, and their university supervisor from each participating school reflected about lessons guided by the student teacher. Two to three children, who had participated in the lesson, were invited to share their ideas for a few minutes after student teachers taught lessons in content areas or literacy using the children's home language for instruction.

RESPONDING TO CHILDREN'S VOLITIONAL ACTIONS

The review of the post-lesson conversations showed that children took multiple volitional actions manifesting agency, and that some conversations mediated children's agency more than others. However, educators did not always use the opportunity of having the children in the collective conversations to learn from them. That is, the children's expressions of wills were not always consequential at the collective level. Rather, at times, the educators situated the children as the novice, less knowledgeable members of the group, hence mediating fewer actions (Young-Bruehl, 2012). When children were able to take more volitional actions, educators did not always readily accept their efforts to critically reflect on and/or propose changes to the lessons. Two vignettes are used to illustrate these observations.

1. The Journey to Critically Reflect and Learn from the Children

There were post-lesson conversations when children were encouraged to enact agency and took multiple volitional actions. Even in these instances, however, the process did not automatically result in the student teacher's commitment to transform the learning space. This was shown during Rachel's first post-lesson conversation, a discussion with a high number of agentive turns. During the lesson, Rachel invited the children to complete a worksheet showing the distributive property of multiplication. Whenever Rachel, a white student teacher who spoke Spanish as a second language, wanted the children to pay attention to her, she would musically recite the following words: "¡Bajen sus lápices! ↑ ¡Manos arriba! ↑ ¡Ojos al frente! ↑ " (Put down your pencils! ↑ Hands up! ↑ Eyes in front! ↑). This can be referred to, in Spanish, as a "cantinela" (i.e., a chant, tune, or ditty).

One of the children, Braylon, a Black African American English-speaking boy, who was labeled with a disability, grew increasingly annoyed during the lesson with this "cantinela" as he visibly puffed and rolled his eyes every time Rachel recited it. Braylon was invited to stay for the collective conversation along with Gracen, a Black African American English-speaking girl with a disability label. During the discussion, I asked Braylon about his reaction:

Patricia: You remember when you were working and all of a sudden it was time to stop? And you had to leave your pencil?
Braylon: Yeah.
Patricia: ¡Lápices al centro! ↑ ¡Manos arriba! ↑ ¡Ojos al frente! ↑ (Pencils to the center! ↑ Hands up! ↑ Eyes to the front! ↑)
Braylon: [Interrupting the speaker] Do we have to . . . do you have to say this every day? Manos arriba ↑ on and on.
Rachel: [Laughter.]
Patricia: ¿No te gusta mucho eso, no Braylon? (You don't really like that, do you Braylon?)
Braylon: No!
Patricia: ¿Qué paso allí? ¿Querías decir que no habías terminado? (What happened here? Did you mean to say that you weren't done?)
Braylon: S::í [softly] (Y::es.)
Patricia: ¿Cómo te sentiste? ¿Nos quieres contar? (How did you feel? Do you want to tell us?)
Braylon: [Head nods up and down.]
Rachel: When you have to stop working on a problem, how do you feel?
Braylon: Mmm [hand motion indicating not so good.]
Rachel: Why do you feel "mmm" [imitating Braylon's hand motion]?
Braylon: Because I don't have to see the hard stuff.
Patricia: You don't have to see the hard stuff?
Braylon: Yeah.
Patricia: What do you mean by that?

Braylon: The hard problems.
Rachel: So, do you like stopping in the middle of the problem, or do you like to finish it?
Braylon: I like to finish it most of the time [. . .] Because, because when you say it all the time it's so annoying!

In this part of this vignette, Braylon took a volitional action, even interrupting the speaker, to express his annoyance toward the cantinela by saying, "do you have to say this every day?" and rolling his eyes. Initially Braylon's action was taken by the collective in respectful ways that appeared to be trying to understand more about his feelings. This is shown by the open-ended questions asked after his volitional action took place.

However, the teacher candidate then tried to deflect the discussion toward the circumstance of having to stop "in the middle of the problem," while Braylon's words stated the issue as rather being the constant repetition of the cantinela itself. At this point, Braylon took a new volitional action as he answered Rachel's question but then went back to his original complaint with the cantinela, "because when you say it all the time it's so annoying!" The following parts of the vignettes expanded upon this idea.

The mentor teacher then asked Gracen, the other girl in the conversation about her thoughts regarding the cantinela. As Gracen was explaining that "[i]t does help cuz some people, they drop it on the floor, they play with it," Braylon jumped in, "But that noise!" Here, Rachel accepted Gracen's response without further inquiry into it, contrary to what she had done earlier with Braylon.

Toward the end of the exchange, Braylon took another volitional action as he suggested a different way in which Rachel could get children's attention, "[W]hen it's ti[me], you can like talk, and then everyone will pay attention and put their pencils down." Rachel closed the topic as she responded, "Okay, that's nice," a statement without much recognition of the power in Braylon, a child who might be perceived as needing help and guidance in school (due to historical processes related to his label and to him being a child of color), generating an alternative to her controversial cantinela.

As soon as the children left, Rachel explained how Braylon "got in trouble like a minute before coming in here and he was almost sent to the principal's office. . . . So, that probably affected his mood." In providing this information, she suggested that this previous event had affected Braylon's opinion. In this way, she appeared to be trying to discredit his negative evaluation of the cantinela.

In this vignette, Braylon's disability and racial identities are reflected in his way of expressing ideas. Since Braylon is labeled with a disability, he at times expressed things in direct ways that might not always have fully observed social implicit norms (i.e., saying you do not like something about the other person's teaching as he did here for instance, or focusing on the sensorial aspects of the event—"But that noise!"). Black children's cultural ways of expressing needs and wishes and enacting agency in classrooms might also be perceived in negative ways. Particularly, Black male students have historically been situated by educational systems, where teachers are mostly white, as aggressive and as not being interested in education (Connor et al., 2008). The overrepresentation in special education categories ensuing from these historical processes manifests the ways Black children's actions are perceived as emotionally inappropriate or as a sign of having lower ability to learn.

However, Braylon's actions should have been situated as an asset in this context where the group wants to receive feedback from the children so that the teacher candidate can learn to create more inclusive bilingual education contexts. It is not immediately clear that Braylon's sincerity is perceived as an asset by the student teacher, who tried to avert the problem onto a different direction.

The educators' conversation shifted after this onto different topics, but eventually Rachel brought back the issue with the cantinela:

> *Rachel:* I think [the cantinela] kind of worked. At least for the first like two-thirds of the lesson, most of them were putting their pencils in the middle . . . if he [Braylon] hates it, I don't know why he's helping me so much with it.

These words once again point to Rachel's resistance in, not only accepting that the dynamic was annoying for Braylon, but in more deeply reflecting on her instruction and on potential changes she could do to allow him to be a better learner. Rachel, a teacher who is familiar with FoK theories, could have been inclined to accept knowledge more directly connected to Braylon's home and community cultural experiences. On the contrary, she did not recognize his volitional actions as part of Braylon's assets or cultural knowledge.

2. Situating Children as the Less Knowledgeable Group Members

There were several instances during the post-lesson conversations where the educators fostered the identity of less knowledgeable group members on the children. These are illustrated using Tung-Mei's (a Chinese student teacher of color) first post-lesson conversation. Children were creating and solving subtraction word problems in the context of mooncakes, traditionally enjoyed during the Chinese Mid-Autumn festival. Examples included subtracting zero from a number.

Two Chinese American children were invited to share their ideas about the lesson. Weici, a Chinese student of color, spoke mostly Cantonese Chinese at home, and Tingzhe, also a Chinese student of color, spoke mostly English at home. While they did not have a disability, these children were atypical in this context in that, while they were racially Chinese, they did not speak Mandarin Chinese (i.e., the lesson's language of instruction) as a home language. In this sense, the vignette speaks to volitional efforts at the intersection of race and language, and the potentially disabling consequences of language competence expectations. The following excerpt shows how the mentor teacher tested and lectured the children, rather than listening to them, during the discussion:

> *Mentor Teacher:* 你学了什么数学？ (What did you learn in math class?)
> *Weici:* If you delete a number by zero, it would be zero.
> . . .
> *Mentor Teacher:* 你刚刚说你如果有一个数字对不对？你减去一样的数字，等于零吗？对不对？那刚刚那个是减去全部还是减去零？
> (You just said that you have a number, right? You subtract it by the same number, is the result zero? Right? Then was that number subtracted by the whole or by zero?)
> *Weici:* . . . [No answer.]

In this part of the exchange, the mentor teacher asked Weici to provide an example of what they had learned during the math class. Weici provided a general description—"If you delete a number by zero"—of what the lesson had been about. However, in the answer Weici stated that "it would be zero," which would be erroneous because when deleting zero from a number, the result would be the same number. As the mentor teacher noticed this, she reformulated Weici's statement to match the answer zero rather than trying to stay with Weici's original idea that corresponded with the focus of the lesson.

At this time, Weici probably felt a conflict because while her statement was about subtracting zero from a number, the mentor teacher now had switched to a number subtracted by itself so that it would have zero as the answer. Weici stayed silent, which *was* a volitional action.

This beginning segment of the vignette manifested how the mentor teacher did not really follow the knowledge that Weici was putting forth about the lesson, but rather restated the problem in a radically different direction. Given that Weici was speaking in English, and she is a child of color who speaks Cantonese Chinese,[2] the complexity of the language in the content of mathematics appeared to also play a role. In fact, Weici stated knowledge about the math class in a way that the mentor teacher might not have immediately recognized as she stated "delete a number by zero" rather than the more canonical form of "subtracting a number from zero" or the form the teacher later stated in Mandarin Chinese of "subtracting it by the same number."

With the best of her intentions the teacher hence, rather than carefully listening to Weici and following her thinking, reformulated Weici's ideas onto a different one so radically that the new example no longer directly represented the learning in the math lesson they had completed. This process resulted in Weici staying silent.

A more inclusive space for Weici's ideas could have taken place if the mentor teacher had, instead, recognized the statement as, while being unusually expressed, perfectly understandable, and if she had moved onto trying to follow Weici's idea of "delete a number by zero" (i.e., subtract zero from a number). The conversation would have also gone in a direction more aligned with what the children had learned in the math lesson. Instead, as shown next, the conversation stayed in this idea of subtracting a number from itself.

The following segment took place next in this vignette:

Mentor Teacher: 好，那 Tingzhe 帮忙。Weici 刚刚讲的例子是减去全部还是减去零？(Ok, Tingzhe can help. In the example Weici was just talking about was the number subtracted by the whole or by zero?)

Tingzhe: 减去全部 (By the whole number.)

Here, the teacher is dominating the direction of the conversation toward her own restatement of Weici's idea and how Tingzhe decided to agree with her reformulation. She is also almost giving up in continuing the exchange with Weici. While we here see Tingzhe enacting actions, the direction of the discussion is dominated by the mentor teacher and her own idea.

The conversation continued as the mentor teacher asked Tingzhe to formulate an example following what they had learned in the math lesson (subtracting zero from a number):

Mentor Teacher: 那 Tingzhe 给老师一个例子，一个减去零的例子。讲月饼吧，知道你很喜欢吃月饼 (Then Tingzhe give the teacher an example, one with which the number is subtracted by zero. Tell me about mooncakes, I know you enjoy mooncakes very much.)

Tingzhe (student): 我有五个月饼，你吃了五个月饼 (I have five mooncakes. You ate five mooncakes.)

Tung-Mei (student teacher): 那我还有几个月饼？(Then how many mooncakes left?)

Tingzhe: 你还有零个月饼 (You have zero.)

Mentor Teacher: 刚刚那个是减去全部还是减去零？(That was subtracted by the whole or by zero?)

Tingzhe: 减去全部 (The whole.)

In this final segment of the vignette, Tingzhe stayed in the direction the mentor teacher (supported by Tung-Mei, the student teacher) had marked, even though the teacher wanted them to give her an example that would resonate with the math lesson. In a sense, the actions Tingzhe, a child of color who speaks English at home, took can be described as efforts to comply with the teacher's expected answers.

During this conversation, which continues in the same direction for several additional exchanges, children had little room for enacting meaningful agency in ways that could alter the direction of the conversation. As the mentor teacher asked multiple questions in a row, the children either stayed silent or answered the educators' prompts. However, the conversation ended, deviating from what the teacher had initially requested. Furthermore, this conversation was meant to be an opportunity for the teacher candidate to learn about the children's impressions about her lesson and obtain suggestions to make her teaching more inclusive of bilingual children with and without a disability directly from the children. Instead of bilingual children being at the center, and the adults following their volitional actions collectively, the opposite ended up taking place.

It is at the very end of their time in the conversation that Weici enacted a volitional action that could have potentially shifted some of the established power dynamics, when she said before leaving the group, "I need my sweater." As she expressed this unprompted need, Weici could have been sensing that the embedded rule (i.e., teachers are in charge) could now be altered. However, the mentor teacher responded, "不用 sweater 了啦" (You don't need your sweater), and in this way, she still retained the control, and the power hierarchies were once again sustained, leaving little space for these children's ideas to be included meaningfully in the classroom space.

LEARNING FROM BRAYLON, WEICI, AND TINGZHE

The perspective of Vygotsky's (1978) double stimulation helped elucidate and contextualize children's volitional actions in this study. All the volitional actions children took can be understood as efforts from children to break away from conflicts of motives they encountered in their experiences and efforts to transform the situation to their advantage (Sannino, 2020). Their actions demonstrate the potential in nurturing hybrid spaces where children can experiment with different identities, a space for being "in-between" otherwise dichotomized binaries such as ability/disability or bilingual/language learner (Martínez-Álvarez, 2020).

This study also manifested how, even when spaces are choreographed to hear from bilingual children with and without a disability, they can continue to be relegated to the condition of needing help (Tronto, 1993). This was shown, for example, in the way Weici and Tingzhe were positioned during the collective conversation. While the children demonstrated their understanding by giving the correct answers as well as generating novel word problems, their actions were highly dominated by the educators' initiations.

Such dynamics showed how traditional rules and power differences guiding teaching and learning can remain stubbornly intact.

The journey shown in the first vignette as Rachel hears from Braylon and Gracen, both Black African American children with a disability, also manifested similar power differences. In the data from that conversation, we witnessed how difficult it was for Rachel to take into consideration, and to center, Braylon's needs as she instead prioritized the average learner (i.e., "most of them were putting their pencils in the middle"). While Braylon's unique perspectives were disregarded, "culturally normative ways" of being in the class were privileged (Greenstein, 2014).

IMPLICATIONS AND CONCLUSION

Having children join the collective discussions with the multiple educators was organizationally very complicated. However, even when the educators managed to have children stay for the conversations, they did not always use this opportunity to learn from them nor showed respect for the different ways the children were responding, either due to their bilingualism or to their disability cultural aspects. At other times, children's individual efforts were not fully taken upon the collective and their potentially transformative effect was wasted.

This chapter has several implications for those working with bilingual children with and without a disability. As shown in the vignettes, there is learning potential in nurturing hybrid spaces where children can experiment with different identities. Children with a disability need to feel that their contributions are recognized and taken seriously. For those who carry both bilingual and bicultural and disability layers of difference, it is even more important that teachers, teacher educators, administrators, and/or community members foster a space for being "in-between." That is, a space where otherwise dichotomized binaries such as ability/disability or bilingual/language learner are part of the same continuum, and where these twofold dimensions, and those in between, are perceived as assets for learning (Martínez-Álvarez, 2020). This idea can be enacted by promoting conversations where children speak to their own learning experience, and where their responses are carefully documented and taken up by the collective for radical transformation. Children must experience follow-up action taken upon their contributions so that they do not lose faith in the power they have in transforming their learning experience. Finally, it is important that those working with children who learn at the intersection of languages, cultures, and abilities understand a range of APs and apply them in balanced ways to the different layers of difference children embody.

Part III

ON NURTURING TEACHERS AND EDUCATIONAL LEADERS

CHAPTER 9

Of the Insubstantiality of "Special" Worlds

Curricular Cripistemological Practices as Asset Pedagogy in Teacher Education

Linda Ware, David Mitchell, and Sharon Snyder

In this chapter, the authors consider the potential for disability studies in education to inform asset-based teaching and learning within the context of teacher preparation, as it currently exists. We contend that the persistent failure of teacher education to respond to students with disabilities outside the historic and systemic framework of remediation and repair all but ensures that an asset pedagogy (AP) approach to teaching and learning will fail. We have written elsewhere (Mitchell et al., 2014) of our own efforts to advance what we have termed "curricular cripistemologies" based on several national and local projects wherein our collaboration sought to reform pedagogical content for teachers informed by the lens of disability studies. Our goal in this chapter is to demonstrate how deficit-based approaches in special education deliver disabled students into the shadowy worlds of insubstantiality that it wishes them to inhabit. In occupying this shadowy terrain of shadowy schools operating below the surface to survive, disabled students learn to understand themselves as a kind of plankton that bigger fish devour. Instead, our approach argues that these shadowy worlds are made up of the discarded critiques of normative ("typical") worlds that disability brings to the surface and provides the basis of what "special" people think of the devalued assets to which they are consigned and those who would consign them there.

MAKING IMPOSSIBILITIES: FORECLOSURES ON SOME LIVES AND DESIRES

Each of us brings to this conversation experience as academics who cross institutional borders in our efforts to support educators. We have long advanced the need to expand teacher preparation in schools of education through rigorous and systematic disruption of status quo approaches to understanding disability. This decades-long partnership is succinctly encapsulated by Snyder in the excerpt below (2002):

> We need curricula that engage disabled students about their own history and culture. If our educational establishments neglect to promote those with disabilities as capable individuals, then disabled students will not succeed. Unfortunately, our public schools regard educating students with disabilities as a remediation issue.

This text appeared in the national call for participation in the first National Endowment for the Humanities (NEH) seminar on disability studies in 2004. At the time, we had prior experience with teachers in Rochester, New York, supported by grants received by Ware. Informed by the success of those projects, we developed a 5-week NEH residential seminar for teachers funded by the NEH that aimed to foreground the problem of an exclusively remedial approach to the education of disabled students. The seminar provided educators the opportunity to design collaborative curriculum projects infused with interdisciplinary disability content. We encouraged educators to pivot away from an emphasis on disabled students as the target for remediation, and to instead recognize the value of their own remediation as they confronted the consequences of the historic construction of disability as a problem posed to education systems (Biklen, 1992; Bogdan & Taylor, 1989; Connor & Ferri, 2020; Connor & Valle, 2019; Connor et al, 2016; Ware & Valle; 2010; Ware, 2001).

In this chapter, we revisit this work to make a further case against the remediation framework that is so deeply embedded in P–12 education through an address of teacher education training and strategies (particularly exposure to curricular content development about disability). We work from the assumption that teacher preparation, as it currently exists, cannot meaningfully respond to students with disabilities given its reliance on the historic and systemic framework of disability remediation as the default paradigm. The remediation approach cuts off disabled students from exposure to a more suitable academically based curriculum and pedagogy that all but assures the end of their learning careers after high school (if they make it that far). Rather than anticipate a diminished capacity for disabled students that is largely addressed through time-consuming practices that cannot be turned into future capacities, the remediation framework must pivot away from low-expectation outcomes for disabled students. Instead, we should reverse focus and develop teacher training in which educators need remediation themselves with regard to developing more productive, agential, and vitalist approaches to education. We need to support future teachers to confront the consequences of the historic construction of disability as a problem posed for education systems to cure, fix, wish away, or even more likely waste away the time until these less desirable bodyminds can be pushed off on other institutions.

RECOVERING HISTORIC ABSENCES AND PRESENT REFUSALS

Our work foregrounds disability as a cultural phenomenon with myriad links to histories across time and into the present, and as such, this content merits consideration as instructional content wherein disabled students and their nondisabled peers explore new understandings of disability together. Such an endeavor that could establish the richness of the human story inclusive of the dignity of disabled lives is far more promising than the lens of remediation. We argue that rather than going against the grain of assets-based approaches, and undermining their promise and potential, such an orientation would be strongly compatible with an assets-based approach to teaching and learning.

Absent such a strand in teacher education, one in which disabled students are viewed and valued as unique and welcome members of the classroom and the school, an asset-based orientation to teaching and learning will likely prove unrealizable. There is a defining precarity that grounds disabled students' experience in public education settings for they are often treated as auxiliary to the educational process. Such exclusion is based, ironically, on their perception as being the bearers of devalued ontologies while, perplexingly, existing as ghosts (forms of "unlivable lives" and lives of nonbeing) who frequent parts of the school with which other students have little contact (Butler, 2004). They are, paradoxically, too much and too little of a body for schools to address directly and meaningfully.

Thus, disabled students feel their exclusion more intensely, and concern over the stigma that their educational lives entail ranks high when there is an absence of direct address of their lives. In this atmosphere disabled students have problems developing even a collective sense of their outsiderness let alone an accomplishment of inclusion. The point of cultivating solidarity is not to produce injury-formed identities where they bond over the wounds they have received from others in educational settings (both literal and metaphorical), nor is to evaluate which wounds are more aggrieved in the larger scheme of things. Rather, it is to make space for undoing, in Athanasiou and Butler's (2013, 185) words, "the social conventions and foreclosures that make some lives and desires impossible."

Thus, our approaches have featured two critical components that can be understood in the terms of this volume as asset-based approaches: (1) offering content that brings all students involved in contemplating disability as a socially depreciated existence that can be rewritten and reimagined to make a more just world of habitation for all (the social justice asset of our offerings) and (2) offering content about disability that is more than a question of remediation. Disability then becomes a way of viewing the world through the standpoint epistemology that disability experience offers, and this, in turn, allows disabled students to recognize the experience of their bodyminds as a source of expertise from which they might draw to make the entire classroom into a learning opportunity (the disability curricular content offering). This near complete reversal of disability education pedagogy results in making disability more integral to how all students understand human differences. Within this framework, disability becomes not something to be shunned within schools of in(ex)clusion but rather a social condition that directs students to ways of imaging more productive forms of world-making (Berlant & Edleman, 2013).

OVERVIEW OF OUR CURRICULAR CRIPISTEMOLOGIES: FINDING FUTURES IN NO FUTURE

Each of us brings to this conversation experience as academics who cross institutional borders to underscore the study of humanities content focused on disability within schools of education and teacher training curriculum. We also share insights informed by the unique knowledges we possess as parents of disabled children who are now adults. Our insider status led to recognition of and resistance to the constraints of a system that is too often unresponsive to the needs and desires of disabled people. Disability proved a limiting form of diagnosis that prophesied no future and thus let teachers, schools, and educational systems off the hook for thinking more productively about what the inclusion of disabled students might offer to their institutions, classrooms, and social solidarity networks. As insiders, we were well-positioned to push back on unresponsive systems and the limits of educational and social exclusion. We were quick to point out the underlying bureaucratic and ideological forces that work against progress for disabled children and youth in schools—and quick to realize that these circumstances were accepted without interrogation by educators, administrators, service providers, and a litany of credentialed helping professionals.

One of us (Ware) brought to our project her own training as a former special education teacher in public schools and decades of experience as a teacher educator for both general and special education pre-service, master's, and doctoral students at several universities from New Mexico to New York. Her expertise served as well, to shape the belief that the task before us—the remediation of teacher education—take center stage in opposition to the remediation of disabled students. This is courageous work that need not turn on accusation as much as it turns on understanding how much is missing from the core curriculum for teacher educators. And it turns on significant reform of federal- and state-mandated protocols that revert to the status quo understanding of disability.

In the case of Mitchell and Snyder, they brought their humanities-based expertise of disability history, culture, and theory to the augmentation of curriculum. Their objective was not to simply supplant a derogatory understanding with "positive images" of disability as so many disability studies scholars had done previously, but rather to offer disability as part of the diverse constellation of perspectives and experiences that disability experience entails. Thus, they turned attention to literature, film, and media as points of contact for complicating our understanding of disability. As scholars trained in literary and cultural studies, they sought out not just an articulation of how disabled people had been treated in the past but also imagining ways that we might create justice for disabled people into the future. As with disability studies key understanding of barrier-free access as a pathway to ease of access for all bodies attempting to navigate the complexities of public space, we took up projects to rewrite curricular content as the most formidable way that disability might be taken up as a collective project of renewal.

This "renewal" as we called it sought to address the material conditions of so many disabled peoples' lives through an address of foundational social problems such as homelessness, the need for shelter, employment exclusions, access to appropriate diets (the destruction of hunger, for instance), and the social refusal of recognition that so many disabled students endure. Disabled people in this alternative curricular formation had been dispossessed by cultures that promised to care for and cultivate vulnerable citizens. The political situation offers a precarious living—refugees and stateless exposed to the debilitating conditions of immigration and climate change; those dispossessed of land, rights, and livelihood through military coercion, community neglect, and economic deprivations; those who were "without papers" and yet also, mysteriously, made up reserve armies of labor pressuring wages downward; as well as those driven into the precariousness of social disapproval with respect to demands to conform with regimes of gender and sexual normativity. Our most significant challenge in addressing this history of dispossession was to ask whether the identification of the sources of precarious life could be used as a means by which to gesture toward and, ultimately, displace the violence that disabled people encounter.

To answer this massive—but necessary—question, we turned to some of the most contemplative yet accessible texts in English that might be imported directly into the classroom. Such works used disability as a foundation for challenging instinctive social responses of dislocation, sequestration, dispossession, and diffusion, those patterns of social organization that cordoned off disabled people from others and from one another. Our cultivation of pedagogical cripistemologies examined ancient Greek drama such as "Philoctetes" to discuss the social decision of his fellow community members to banish him to an isolated island due to possessing a leg wound that was offensive to look at and odious to others' sense of smell. Lack of access to medical care resulted in social abandonment that was believed to "belong" to the wounded individual rather than communal inadequacies.

Our cripping of the curricula used Foucault's (2009) history of disability to understand how institutionalization (and other forms of the carceral state) became a dumping ground for all types of social undesirability and therefore constituted a model site for bridging collectivities of the excluded. Such approaches searched out opportunities for fashioning alternatives worlds even within the institution itself. Charity networks of the Middle Ages exposed the ways in which helping disabled people often redounded to the merit of the giver even if the receiver was ostensibly the object of the assistance offered. Such insights we hoped would help teachers and administrators to see why today's charity networks operate on the grounds of conspicuous contribution that undermine, rather than enhance, disabled peoples' autonomy and well-being. The 19th-century clinic in works such as Harriet Martineau's *Life in the Sick Room* (1845) focused on ways that even in the midst of sequestration disabled people opened up their faculties of scrutiny to the microcosm that teemed with activity and life and cultivated opportunities for philosophical reflection. We introduced teachers to the disability history writings of the French anthropologist Henri-Jacques Stiker to think about how 20th-century rehabilitation had set out goals for disabled people to become more like able-bodied people and thus participate in the masking of their own defining differences.

NOT A DISCOURSE OF SPECIALNESS

When the editors of this volume invited us to extend the arguments expressed in an earilier essay, "[Every] Child Left Behind" (Mitchell et al., 2014), we welcomed the opportunity to further advance the construct of "curricular cripistemologies" and turn a critical eye to its relationship to an asset-based approach to teaching disabled students in public education. In 2014, we expressed concern that "rather than expect that disabled students submerge their disability experience in order to pass as non-disabled (the primary aim of inclusionism), a curricular cripistemologies methodology draws upon the latent disability knowledge available in the classroom . . . through readings of long-taught texts whose stories turn on disability insights" (p. 301). Curricular cripistemologies could be used as means to enable educators to (re)set the stage for disabled students to claim their experiences as something to be "cultivated as a form of alternative expertise rather than as useful only to the degree that disability can be disguised and hidden away." Curricular cripistemology we insisted, "operationalizes disability into an active, unabashed, and less stigmatizing part of classroom discourse from which all can learn" such that, in practice, "disability is positioned as the "site for active learning" (p. 301).

This approach is not a "discourse of 'specialness' wherein we learn to value disabled people as 'human' too, nor tolerate their incapacities when we discover them scraping out an existence alongside others" (Mitchell et al., 2014, p. 303). Further, we do not advance understanding disability as an "opportunity for political correctness wherein all bodies are valued for 'diversity' in a relativistic equation of multicultural differences" (p. 304). We called for a commitment to unpacking the paradoxes of inclusionism and its goals that amount to little more than "culturally rehabilitating disabled people's experiences" (p. 304). We hold that inclusionism "covers over an unethical promotion of the successes of the few based upon normative standards of achievement for the inadequacies of the many" (p. 307). Without apology, we continue to encourage "approaches to the teaching mission that force an encounter with the often-discomforting content of living interdependently with others" (p. 305). Curricular cripistemologies imagine another kind of inclusion that entails an approach to making crip/queer subjects not just integrated but integral to the contemporary curricular knowledge base (Stiker, 1999). With this as a backdrop we continue to explore the ways our earlier critique melds with an asset-based approach outlined in this edited volume.

INTERRUPTING RITUALISTIC PROCEDURAL PERFORMATIVE COMPLIANCE

In order to determine the ways in which we might situate our work against the backdrop of an asset-based context, we found a synopsis by Lalor (2020) that calls for the expectation that teachers:

> [B]egin to look at what students understand, know, and can do, [such that] it changes the way the teacher and their students approach learning. The teacher begins to leverage what students know as a means for moving learning forward. For students, small successes lead to larger ones and help develop belief in their own capability as well as the willingness to engage when learning becomes difficult. When students are made aware of how they can learn, they take another step toward being independent, self-regulated learners.

As Lalor notes, and we concur, any such endeavor must begin with the teacher and learning expectations. The focus remains on the individual teacher who must contend with their individual students in the individual context of their individual classrooms. This seemingly obvious mandate, in practice, often proves quite challenging for educators to enact even though "individualization" was integral to service provision mandated by the

Individuals with Disabilities Improvement Act (IDEIA). Further, "individualization," "free and appropriate public education" (FAPE), and "least restrictive environment" (LRE) are all foundational terms that teachers know as central to the "procedural safeguards" associated with IDEIA compliance. Enacting these policies and procedures in the absence of recognizing the spirit of the law too often amounts to little more than performance and ritualistic compliance.

To explain why this neglect of the spirit of the law proved so egregious, we mined the experiences of our disabled children as they navigated their way through education systems. Our children span an age difference of 25 years. Justin, just turned 50, and Emma just turned 26, suggesting that their educational experience would be distinctly different—yet our children experienced very much the same system that inherently excluded them and their lived experience. Justin navigated the earliest years of the implementation of P.L. 94–142 (the Education for All Handicapped Children Act), and Emma experienced a system that was purportedly upgraded through the bureaucratic mechanism of congressional "reauthorization." Our critique followed to show that these were not merely academic solutions for real-world problems but also had material effects on disability education and the participants who found themselves more excluded within the institutionalized-inclusionist-education edifice. We marked the IEP process as one of the most debilitating, legalistic, and fruitless processes that ate up every administrative, professional, parental, and student obligation with the production of a document that almost no one read and fewer followed. We discussed the exclusion of our disabled children and those of others from activities that presumably embraced all and were not about meritoriousness but rather collective experiences such as access to choir, musical instruments, sports, and so on. Disabled students we observed were treated as excessively fragile and untalented, although such evaluation did not apply to others without disabilities but with similar characteristics who nevertheless found themselves included in those collective expereinces. We noted how accessibility on exams and homework proved superficial and that teachers were more interested in enforcing a one-size-fits-all standard that almost no one in the class benefited from except to most privileged.

Crip temporalities had no place in the educational system, because if you couldn't perform an exercise on the normative timeline the exercise wasn't worth doing in the first place (Samuels & Elizabeth, 2021). Our children developed their assignments based on worlds that they knew rather than those that were automatically assumed to be valuable—long-term hospitalization stints rather than summer camp; disabled peoples social predicaments rather than histories of nondisabled people which left behind those who couldn't possibly qualify as "history-making" in their endeavors; the production of disability and death on slave plantations; the cultivation of disability languages among institutional residents that allowed them to converse beneath the uncomprehending radar of the surveillance state; the intersections of disability and race (more than 50%) in the chronic police shootings that have plagued the country for decades; and finally, the demonstration projects that showed how accessibility in pedagogy was beneficial to all and significantly lowered the anxiety and stress levels for students in every situation.

THE "POWER OF THE NORM"

We believe that educators and the university-based teacher educators who train them must grapple with the mindset that would enable them to enact asset-based practice in the first place. General and special educators will need to evaluate their commitment to that which Foucault (1995) identified as the "power of the Norm" (84)—a phenomenon intrinsic to the disciplines. Foucault is no stranger to education and to the preparation of teachers, yet few programs center his work in their programs. A mere handful of teacher educators draw from Foucault to position educational theory (Baker, 2002). Certainly far fewer educators would be able to critique institutional norms and the trappings of power in contrast to those who could defend the tenets of behaviorism. Behaviorism has been dominant for so long in education that any program which might assert training free of norms and standards reified and sanctioned by district and state policies and procedures is nothing short of unimaginable and unrealizable. The forms and checklists that have long served institutions, and education in particular, to construct disability as a problem identity in need of repair remain indifferent to the potential for the meaningful embrace of individual difference. Impotence follows then when inviting educators to consider a student's assets in the absence of a formal assessment derived of institutional norms and rooted in reductionism. The student as well as the learning context are contrived by conformance with the standards of practice and the policy mandates that inform institutions.

Consider one of special education's central tenets designed to ensure access to a quality education, the LRE. Steven J. Taylor (1988), educational sociologist and disability activist, early on pointed to the paradox of the least restrictive environment (LRE), which he viewed as inherently problematic, too often resulting in exclusionary policies and practices that impede the integration of disabled students. Taylor's decades-old critique of the LRE has endured as mightily as has the LRE. His analysis figured into a recent essay citing the continuum of services as a "trap" that catches disabled students, particularly those with intellectual disabilities (Sauer & Jorgensen, 2016 Ware & Sauer, 2021). Teacher training programs, both general and special education, are littered with behaviorist literatures and "empirically based" research that serve to document human difference as a problem orientation. Long-taught texts amount to uncontested literatures that offer interpretations of disability that do not fold into the curricular cripistemology we advocate, but fold easily into the standard policies and practices that work against the development of a critical mindset among educators. Yet it bears recognition that numerous works by disability scholars have challenged the inherited narrative that positions special education as impervious to contestation (Baglieri & Lalvani, 2019; Brantlinger, 2006b; Connor & Bejoin, 2007; Ferri et al., 2001; Ferri et al., 2005; Mukopadhyay, 2015; Smith, 2009; Ware 2001; Ware & Valle, 2010). Among the earliest scholars of these critiques, Douglas Biklen (1992), Lous Heshusius (Ware & Nusbaum, 2021), Hugh Mehan (1996), Thomas Skrtic (1987, 1992), Christine Sleeter (1986), and Steven Taylor (1988) were powerful voices who paved the way for what became the foundations of disability studies in education (Ware & Nusbaum, 2020; Ware & Sauer, 2021; Ware & Slee, 2020). We wonder then, how will the literatures of asset-based approaches tackle this uninterrogated giant that is institutional special education?

Schools of education are slow to transformation, and except for one or two courses in any teacher training program, reification of norms rather than the creation of new knowledge of disability persists (Connor & Valle, 2019; Connor et al., 2016; Kincheloe, 1993; Ware, 2010, 2013; Wilgus 2013). Reflecting on her own teacher preparation program at City College/ CCNY, City University of New York/CUNY, Wilgus (2013) offers a critique that considers the ways that anti-intellectualism among teacher educators prevails and how "teachers as intellectuals" need not remain an oxymoron. Her edited volume featuring the research, scholarship, and program development authored with her CUNY colleagues notes "disturbing propensities . . . both conspicuous and concealed" that serve as institutional incentives to actually discourage teachers from "critically evaluating the educational ideologies, curricula, and classroom practices to which they are exposed in teacher education" (2013). Wilgus further notes:

> Teachers, children, administrators, and university teacher education faculty alike have been indiscriminately and routinely targeted by those who advocate for increasingly diminished possibilities to "think for oneself" within school settings. The challenge becomes how to encourage teachers to investigate the philosophical and ideological underpinnings of various curricula, and to then consider "what is deemed worthy of knowing and why" (Aronowitz, 2002) and of the pedagogical approaches through which these curricula are realized.

The imperative for transformation in education, according to Wilgus and others, demands that we revisit the early work of eminent educational theorists (e.g., Stanley Aronowitz, Pierre Bordieu, Jean-Claude Passeron, Paulo Freire, Henry Giroux, Joe Kincheloe, Peter McLaren, and Ira Shor). We acknowledge that none of these educational theorists actually considered disability in the manner we consider it in our work; however, they endorsed the very kind of thinking and pedagogic reimagining we advance relative to disability.

Asset-based learning and teaching relies upon what the teacher brings to the conversation when attempting to understand the construct of students' abilities. It would seem an extension of the question we previously asked: how might schooling promote a "growth mindset" for those students who vex the system as it currently exists? How aspirational will it prove to be? Remediation of such a system would locate the intellectual project whereby disability embodiment and disability experience serve as the potential sources to inform the foundation as valued "assets." Our multiple efforts have engaged teachers in such conversations that challenge them to explore disability throughout history and the arts, and not exclusively through the established categories and modes of knowing disability perpetuated by institutions, attitudes, and social and historical understandings that haunt teacher education. In brief, curricular cripistemologies call teacher education programs to move beyond behaviorism and reductionist remedies to repair and remake disabled bodyminds.

"DIRECT CHALLENGE" LITERATURES TO DRAW UPON

Hunt (2017) called out the direct challenge posed by disabled people who fall outside the comfortable consideration by nondisabled people in society. Writing in a time when a disability studies perspective was generally unknown, Hunt advanced the notion of understanding how disabled students come to know what they know and why what they know might fall outside the normalizing discourse of schooling. Such accounts were underreported and few. It is rare to find first-person, unmediated voices in the pages of the glossy texts that teacher educators rely upon in their coursework (Brantlinger, 2006a).

Most recently, qualitative researchers and disability studies scholars Lester and Nusbaum (2021) edited the collection *Centering Diverse Bodyminds in Critical Qualitative Inquiry*, a project centered on whose disabled lives we research, how we research disability, and how authentic authorship in the example of disability merits exploration. The collection directly responds to the "call for engaging in a new critical qualitative inquiry with consideration to issues related to power, privilege, voice, identity, and agency, while examining the hegemonic power of ableism and ableist epistemologies" (Lester & Nusbaum, 2021, p. x). It features diverse contributors whose lived experience as disabled academics, advocates, and researchers center disability in their work to "complicate the normative desire to create method/methodology that is 'standard,' versus thinking about method and methodology as fluid, emerging, and disruptive" (p. 1). The biographical notes of one of the volume's contributors, Briana Dickens (preferred pronoun, they), a PhD candidate in special education and disability studies at Syracuse University, offered:

> They teach courses to preservice special education students, as well as graduate level courses related to disability and theory. Brianna works on research teams that center the perspectives of disabled people and expand who is a research participant, how research is done, and how it is disseminated. Brianna is an autistic self-advocate who works to bring together their neurodiverse ways of being, their educational systems and structures to supporting educators in both K-12 and higher education to think about pedagogy and practice in ways that center multiply marginalized students and support a more just and equitable educational system.

Lester and Nusbaum (2021) foreground what it might mean to center disability as Dickens notes, so that critical qualitative researchers can imagine disability beyond quantitative, reductionist frames utilized in general and special education. The volume borrows from Athanasiou and Butler's (2013) notation of "illegible" bodies, and Kafer's (2013) extension regarding "the need for disability to be *legibly* read on the body—a discussion that has implications for the ways in which qualitative research and researchers have responded to considering disability/disabled participants through accommodation and/or protecting a population deemed 'vulnerable'" (p. 11). The contributors to this volume, render "thinkable" portrayals of life that captivate readers to recognize "imaginable lives" that center disability, and for purposes of this chapter, could orient assets-based educators to center disability as "legible" and "livable."

Informed by Kolárová's (2014) "crip horizons" in which disability is "rendered desirable, and the structures which surround it, profoundly contested" (p. 257), Lester and Nusbaum provide the grounding for educators to, as Lalor (2020) noted in the example of assets-based education, "begin to really . . . look at what students understand, know, and can do, [such that] it changes the way the teacher and their students approach learning." Such an orientation, based on our project experience and working from a cultural lens with a range of literature and arts exemplars alone has proven unthinkable and unrealizable by educators. However, the deployment of research reimagined as Lester and Nusbaum have provided extends the archives of disability culture and wisdom in an immediate context readily translated for teachers. To read Dicken's co-author, Holly Pearson, reflect on the strategies she designed in the data collection of her research as a deaf doctoral student, reveals the otherwise unrecognized ableist assumptions built into her doctoral coursework—in much the same way that ableist assumptions are built into public school instruction (Pearson & Dickens, 2021). Pearson recounts her "hypervigilance" when attending to the interactional processes of her research participants. Pearson explains, "I felt conflicted in my participation in masking or rendering disability invisible and perpetuating neutrality by upholding the dominant ideologies of what constitutes research/er" (p. 88). Pearson's experience as a researcher who required nonnormative strategies to engage with her participants was powerfully encapsulated when she wrote:

> The absence of alternative ways of engaging—such as discussion of how to navigate interviews with hearing participants in ASL with an ASL interpreter who revoices what you are saying, conducting participant observations as a Deaf Asian female in a predominantly hearing white institution, or a BIPOC transgender individual who wants to conduct research on white supremist attitudes in a small town that strongly embraces Catholic homophobia—is a problem, period. When raising these kinds of questions, often, blank stares are the outcome. (p. 88)

Pearson had prepared for her research informed by many of the top resources for conducting qualitative research (e.g., Creswell & Poth, 2016), but her disability did not figure into that preparation. It presented as something of an afterthought until her fieldwork began, as she slowly realized she had been pigeon-holed into a research project that was not fully of her choosing.

PUBLIC EDUCATION PLANKTON

Pearson's experience is common to many disabled and disability researchers who attempt to draw upon discredited experience. Their fieldwork and findings are often disqualified as "too close," or "insufficiently empirical," or "excessively devoted to the well-being of the subjects." This disqualification, ironically, often comes at the expense of children/students with disabilities who are not deemed credible or qualified because they have been diagnosed with disabilities and disability throws one's perspective into dispute as noncredible. This disputation of the credibility of disabled people as irrelevant or tarnished in some way is often the result of a lack of an asset-based approach to pedagogy. Disability is a land of shadows rather than *terra firma*. At the conclusion of Tito Rajarshi Mukhopadhyay's book, *Plankton Dreams: What I Learned in Special-Ed*, he comes to an epiphany about why disabled students are so commonly discounted by the educators paid a salary to teach them:

> At the lake I had an epiphany. There is a pristine world above the water and a murky, reflected one below. There is the typical domain of typical beings who aren't doubted or tested repeatedly, and who have a real place in education, work, and decision making. And then there is the "special" domain of "special"

beings, where all is shadow, formless and wobbling, and hope itself lies sodden and submerged. The ducks [i.e. disabled people in special ed], as social as fowl can be, dismiss their own reflections. Who needs illusory wings? Standing there, watching the ripples on the surface of the lake. I learned the biggest lesson of all: nothing will create substance out of shadows. (p. 83)

The curricular cripistemologies we have discussed intend to make substance out of the shadows of special education as the world of disabled people is not a poor reflection of the substantive world of the "typical beings." Rather, AP helps to solidify the shadows that education has striven to make of its disabled charges so that their worlds ripple away and become "sodden and submerged." We must surrender this failed pedagogical construction of "typical" people teaching "special" people as it demeans both parties involved in the learning struggle. Why would special educators continue to want their pedagogical labor to be reduced to the "murky, reflected [world] below?"

The opening line of Tito's book begins, "[E]very educational approach has a life span" (p. 7). An AP could do the field a service by calling on special education researchers and teachers to bring the special education approach of deficits and consumption of time to a crashing, imminent, and inevitable end. The reductive repetitions of special education have become a kind of perseveration behavior, and we need to be brave enough to realize that the object that students with disabilities can teach us about is the performances of the substantive, "typical world." They expose it as ruse, and, in doing so, turn the typical world and those who believe they inhabit it into the shadowy world below. In an asset-based curricular cripistemological approach, "special" switches places with "typicality" and surfaces with what the murky depths represent as out of bounds and inappropriate for discussion: "the difference[s] that disability makes" and the hard truths of human variation that it allow us to contemplate rather than wish away into the insubstantiveness to which it has been consigned (Michalko, 2002, p. 6).

This alternative swapping of places is also a key formation of "crip temporalities" in that, as María Elena Cepeda (2021) argues, we crip time by "re-calibrating speed and intensity, slowness and rest" (311). It not only turns the typical world into an object of study but also promises the creative alternatives that paying attention to disabled students' unique modes of interacting with the world can bring to our notice. Right now, our pedagogy devalues disability because it consigns their insights and worldview to "dustbins for disavowal" (Shakespeare, 1994, p. 283)—their attention to what is not working for themselves and other "special" people. Curricular cripistemology practices the "slow burn" of crip temporalities in that it refuses compliance with the public education demands of timeline, deadline, overproductivity, work-is-the-only-valued human capacity, consumption-ridden naturalization of the typical world.

In describing the American ingestion of the Hawaiian Islands into an annexed territory of colonial possession, Sarah Vowell (2011) quotes the 19th-century Hawaiian historian David Malo on the danger from below: "If a big wave comes in large and unfamiliar fishes will come from the dark ocean, and when they see the small fishes of the shallows they will eat them up. . . . They know our people are few in number and our country is small, they will devour us" (138–139). The shadowy lives of little fishes threatened by "the large and unfamiliar fishes of the dark ocean" can be understood in the naming of Mukhopadhyay's book with the mysterious title *Plankton Dreams*. Those who practice special education as remediation of weaker little fishes threaten to consume disabled students' lives like public education plankton until mandatory education is over; a good portion of their lives are used up in meaningless, rote repetition, until they can be released back into the depths without particular skills to survive in it.

As Mukhopadhyay (2015, p. 7) points out, "I did learn things in special education—not what I was supposed to learn but important things all the same." Tito exposes the ways that he comes to view the helper professionals as endangering rather than rescuing. This is an enactment of curricular cripistemologies in that it turns the tide of the outcomes of remediation-based pedagogy on its head. The remediationists of the pedagogical world are those who are pressed (or who accept, rinse, and repeat) their service of further rendering those who cannot abide by these terms of human value into less substantive versions of themselves.

CHAPTER 10

Mothers of Color of Children with Dis/abilities

Centering Their Children's Assets in Family as Faculty Projects

Cristina Santamaría Graff

Over the past 5 years (2016–2021), I have had the honor to work with families of children with dis/abilities, and, specifically with many mothers who have, with gentle force, guided my unlearning of what counts as knowledge within my discipline of special education. As a self-identified nondisabled, biracial Mexicana, mother/scholar, I have had to be conscious of my multiple identities to respectfully and compassionately navigate complex landscapes involving the mothers who collaborate with me on family-centered projects, specifically those that integrate family as faculty (FAF) approaches. Over the past few years, several family members, including fathers, grandmothers, and siblings of individuals with dis/abilities, have participated in FAF projects embedded within the family-focused special education teacher preparation courses I teach. Often, however, most of those who coplan, coteach, and coresearch through FAF approaches are mothers. Over thirty have participated to varying degrees over the past 5 years.

I have learned from these mothers, specifically Black and Latina mothers, that they confront wide and deep layers of oppression consistently and exhaustively. In comparison to the white, monolingual English-speaking mothers with whom I have worked closely and who also deal with systemic oppressions related to disability, educational level, or class status, the mothers of color I have gotten to know resist additional marginalization because of their race, language, or immigration status. Rarely are their assets noticed or valued at student-centered meetings, including individualized educational planning (IEP) or transition meetings.

In my own scholarship, I have been involved in research projects that focus on family members of children with dis/abilities and specifically Latino/a/x immigrant families. Here, and within specific contexts not related to disability as an eligibility category per se, I use the slash (/) in dis/ability to emphasize the importance of *disability* as a social construct. In this context, the individual's dis/ability is perceived as variance within the human experience rather than as a fixed, indelible trait limiting the individual to a static caricature of who that person is, has been, and/or desires to become (Davis, 2013; Gillborn, 2015). In the past few years, I have explored FAF approaches that are derived from health care models or adapted for special education teacher preparation programs (Heller & McKlindon, 1996; Johnson et al, 2006; Macy & Squires, 2009; Patterson, et al., 2009; Williams, 2012). What I appreciate about FAF is that, at its core, it reconceptualizes, repositions, and redistributes power so that the knowledge and insights of family members of children with dis/abilities are valued alongside other epistemologies traditionally used to prepare special education teachers (Santamaría Graff, 2021). In practice, as I will explain, FAF can provide a structure where families share expertise and practical experience so that future teachers can learn to better work with, listen to, get to know, and teach students with dis/abilities.

In this chapter, I center four mothers of color who have been a part of FAF projects and whose stories highlight how they inform preservice special education teachers (PSETs) about their children's and families' inherent assets at intersections of dis/ability, race, language, and other identity markers of difference. I use an interdisciplinary framework (Thorius et al., 2018; Waitoller & Thorius, 2016) alongside an existing FAF framework currently being developed with the following essential understandings (EUs): families are experts, positionality is relational and contextual, and "normative" power dynamics in school settings are uneven (Santamaría Graff et al., 2020). I incorporate traditional qualitative methods and use a deductive approach to analyze data collected from different FAF projects. I conclude by discussing the findings in relation to asset pedagogies (APs) inclusive of *dis/ability* as both culture and identity.

FAMILY AS FACULTY

My orientation to FAF was derived from empirical studies in health care and in education that valued families' narratives as part of the pedagogy used in the preparation of health care practitioners or pre-service special education teachers (PSETs), respectively (Heller & McKlindon, 1996; Johnson et al, 2006; Patterson, et al., 2009; Williams, 2012).

The underlying premise of FAF approaches is to (re)position families as leaders to help transform individuals' perceptions of families of children with dis/abilities from deficit to asset based. In health care, FAF has targeted health care practitioners and in special education FAF has focused on PSETs. In my own work, I emphasize FAF as a vehicle through which family members are coeducators and teach PSETs in university or college courses as "faculty" (Santamaría Graff, 2021). Their status as faculty or coeducators means they contribute directly to both the pedagogical decisions impacting courses I teach as well as the research choices shaping FAF projects.

In FAF approaches, where family members are valued contributors to the decision-making connected to course content and instruction, family members model for PSETs ways to center students' strengths in student-centered meetings. My rationale for embedding FAF into special education courses parallels that of special education law, the Individuals with Disabilities Education Act (IDEA), which stipulates that families of children with disabilities not only are afforded rights in decision-making about their child's education but also are encouraged to "work together with school personnel" in the child's best interest (U.S. Department of Education, 2006, §300.306). FAF provides concrete avenues for family members to interact with, teach, and share important knowledge with future PSETs who will be working with students with dis/abilities not unlike their own children. Structurally, FAF shifts traditional power dynamics that often situate educators' experience and status *over* families by (re)positioning family members in important leadership positions where future teachers learn *from* them. In the spirit of IDEA, this shift creates more opportunities for families to be valued as important contributors at student-centered meetings where their decisions impact the trajectory of their children's educational futures.

INTERWEAVING A FAF AND INTERDISCIPLINARY FRAMEWORK

FAF models have provided me with guidance for how to cocreate learning activities in special education courses with families as well as ways to integrate family members as part of the research team in collecting, analyzing, and disseminating data. However, in adapting these models for my own research projects, there is limited information on what it means to collaborate with multiply marginalized families who experience systemic oppression. Though some FAF and family-centered models mention the importance of including "diverse" families (Heller & McKlindon, 1996, p. 469) and developing cultural competency among PSETs (Shartrand et al., 1997), existing models do not explicitly discuss dis/ability at the intersections of race, language, gender, and other minoritized identities. Therefore, I have been working on developing a FAF framework with EUs that consider (1) families' background knowledge, expertise, and ways of knowing; (2) positionalities of those interacting together within FAF projects; and (3) power relations among and between FAF stakeholders, including families, educators, and PSETs.

Along with these EUs, and in relation to this chapter, I consider an interdisciplinary framework informed by Thorius, Waitoller, and colleagues (Thorius et al., 2018; Waitoller & Thorius, 2016) rooted in APs to draw attention to the ways the four mothers signal to and inform PSETs about their children's and family's inherent assets at the intersections of dis/ability, race, language, and other identity markers of difference. This interdisciplinary framework "for countering ontological stances on culture in special education" (Thorius et al. 2018, p. 13) includes three grounding assertions: (1) culture is dynamic and intersectional, (2) normalcy is debunked and racism and ableism are disrupted, and (3) disability is understood as culture. In the next sections, I describe ways that Thorius and Waitoller's framework interacts with FAF's EUs (see Figure 10.1) to highlight assets of families with multiple intersecting identities.

Figure 10.1. Interacting Frameworks

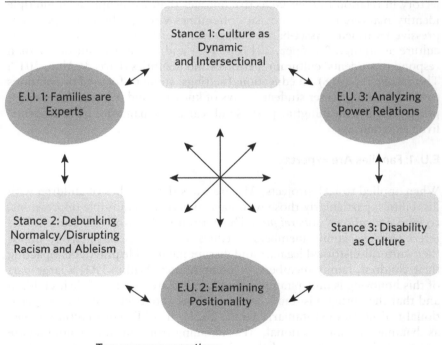

Stance 1: Culture as Dynamic and Intersectional

According to Thorius et al. (2018), "culture" is a term in educational literature that has often been used as proxy for sociodemographic markers such as ethnicity and class. Culture is generally presented as a static, monolithic trait applied to large swaths of P–12 student populations for the purpose of investigating low academic achievement, cognitive differences, and behavioral challenges. Disability in relation to culture is oftentimes relegated as an afterthought and generally defined through deficit-driven frameworks emanating from the medical model perspective. Thorius, Waitoller, and colleagues reframe culture as dynamic and intersectional to center students' assets. This dynamic view allows for variance in how an individual may express aspects of self that spring from identity-formation and identity-exploration in connection to familial/communal histories that are alive and constantly evolving (hooks, 1994). Culture as intersectional considers how multiple identities interact to form, influence, or shape an individual's trajectory in relation to their collective lineages that, for people with multiple identity markers of difference, are oftentimes wrought by histories of oppressive treatment. Asset-based pedagogies are those that view "students' culture as strength" (López, 2017, p. 193) and aim to sustain rather than respond to students' cultural repertoires and identities (Paris & Alim, 2017; Thorius, et al., 2018). In educational settings, strength-focused orientations toward teaching center students' ways of knowing and being and create opportunities for meaningful, purposeful learning emanating from students' lived experiences.

E.U. 1: Families Are Experts

When applied to FAF projects, APs are ways that families of children with disabilities, particularly those who have experienced multiple oppressions, reclaim *educational sovereignty*. This term used by Moll and Ruíz (2002) refers to ways family members in education settings can actively honor their cultural-historical legacies and disrupt inequitable practices impacting their children, family members, or communities. Within FAF, a large part of this honoring is understanding that families are experts of their children and that they bring wisdom to conversations about their children's educational trajectories (Santamaría Graff, 2021). In FAF, when culture is seen as dynamic and intersectional, APs stemming from this understanding are constructed with intentional thought to uphold and sustain families' dimensionality, including cultural, linguistic, educational, and economic repertoires (Gutiérrez & Rogoff, 2003). Importantly, dis/ability is valued as a contributive facet of families' dimensionality. Dis/ability in FAF is accepted as one aspect of identity interacting and intersecting with others that, when viewed holistically, provides richness and depth to understanding the individual's multifaceted humanity. In FAF, family members communicate to PSETs the different ways in which dis/ability is conceptualized, understood as a social construct, and contextualized through individual lived experiences.

Stance 2: Debunking Normalcy/Disrupting Racism and Ableism

A core assertion of Thorius and Waitoller's interdisciplinary framework is to reject the pathologization of students' abilities by recognizing the false belief that physical, cognitive, psychological, and other differences—both visible and invisible—are automatically in need of fixing, remediating, or treatment because they present as "abnormal" in relation to a medicalized "normalcy" (Baglieri et al., 2011). In special education, students with dis/abilities with other intersecting marginalized identities, such as race or language difference, have been assessed through norms pertaining to and benefiting white, English-speaking, nondisabled persons (Artiles, 2003). Oftentimes, when compared to these norms, these students have been found lacking, behind, and "less than" and, consequently, have been disproportionately labeled in specific special education disability categories and/or placed in more restrictive learning environments (Tefera & Fischman, 2020).

E.U. 2: Examining Positionality

In FAF approaches, families of children with dis/abilities are in leadership positions as coeducators to counter, debunk, and disrupt "normalcy" narratives. In alignment with Thorius and Waitoller's framework, when family members share insider perspectives about their children with PSETs, they often are rejecting deficit mythologies perpetuated in mainstream society surrounding labels like *intellectual disability*, where students' capabilities and knowledge are oftentimes undervalued and underestimated. Family members (mostly mothers in my FAF projects) have disrupted deficit-based assumptions by PSETs who, though well-intended, have insinuated that, because of their credentials, they need to teach parents how to work with their children (Santamaría Graff et al., 2020).

FAF family members' shared narratives are powerful because they position family members' identities and lived experiences as contributive knowledge in the formation of PSETs. In FAF contexts, positionality is important. Positionality refers to who the family members are in relation to the PSETs and within the context of educational structures that generally privilege teachers' over families' voices (Connor & Cavendish, 2018). In FAF, family members are (re)positioned centrally to be seen by PSETs as active advocates, partners, and forces of change rather than as passive or "uninvolved" bystanders (Santamaría Graff, 2021). This (re)positioning is essential because the majority of PSETs in the courses I teach are predominantly white, middle-class, monolingual English-speaking females who have limited experiences working with students of color with language differences and/or dis/abilities. When family members, particularly family members of color, enter special education teacher preparation courses as coeducators and speak about their children's assets, PSETs actively listen and are engaged by their stories. Through this engagement, family members present to PSETs a different perspective, often one that is completely foreign to the PSETs (Santamaría Graff et al., 2020). This perspective is one that disrupts racist and/or ableist thinking about students with dis/abilities with intersecting minoritized identities. For example, in FAF projects, family members of color often share the ways they are highly involved in their children's education, debunking the myth that they are uninterested (Santamaría Graff et al., 2020). They talk about their child's dis/ability as a facet of that child's overall humanity rather than as a deficit. Further, they provide examples of ways special education systems and practices often marginalize and disable students whose "differences" do not adhere to a dominant, able-bodied understanding of physical, cognitive, social, behavioral, adaptive, or functional "normalcy."

Stance 3: Disability as Culture

Thorius and colleagues (2018, p. 17) assert that "disability cultures . . . are worthy of and must be sustained" as important cultural repertoires. They explain that within special education contexts disability often is framed as deficit leading to institutional practices that silence through exclusion or restrictive placements. This silencing, specifically referred to as disability-culture silence, is one in which assets of students with dis/abilities are rarely valued as contributive to the classroom or school community. Disability-culture silence creates outsiders by locating students with dis/abilities in peripheral spaces where dis/ability identity is repressed or made invisible. For students with dis/abilities, disability culture and other cultures of difference to which they hold membership interact in dynamic ways oftentimes not understood or accepted by dominant, mainstream culture (Annamma & Morrison, 2018). Students with multiple cultural repertoires of difference are likely to confront increased oppression because of their intersecting identities that, within systems privileging a white-dominant norm, are considered problematic, less valuable, or in need of silencing (Erevelles & Minear, 2010).

E.U. 3: Analyzing Power Relations

In FAF, uneven power dynamics are considered to privilege the voices of family members of children with dis/abilities, specifically family members of color with intersectional identities of difference. In FAF projects, *analyzing power relations* is taking action to ensure that family members entering into FAF projects are given control of their stories so they can share their narratives freely and unencumbered. In alignment with Thorius and Waitoller's framework, dis/ability in FAF is honored as a culture that enriches the dimensionality of the families' overall lived experience. For example, many of the families who participate in my FAF projects belong to parent-support networks focused on a specific disability (e.g., Down syndrome, Autism). During their regular meetings, of which I have been a part, they often discuss how they have benefited from both the challenges and high points of being parents/caregivers of a child with a dis/ability. These conversations focus on unique ways that dis/ability is an additive and dynamic facet transforming the landscape of the family's deepening and evolving awareness of the ways their child's dis/ability interacts with other aspects of their personality over time.

In FAF, family members' stories that locate dis/ability as culture act as counternarratives to traditional ways of understanding students with dis/abilities. Often, when family members of color with other minoritized identities talk about their children, dis/ability is an interacting identity that informs the complex layers of *how* and *why* they and/or their children have been silenced within special education systems (Santamaría Graff & Vázquez, 2014). In my experience, PSETs sometimes arrive to special education programs with un/conscious biases against family members of children with dis/abilities and, specifically, families of color (Santamaría Graff et al., 2020). Many such biases have been formed through negative media portrayals of individuals with dis/abilities, lack of interaction with individuals with dis/abilities, or a superficial perception of people with dis/abilities formed through an unconscious ableist lens. Dis/ability as culture, framed as an asset by family member coeducators, can begin to change PSETs' deficit orientations about dis/ability by bringing awareness to their unconscious or hidden biases (Santamaría Graff, 2022).

DESCRIBING A FAMILY AS FACULTY PROJECT

This qualitative study is based on a larger longitudinal FAF project with data collected from 2016 to 2019. Each FAF project is one semester long and occurs in both a university classroom and on site at a nonprofit parent-to-parent organization near campus. In this study, I focus on four mothers of color who have participated in FAF projects as coeducators. I specifically am interested in the ways they talk about and inform PSETs about their children's and families' inherent assets at the intersections of dis/ability, race, language, and other identity markers of difference. In the next sections I detail methods used to examine how the four mothers signaled to and

Table 10.1. Descriptive Information About the Mothers Highlighted in This Study

Mother/Coeducator[a]	Country of Origin	Race/Ethnicity	Child's Disability
Janice	United States	Black	Autism Spectrum Disorder[b] (Asperger's syndrome)
Patricia	Mexico	Latina	Profound sensorineural hearing loss
Lizette	United States	Black	Autism spectrum disorder (PDD-NOS[c])
Dolores	Nicaragua	Latina	Down syndrome

[a] Pseudonyms used
[b] DSM-5 classification used
[c] Pervasive developmental disorder—not otherwise specified

informed PSETs about their children's and families' assets using the interacting framework (Figure 10.1) to ground the analysis.

Participants and FAF Participation

Participants in this study included four mothers (two Black, two Latina) of children with dis/abilities (see Table 10.1). All mothers participated in at least two FAF projects embedded in a special education course on families. Each mother met with me to coplan the classes they cotaught. Coplanning sessions included going over syllabus topics, making decisions about course content, and cogenerating instructional activities aimed to bring deeper understanding to the ways that families experience dis/ability within the special education system. After coplanning, the mothers/coeducators cotaught and/or led at least one 2½ hour class by (1) sharing their stories, (2) engaging students in mock IEP meetings, (3) presenting case studies they wrote, and (4) interacting with PSETs in question-and-answer sessions.

Data Collection

Data collected from 2016 to 2019 was extensive. For this study, I singled out audio- and video-recordings of coplanning sessions and family-led classes involving the four mothers. Because all mothers had participated in at least two FAF projects, I examined 10 coplanning sessions and eight family-led classes by watching and listening to the video recordings and reading the transcripts associated with the recordings. In addition, three of the mothers participated in focus groups and individual interviews that were also transcribed. Finally, I kept and analyzed correspondence approved by the university's human subjects review committee from the mothers that, I believed, shed light on some of their insights in relation to their children's assets.

Data Analysis

I examined the data collected through traditional qualitative methods using a deductive thematic analysis used to identity, analyze, and report patterns or themes within the data (Braun & Clarke, 2006). Because I had already analyzed and written extensively on my FAF research and had a robust "collection and analysis of data" (Pearse, 2019, p. 264), I had a strong sense of the ways the mothers of color in this study understood dis/ability in relation to asset-based framings. However, I had never formally studied the exact manner in which they articulated these understandings to PSETs. I asked the question, *What are the ways the four mothers of color signaled to and informed PSETs about their children's and families' inherent assets at the intersections of dis/ability, race, language, and other identity markers of difference?*

To answer this question, I drew from two frameworks to inform my analysis. Because the mothers were participating in a FAF study, I used the developing FAF EUs to account for relational and contextual orientations embedded within the research study design and implementation. In addition, I wanted to examine specific ways the mothers signaled to and informed PSETs about their children's and families' assets. I used Thorius et al.'s (2018) interdisciplinary framework to make sense of the ways the mothers centered their children's strengths through the framework's three stances: (1) culture as dynamic and intersectional, (2) debunking normalcy/disrupting racism and ableism, and (3) disability as culture. By analyzing the commonalities between the frameworks, I discovered several ways these two frameworks interacted (see Figure 10.1). Though there were many similarities, specifically in the way both frameworks aimed to disrupt deficit perspectives of dis/ability, I decided to focus on two main areas of synthesis between the frameworks. These areas provided clear guidance through which I could answer the research question and ground my data analysis. These areas of synthesis I name "assertions" to convey the convergence of "stances" essential in dismantling ableism and racism when working with families of color of children with dis/abilities:

Assertion 1: Families' cultures—including expertise and strengths—are dynamic and interactional.
Assertion 2: Racism and ableism cannot be disrupted unless positionality and power are addressed or confronted.

Using these two assertions, I created codes and operationalized each code's meaning. I followed a deductive thematic analysis approach to answer the research question by drawing from the two assertions as a point of departure from which to code the data (Pearse, 2019). The codes included strengths, assets, asset-based understandings, expertise, culture, identity, race, class, dis/ability, language, ethnicity, intersectional, racism, ableism, power, privilege, positionality, speak out, advocate, address, confront, and disrupt. An example of an operationalized term for "asset-based understandings" was beliefs/perceptions that affirm an individual's lived experience and include culturally sustaining attitudes of families' cultural-historical legacies and traditions. I analyzed the data through the codes and the ways that the codes brought insight to the mothers' action or speech through the operationalized definitions created (Fereday & Muir-Cochrane, 2006). Next, I reviewed, revised, and confirmed the codes by finding concrete examples (Yukhymenko et al., 2014). I found that I needed to add the code "behavior" as understood through either the lens of "appropriate" or "inappropriate" in relation to the ways the mothers spoke about their children's behavior in school. I then identified "themes looking for evidence in the data of the patterns . . . articulated" (Pearse, 2019, p. 266) in the common assertions derived from the interacting framework. These themes emerged from connecting codes and identifying patterns represented through mothers' statements in the data.

CENTERING CHILDREN'S AND FAMILIES' ASSETS IN FAF

After conducting a deductive thematic analysis, three specific findings surfaced. The mothers/coeducators in speaking to and teaching PSETs centered their children's and families' assets in the following ways: (1) by explicitly naming the assets and strengths of their children with dis/abilities, (2) by contextualizing or reframing their children's behaviors, and (3) by calling out educators' misinterpretations of their behavior or their child's as racist or ableist. Under each finding heading, I focus on at least one mother's stories. These findings will be analyzed or discussed in relation to the two common assertions derived from the interacting frameworks (i.e., FAF's EUs and the interdisciplinary framework's stances). To be clear in my analysis, I add "Assertion 1" or "Assertion 2" after specific statements or sections to draw attention to the ways I am interpreting the findings.

Naming Assets and Strengths

One important finding was that all four mothers were conscientious to frame their presentations to the PSETs around their children's strengths. Each took time to describe their child through a positive, humanizing lens. These descriptions were important because all their children had experienced negative consequences for being perceived by educators as "unable to perform," "too immature," "not capable," or "challenging." Janice, whose son with autism was in high school during one of her presentations (fall 2017), began by describing him as "mild-mannered," "doesn't speak loud," "easy-going," "kind-hearted," and "the type of kid that won't kill spiders" (Assertion 1). Patricia described her 5-year-old son with profound sensorineural hearing loss and hypotonia in this way: "He talks. He truly talks. [Voice breaks due to emotion] I never thought he was going to survive [Assertion 1]. And he talks and he runs!" Lizette, whose daughter with autism was a young adult during the study (fall 2016), recalled her daughter's pre-kindergarten teacher who told her, "This one [referring to Lizette's daughter] isn't going to make it." Lizette told the PSETs how she countered the teacher's deficit notions by responding (Assertion 2): "She needs to be in choir. She needs to be a cheerleader. She needs to be on the Best Buddies Basketball team. She needs to be in Special Olympics. She needs to learn how to cursive write her name because she is going to have a checking account!"

Finally, Dolores, whose daughter with Down syndrome was 9 years old during one of her presentations (fall 2016), told the PSETs firmly (Assertion 1): "My daughter is in fourth grade. She is reading at the second-grade level. She is able to identify main idea, characters, setting, and details. She is able to do math. She is also able to communicate her needs and wants. She is a happy girl."

Through these affirmative accounts, the mothers foregrounded their children's strengths as central to how they wanted the PSETs to be "introduced" to their children. For Dolores, these introductions were particularly important because of the ways her daughter had been perceived negatively at her school for being both an English learner and having Down syndrome. Dolores took time to present to the PSETs her daughter's many academic accomplishments as a way to juxtapose her daughter's true abilities against the perceived abilities presented to her by her daughter's educators (Assertion 1). In Dolores's narrative to PSETs, she told them how on the 1st day of school, when her daughter was in 1st grade, she had been placed in a life skills classroom without Dolores's consent. Dolores recalls being frustrated because she was unable to advocate well for her daughter to have her placed in a general education classroom. She believed she was not consulted prior to her daughter's restrictive placement because of her and her daughter's positionalities. She was a Latina immigrant. Her daughter had a dis/ability and a language difference. Neither were proficient in English at that time. She also understood during meetings with the school assessment team that they "had low expectations of my daughter's ability . . . due to her diagnosis" (Assertion 2). Further, when her daughter was provided with initial special education services (speech and language services), she received "a minimum fifteen minutes per week in a small group of three."

In the classes Dolores cotaught and cofacilitated, she described her daughter's assets in an explicit manner in front of the PSETs as a way to signal to them the importance of centering and prioritizing students' abilities and strengths (Assertion 1). Dolores was adamant that teachers should not lower expectations for children with dis/abilities because of assumptions around a specific label (Assertion 2). She believed her daughter's dis/ability, at the intersections of race and language, caused educators at the school to place her in more restrictive environments and reduce the amount time given for services. Moreover, at IEP meetings she found that there was an overall lack by IEP team members to acknowledge her daughter's ability to communicate her needs, which were constantly strengthening and evolving. She emphasized to the PSETs that her daughter's ability to effectively express what she desired or needed was significant particularly because she experienced language challenges as an emergent bilingual and, as an individual with Down syndrome, struggled with phonation, respiration, and articulation (Assertion 1).

Contextualizing or Reframing Their Children's Behaviors

The four mothers shared several stories with the PSETs describing their children's behaviors in relation to their intentions versus how the actual behaviors were interpreted by teachers. One purpose of these stories was to demonstrate to the PSETs how quickly certain assumptions about their children's actions could lead to negative consequences for their children. The other purpose was to explain to the PSETs the importance of knowing each child, including their desires and triggers so that instead of automatically reaching unfavorable conclusions, PSETs could learn to see their students' behaviors as purposeful. For an example, I focus on Lizette's story.

In one of the classes Lizette cotaught, she shared a time when her daughter was 6 years old. The main point of her story was to emphasize to the PSETs not only the importance of knowing their students well but also understanding the ways teachers can limit students' growth by maintaining low expectations of them. Specifically, Lizette framed her narrative around her daughter's intelligence and juxtaposed it against her daughter's teachers' deficit-based and limiting perceptions.

In her account, Lizette described going to her daughter's school in the second half of the school year and being surprised at finding her daughter and her daughter's special education teacher sitting on the floor of the classroom. The teacher was buttoning up her daughter's jacket and tying one of her shoes. Lizette recalled looking at her daughter and exclaiming, "Excuse me!" whereby her daughter, who rarely spoke, glanced toward Lizette, replied "Oh," and quickly proceeded to tie her other shoe. The teacher, in shock, stated incredulously, "She knows how to tie her shoes," as if allowing the information to sink in. Lizette then turned to teacher and asked, "How long have you been doing that?", to which the teacher replied, "Since the first day of school." Lizette looked at her daughter, then at the teacher, and said matter-of-factly, "Girl, she has been playing you."

Without additional context, the gravity of Lizette's story may not be apparent. However, this account within the scope of other experiences where Lizette's daughter was not provided opportunities to expand upon or practice her skills is consequential. Being a young Black girl with autism who has difficulty with verbal articulation made Lizette's daughter "a target" for being "pushed out" of the general curriculum, cheerleading, and other school-based activities she enjoyed. In the example Lizette provided, she wanted to make clear to the PSETs that her daughter's intersectional identity was part of the reason why, in this case and in others, her daughter's teachers did not encourage her to do more and did not get to know her well. At an IEP meeting, Lizette recalled IEP team members refusing Lizette's request to teach her daughter cursive writing because they did not believe she could write. Upset, Lizette responded, "You guys refuse to teach her. . . . As long as that sign out there says 'school' on it, you will teach her. I don't care what her diagnosis is" (Assertion 2). When they continued not to teach her daughter cursive (something the Lizette valued greatly), Lizette realized: "[They] assumed I was going to be a Black female, single mother that never came to the case conference. I was at every case conference except for the ones that they had without me and there were case conferences without me being there."

In addition, Lizette told the PSETs that she chose to tell this story of her daughter to demonstrate that when teachers gave up on her daughter, her daughter began to give up on herself. According to Lizette, though her daughter "was playing" the teacher by having the teacher help her with adaptive tasks (e.g., tying shoes), she was also losing out on important opportunities to demonstrate and practice her independence, which at home was highly valued (Assertion 1). Lizette believed that her daughter's dis/ability at the intersection of race as well as Lizette's status of being a "single mother" caused many of her daughter's teachers, over the years, to greatly reduce their expectations of her daughter and, thus, stifle her daughter's potential and growth (Assertion 2).

Calling Out Educators' Misinterpretations

FAF approaches provide family members opportunities to share their narratives reflectively and reflexively. To share stories in these ways means that family members can recall moments from the past by infusing reflective understanding of the multiple contexts, agendas, or intentions occurring at a given time and place. They can also provide reflexive, critical perspectives that account for their own positionality in relation to status, privilege, or power of all those involved in a situation within the systems through which interactions were mediated. Each of the mothers in this study discussed moments within the school system when they were discriminated against because of race, ethnicity, language, disability, or class. From Patricia being referred to as "the Mexican" to Dolores and Lizette not being valued for their contributions at IEP meetings, all mothers shared with PSETs the way schoolwide systems, rooted in dominant wite, Eurocentric ideologies, supported inequitable practices.

Of all the stories shared, Janice's was the clearest example of the way educators' implicit biases showed up at an IEP meeting and directly impacted her son's educational trajectory. She was slow and deliberate in narrating her account of what occurred to demonstrate to PSETs the ways racism and ableism manifest in school spaces meant to support, rather than further marginalize students of color with dis/abilities and their families. Here is an important excerpt from her account:

> One of the things that really bothered me about the meeting was, during the meeting they started asking me—now, mind you, everyone in the room knows that my child has Asperger's—but they asked me, "Well, are you married? Is his father in his life? Is there anything going on in his household? Drugs? Alcohol?" And, I'm thinking, "Why is that even a question?!" He's not acting out in school. He's not throwing fits. He's not fighting, he's not cursing, he's not cutting school. He's displaying the normal behavior of someone with Asperger's Syndrome. So, what would cause you to ask me questions like this in a meeting? And, if you wanted to ask me these types of questions, why would you do it in a setting where's there's 8 to 10 other people? And, if I did have an issue, I wouldn't feel comfortable talking to you about it. And so, those kinds of things can really make working with a parent . . . very, very difficult.

Through this example, Janice provided a snapshot to the PSETs for the reason behind a school's decision to request that Janice find a different school for her son. The school had claimed that her son was being disruptive in class. However, in this IEP meeting, where Janice was met by approximately 10 teachers and administrators who strategically sat away from her, she found out that these "behaviors" were ones directly related to her son's Asperger's condition (Assertion 2). For example, the main "inappropriate" behavior the IEP team cited repeatedly was her son's tendency to twirl string in his hands during math class. When Janice argued calmly that the string twirling was directly related to his condition and was a behavior addressed in the IEP goals, the IEP team members began a different line of questioning (Assertion 2). They shifted from focusing on her son's "disruptions" in class to what they perceived was occurring in the home and causing these distracting behaviors at school.

Here, Janice pointed out to the PSETs that the IEP team members "crossed a line." Here, she believed that her son's dis/ability at the intersection of race became the salient issue. She reiterated that her son's string twirling was not a result of instability at home, but rather that, when he got bored, he tended to play with string to keep himself stimulated. Playing with string, she made clear, had nothing to do with his race. Though he struggled in math, it was not that he could not do the problems; it was more that he needed extra supports to guide him through difficult areas (Assertion 1). She made clear that her son was not the problem, nor were his behaviors the issue. The main issue was that the school did not want to invest in the required resources to provide her son with FAPE (Free and Appropriate Public Education) and, instead, sought to blame her son and her family for his lack of adequate performance and "appropriate" school behaviors (Assertion 2).

TEACHING PSETS THROUGH STORIES

The four mothers in this study were intentional about how they wanted to present who their children were in relation to how they were perceived by educators. They signaled to the PSETs that carrying implicit, deficit-driven biases about children and their families was a detriment to students' ability to evolve and to become more independent. They emphasized the need for PSETs to actively listen to and observe the students whom they will be teaching to understand their needs and desires. They modeled for PSETs how to begin advocating for students with dis/abilities by centering their strengths. This was an important step toward arguing for appropriate placement in the students' least restrictive environment, which, for the mothers, was the general education classroom for the majority of the school day. Moreover, they each provided clear examples of ways their children's diagnosis was given more importance over the assets they readily displayed and, through these examples, challenged PSETs to confront their preconceived notions of dis/ability. In addition, the mothers discussed ways that racism, ableism, and other discriminatory practices operate in schools as status quo and have a debilitating impact on students with dis/abilities and their families. Finally, they offered PSETs guidance about how they would like both current and future educators to interact and work with them. All four mothers stressed that treating students and families in humanizing ways was at the core of change. They believed that teacher education programs needed to integrate strategic activities to teach PSETs not only ways to become more responsive to students' cultural repertoires including dis/ability, but to recognize manifestations of racism and ableism in order to take concerted action against all forms of oppression.

In this study, the mothers used stories to share their lived experiences to demonstrate their children's assets as evolving, dynamic, and intersectional. Using an interacting framework built on families' assets and the ways that dis/ability is understood at the intersections of other identity markers of difference, these stories were examined within the multiple contexts in which they occurred. For example, it was impossible to separate out school-driven practices such as placing Dolores' daughter in one of the most restrictive settings (i.e., self-contained, life-skills classroom) from the impact it had on her (e.g., reduced exposure to the general education curriculum). Thus, the context for where, when, and how events occurred at the school became as important as the intention—the why—behind certain actions taken by educators that detrimentally impacted the mothers in this study and their children.

Through shared story, the mothers situated and explained both context and intention to the PSETs. Mainly through nonexamples, the mothers conveyed how educators' implicit biases, rooted in racism and ableism, perpetuated deficit-driven myths of their children as *unable to learn* because of their dis/ability, home life (associated with race and/or class), or language (associated with language difference). The mothers also discussed, both directly and indirectly, the ways that power operated within school hierarchies to privilege educators' knowledge about their children *over* their own lived, insider expertise. Specifically, Lizette, Janice, and Dolores experienced marginalization by being told, in different ways, that their minorized statuses (race, language) precluded the dominant majority IEP team members from listening to or acting upon what they had to say.

REEXAMINING THE FRAMEWORK

The interacting framework is a beginning to better understand how families' assets and cultures can inform the ontologies and epistemologies of "schooling" in determining what and whose knowledge matters, what is taught, how it is taught, and what behaviors determine "success." However, in applying the framework to the four mothers in this study, it became clear that, though the mothers began their shared narratives with centering their children's assets, many times they cotaught through nonexamples because so few educators throughout the mothers' experiences had showed that they valued the mothers' knowledge or expertise. At the onset, my intention for the interacting framework was to unearth positive exemplars of how families' cultures were honored by educators in the school system, as described through Assertion 1. These exemplars could then be used to model culturally sustaining behaviors for PSETs. That stated, I was not surprised that most of the mothers' narratives were framed to the PSETs as practices of "what not to do." This leads me to (re)conceptualize Assertion 1 to include the caveat that though families' cultures are dynamic and intersectional, dominant school cultures continue to resist real commitments to inclusion, equity, and diversity by excluding the voices of minoritized families who make up their school communities.

IMPLICATIONS

In FAF projects that actively recruit families of color with intersecting minoritized identities, opportunities to trouble whose knowledge matters in schools and in teacher preparation programs are made possible.

Knowledge-making through families' shared narratives, centering the assets of students/children with dis/abilities with other minoritized identities, can act as counternarratives to pathologized and racialized depictions of these students in textbooks, media, photography, or other mediums. Having mothers like Lizette, Dolores, Patricia, and Janice as coeducators in college/university courses, who position their children's strengths as central to the conversation around dis/ability, provides strong footing for sustaining dis/ability cultures as important cultural repertoires worth embedding within teacher preparation pedagogy.

I argue that individuals with dis/abilities at the intersections of other minoritized identities and their family members can have a major impact on PSETs' formation by teaching about dis/ability from an insider perspective. Their ability to positively impact deficit-driven mindsets is evident (Santamaría Graff, et al., 2020, 2022) and their voices invaluable in shifting whose knowledge and assets count in the larger landscape of systemic educational change.

CHAPTER 11

Practicing for Complex Times
The Future of Disability Studies and Teacher Education

Srikala Naraian

The foundations of teacher education informed by disability studies are typically premised on the idealized principles derived from critical theory in education, including disability studies and critical race studies (Connor et al., 2016). As a field of study that has grown out of a necessary scrutiny of discriminatory practices against historically marginalized communities, teacher preparation for inclusion informed by disability studies has relied on the insights derived from the experiences of those communities to imagine transformation in schools (Slee, 2011, 2019). This has, predictably, produced a strong critique of prevailing forms of practice that encompass both institutionalized procedures as well as micro-level encounters between school actors such as educators, disabled students, and their families. Such critiques have established some fundamental aspirations and commitments that teachers must learn to affiliate with to teach inclusively in schools. Teacher educators who seek asset pedagogies (APs) for socially just practice draw on disability studies to enjoin teacher candidates to imagine schools differently as they work toward change.

For teachers who are disillusioned with the oppressive conditions within which students learn, these calls are compelling, even if they are not easily enacted. Many will successfully go out and challenge the inequities they encounter. Many others will be co-opted into deficit discourses that they committed to dismantling during their programs of preparation. Still others will remain reflective of the inexorable pull of those discourses and consciously make strategic decisions to appropriate or reject them (Anderson & Stillman, 2015; Stillman, 2011). In all these cases, what surfaces as a constant is that teaching inclusively is never an idealized phenomenon. It remains an embedded and embodied process of coming to know oneself alongside teaching-learning in schools. In that regard, the preparation of teachers for inclusion[1] must locate idealized commitments alongside the material and discursive arrangements within which inclusion comes to take form.

The purpose of this chapter is to explore a theorizing of teacher education for inclusion, which is grounded in the knowings of teachers. In focusing on teacher knowledge, I do not turn away from the struggles of scholars in disability studies who, working at the periphery of mainstream educational research, seek to center the knowings of disabled students and families. As a nondisabled scholar, I embrace the learnings of the field of disability studies as foundational to my understanding of schools. As a teacher educator, I am simultaneously and compulsorily drawn into questions of *teacher* learning and its embeddedness within a political landscape in which teaching competencies are continually calibrated by multiple actors that include government representatives, private entities, and community agencies (Cochran-Smith et al., 2012). The preoccupation that underlies my efforts is this: How can an asset-based approach to students' learning also subsume an asset-based approach to teachers' learning?

I begin by first examining the significance of theorizing teachers' practices of inclusion in ways that can disclose its complexity—a task that suggests a greater diversification of our theoretical commitments. I follow this with an example of my journey in pursuing theoretical frames that can provide a complex accounting of teacher agency within material contexts. I then describe how these frames for investigating teachers' practice have deepened my understanding of inclusion itself. Subsequently, I articulate two important directions for disability studies in teacher education, namely, the importance of a narrative stance toward teachers' experiences and understanding inclusion in terms of assemblages. Collectively, they can stimulate an AP of teacher education for inclusion that accounts for the unpredictable confluence of past experiences, present material and discursive contexts, and aspirations for the future (Priestley et al., 2015).

THEORIZING *PRACTICE* IN ORDER TO PRACTICE THEORY

One of the core tenets in the field of disability studies in education (DSE) has been the privileging of the experiences of disabled students/individuals and their families. Many of our courses in teacher preparation for inclusion include personal narratives of experience that can allow prospective teachers to empathize with the ways that the confluence of policies, beliefs, and attitudes can produce oppressive conditions, which then stifle student's capacity to learn. This history of marginalization alongside an awareness of the multiple ways in which schooling structures perpetuate oppressive conditions has largely remained the bedrock of teacher preparation for inclusion. In other words, theorizing of inclusion has tended almost exclusively to the *why* of inclusion—that is, theorizing that begins with a critique of current systems. Theorizing that begins with the practices of teachers has assumed a less significant role within the development of the field. Said differently, teacher *practice* has served of minimal theoretical value to conceptions of inclusion within the field of disability studies in education (Naraian, 2019). There have been many important examples of locating the interests of practice within theory (e.g., Waitoller & Thorius, 2016). What has, however, remained the norm are conceptualizations of inclusion that flow from the academy rather than emerging from the complexities of teaching practice in varied material contexts.

Given the peripheral location of disability studies within the larger field of educational research, particularly in comparison to the more dominant field of special education, an emphasis on securing the rationale for inclusion is understandable and, arguably, justifiable. Still, it has inadvertently deepened the theory–practice divide that researchers are warned against perpetuating (Cherryholmes, 1988). The field of inclusive education has not sufficiently considered how teachers understand and develop their own attachments to idealized principles of inclusion amid deficit-based schooling discourses. When insights about "inclusion" emanate exclusively from the academy, they serve to reestablish the historical hierarchy between theorists and practitioners (Lagemann, 2000), while also perpetuating a form of "damage-centered teaching" in teacher education that inadvertently fosters a deficit orientation to students and schools (Carter-Andrews et al., 2019).

Over the last few decades, scholars in the field of teacher education have increasingly advocated for the centering of teachers "personal, practical and professional knowledge" over a "formalistic" approach that relies on the conceptual frameworks brought by researchers to assess what things are and how they could be different (Clandinin & Connelly, 1996, 2000). Arguing for teacher knowing as epistemically significant, Lytle and Cochran-Smith (1992) advocate for teachers' classroom inquiries as advancing what we know about teaching. Increasingly, scholars are being urged to take up participatory approaches or more specifically supporting practitioner inquiry when researching marginalized populations (Simon & Campano, 2013). Within disability studies in education, too, new ways of describing teacher's practice that acknowledge their complex, agentive work have begun to emerge (Naraian & Schlessinger, 2021; Waitoller & Kozleksi, 2013). They attest to the need for a deeper engagement with teachers and the "systems, processes, and constructs" within schools that impact teachers' efforts toward inclusion (Miller et al., 2020).

An approach that values teacher knowledge, therefore, must also then bring a complex accounting of their agency. Exhortations to teachers to serve as "change agents" that flow from idealized notions of inclusion presume static notions of agency as inherent within people. They give rise to discourses of heroism or compliance that do little justice to the complex negotiations that are warranted by the material realities of schools (Priestly et al., 2015). However, by attending to *practices* as an opportunity to understand agency for inclusion, researchers are inevitably drawn to inquire into the collectivities within which they (i.e., practices) emerge. Such collectivities consist of multiple elements that may include families, school policies, accountability mandates, state and federal laws pertaining to students *and* teachers, the role of community organizations, and the phenomenon of charter schools, among others. Embedded within these collectivities, teachers encounter (and engage with) multiple orientations to schools and learning, some of which may be compatible with their own, and others distinctly misaligned. Each encounter delivers an occasion to both uphold and question what they know. Each encounter also locates them variously along dimensions of race/ethnicity, gender, dis/ability, religion, and linguistic status that inevitably mark their relations with people and ideas. This *multiplicity* (Hames-Garcia, 2000) that characterizes their work in schools presumes a straddling of, and negotiation with, multiple systems that defy facile explanations of inclusionary/exclusionary practice.

ENGAGING DIVERSE THEORIES TO CENTER PRACTICE: MY JOURNEY

Diversifying our theoretical commitments as DSE scholars, many of which have relied on Eurocentric intellectual foundations, may be helpful to begin complexifying our explanations of teacher practice. In this section, I offer a few of my own explorations as an example. As a teacher educator-researcher lodged within a DSE tradition, my interest in a more complex accounting of teacher agency led me to the body of work described as U.S. Third World feminism (Sandoval, 2003). This included the writings of scholars such as Gloria Anzaldua, Chandra Mohanty, and Trinh Min-Ha, who recognized that fixed ideological boundaries were impossible when seeking to achieve collective solidarity around principles of equity (Anzaldua, 1988; Minh-Ha, 2011; Mohanty 2003, 2013). For instance, drawing attention to the everyday oppositional consciousness of poor women in Third World contexts, Mohanty (2003) argues for a politics of engagement rather than an identity politics in the search for equitable conditions for practice. For scholars interested in supporting educators' efforts toward APs, an oppositional consciousness requires that inclusion cannot remain premised on abstract notions of equity but must evoke a framework for action that considers the intersection of multiple needs and desires within any given context (Danforth & Naraian, 2015). Collectively, the work of U.S. Third World feminists and that of other feminists of color, including Alarcon (1991), speaks to the necessity for an epistemological pluralism, which can account for ways of knowing inclusion that are not Eurocentric in their orientations. They trouble frames of resistance that are premised on binary thinking (e.g., oppressor/oppressed, colonizer/colonized, inclusion/exclusion, etc.).

While the writings of Mohanty (2003) and Trinh Minh-Ha (2011) allowed me to fold in the material contexts of teachers' practice in my theorizing of inclusion, spatial theorizing helped me focus more deliberately on teacher identity and practice. Spatial theory (Soja, 1996) I found afforded the opportunity for educators (inclusive or otherwise) to think about student learning without associating it with fixed environments. Spatial theory requires us to imagine the places within schools as not merely containers with fixed stable boundaries within which practices occur. Rather, they are constructed and emergent within the interactions of people, ideas, and practices. Spaces are seen as dynamic that can produce identities even as spaces themselves can acquire particular identities (Massey, 1993). Building on my research with teachers in U.S. public schools, a spatial orientation allowed me to offer a *diasporic* sensibility (Kooy & Freitas, 2007) as a requirement for teachers to navigate the presumably fixed boundaries of special and general education. It permitted a recognition of learning need as a socially constructed concept while also permitting boundaries between locations and disciplinary knowledges to remain fluid in the consideration of those needs (Naraian, 2016).

Collectively, my attempts to focus theoretically on context to understand inclusion as well as *teaching* for inclusion has produced a search for theory that can imbricate social constructionism without disprivileging materiality. Recognizing the risks of appropriating a material-discursive binary, my recent explorations have begun to draw on posthumanist thought to understand inclusion and teaching for inclusion (Braidotti, 2019a, 2019b). Briefly, within posthuamism, matter is not understood as inert; rather it is fluid and dynamic (Coole & Frost, 2019). Alongside humans, matter too exercises agency within collectivities of human and nonhuman entities. Posthumanist theory allows us to see actors, including teachers, as more-than-human, even as it can acknowledge the less-than-human ways in which disability has been understood historically (Goodley et al., 2015). While a posthumanist stance may decenter human intentionality and agency, it can disclose new ways of understanding inclusion as an embedded and embodied phenomenon that can inform how we approach teacher education for inclusion.

The movement I have described thus far through multiple theoretical frames was stimulated by my interest in beginning with teacher practice. The conceptual diversity this offered has continually helped me refine how I understand inclusion. Of course, as theories that do not originate in disability concerns, they also inevitably bear the risk that disability will be either discounted or misappropriated (Goodley et al., 2019). While this admittedly remains an important challenge, recent studies in *ableism* (Campbell, 2009) as well as the work of philosophers of inquiry who make the experiences of autistic individuals central to their own theorizing (Manning, 2016; Manning and Massumi, 2014) offer encouraging routes to explore.

IT'S ABOUT TIME (AND PLACE): AN EXAMPLE OF COMING TO KNOW INCLUSION FROM TEACHERS' PRACTICE

In what ways has a diversified theorized engagement with teachers' practice helped me refine my understanding about inclusion? To illustrate this, I take up one strand of inquiry that focuses on teachers' compulsory engagement with *time* and *place* in their efforts toward inclusion (Naraian, 2014, 2017). My insights are derived from several qualitative studies in schools conducted over the past decade or more. The teachers within these studies taught in U.S. public school settings (elementary and secondary; urban and suburban). Teacher-participants identified either as male or female and encompassed affiliation with different racial categories including Asian American, Black, Latinx, and white. (For more details of these teachers and the contexts of their practice, please see Naraian, 2008, 2011, 2014, 2016.)

Conceptions of time in school are relentless. Not only do they determine the pace of learning through premarked school periods, school days, and the school year, they also force their way into documents such as the IEP (individualized education plan) that then establish how much learning will happen where and with whom. Through these temporal devices, students themselves are variously categorized such that speed is associated with intellectual skill (e.g., a quick learner), and the absence of speed is indicative of deficit (e.g., a slow learner). Associations with time equally showed how teachers in my studies were caught up in a never-ending loop that prioritized physical place—environments inevitably marked as "general" or "special." The idea of special education as *not* a place has been critical to make the shift toward more inclusive practices (Taylor, 1988). Yet it has, inadvertently, also reified inclusion as a *place*—most typically, the general education classroom (Lipsky & Gartner, 2008).

As inclusion became framed as a particular kind of "placement" of disabled students, teachers in my studies improvised in multiple ways to move boundaries within and between classrooms to support the learning of their students, regardless of their labels. This might take the form of learning groups within classrooms or creation of out-of-classroom spaces. Despite the risks such arrangements posed to concepts of inclusion—and such risks *did* sometimes materialize in exclusionary practice—teachers sought to mitigate them through discourses of community to foster greater connectedness among students (Naraian, 2016). Arguably, they were implicitly protesting both the divisions between general and special education as well as schools' attachment to fixed places as marking the status of students as learners. Yet, unsurprisingly, teachers also sustained the institutional separation between special and general education; this was illustrated, for instance, in the ways they assessed student capability for learning as well as their own capability to serve them. Even as they wondered about their professional preparation to serve *all* students, they also seemed to suggest that some students might benefit from the conditions provided by special education spaces.

It became evident that the institutional structures that divided services for disabled and nondisabled students constrained teachers' capability to maneuver time and place in ways that could more readily serve inclusive goals. My inquiries into the conditions managed and/or created by teachers for greater accessibility in the classroom further disclosed that time itself remains deeply undertheorized within inclusive education. While notions of "crip time" are available to us through the work of many disability studies scholars (see, for example, Kafer, 2013), it has been less deeply utilized to understand how it can come to inform the practice of inclusion. Drawing on "crip time" allows us to see that general and special education "times" are made incompatible and accepted as such within school systems, usually to the disadvantage of disabled students. Whether it is the time needed by a student using an augmentative communication device to extend a greeting or whether it is the deliberate configuration of the school day to accommodate "community field trips" (typically, for students with special education labels), time becomes modulated by the particular commitments teachers bring to schools, disability, and learning. In that regard, time as an integral component to the "grammar of schooling" (Tyack & Cuban, 1995) has received minimal attention in the scholarship on preparing teachers for socially just APs.

If time structures the everyday practice of teachers, how can it help us in arriving at a deeper understanding of how teachers can enact their commitment to social justice? The work of disability studies scholars who describe the "strange temporalities" that pervade disability experiences (Kafer, 2013) reminds us not only of the differential ways in which students inhabit school spaces but also the neoliberal values that undergird the typical configuration of the school day. We are returned to questions of *how* much time all students are engaged in doing *what*, *where*, and *when*. Even as "crip time" renders the values of normative schooling practices more visible, the acknowledgement of the variable embodiment that it registers may permit a more nuanced understanding of interventions. *Interventions* have typically been part of mainstream special education discourse and reference practices, which are adopted as a response to individual learning needs that are seen as predictive of failure in schools.

As focused on the remediation of learners, interventions thus conceptualized fail to recognize individual needs as intertwined with instructional practices, and in that regard, they earn the justifiable distaste of scholars in disability studies. Yet, while interventions can, and often do, suggest histories of oppression, approaching it from the perspective of "crip time" can be generative. By acknowledging the complexities of embodiment that constitute disability experiences, "crip time" orients us differently toward individual students' "needs" not as requiring remediation but as indicative of the unpredictable needs of diverse bodies inhabiting inhospitable spaces (Piepzna-Samarsinha, 2018). Simultaneously, it compels us to look outward to the ideologies of ability that frame the work of schools as partly constitutive of the emergence of learning need itself (Siebers, 2010). "Need" then can both be located within the body while also loosened from it such that the remedial character of "interventions" is undermined. In doing thus, we come to know that interventions are also never only oppressive or only reflective of ableist goals (Kafer, 2013). We are released from thinking about interventions as concerned with "fixing" an individual and instead consider what it may accomplish for the individual and how that can be enacted in respectful ways.

A reorientation to interventions through a reorientation to time emphasizes other ways of coming to know teaching practices. An understanding of time that extends beyond the immediacy of the moment relaxes our rigid grip on the idealized principles of inclusive pedagogy every time, all the time—a condition that most would argue is neither practical nor, in some cases, desirable. Instead, it calls for a pedagogy of *deferral* that acknowledges both the imperfect conditions of teaching-learning of the moment as well as wider commitments to individual growth. A pedagogy of deferral means recognizing that students' potential (as well as that of teachers) remains unfinished and always in process. For teachers, it means reorienting to what students are doing in the moment in terms of future possibility. Each act of deferral is an improvisation that draws on multiple elements that are imbricated in that moment. While those elements may include constructivist understandings of learners, they may also work alongside, for instance, behaviorist discourses. But the larger commitments to students and their communities that prefigure those teaching-learning moments allow such acts to be understood as deferring desired inclusive outcomes. Arguably, such deferral remains vulnerable to deficit-based practice and/or ableist norms. However, integral to such a pedagogy is the reflective practice that teachers need to undertake to interrogate those same improvisations as they sustain their commitments to equity (Naraian, 2014; 2019).

THE *BECOMING* OF TEACHERS AND THE CONTINUAL (RE)MAKING OF "INCLUSION"

The qualitative studies referenced in the previous sections and others I have conducted (Naraian, 2008, 2011, 2016, 2017, 2019) register the conceptual gains I have achieved in attaching epistemic value to teachers' experiences of inclusion. Over the last few decades, many scholars have tried to beat back the "scientific" discourses within educational research that have been premised on positivist epistemologies and positioned disabled students' experiences as lesser than their nondisabled counterparts (Giangreco & Taylor,

2003). Those same "scientific" discourses have also been responsible for the marginalization of teachers within the academy (Lagemann, 2000). As a scholarly community, we need to remain attuned to that history and make teachers integral to how we derive important insights about inclusion. In the following paragraphs, I emphasize the directions that have been stimulated by my theoretical explorations for a disability studies-informed teacher education for inclusion. Specifically, I address the importance of narrative to understand teachers' becomings, as well as the potential afforded by recent posthumanist thought to deepen our understandings of inclusion itself.

Thinking Narratively About Teachers

A narrative stance toward teachers does not mean that we simply ask them to share their stories about their experiences as teachers with us as researchers. If we remain attached to meanings of inclusion that we have already presumed are nonnegotiable, then we will merely look for the ways those meanings are/are not reflected within those stories; our orientation to those stories are already predetermined (Clandinin & Connelly, 2000). Instead, it requires us to approach their learning with a *loving* rather than *arrogant* perception (Lugones, 1998) that does not center standards of inclusion derived outside their experience but explores the emergence of tenets through their practice. A narrative stance, therefore, privileges teachers' agency as knowers, rather than seeking a "faithful representation of a reality independent of the knower" (Clandinin, 2013, p. 14). A focus on their experiences presumes that they are continually engaged in the process of coming to know inclusion. Stories allow teachers to make sense of their lives; as researchers, we are called upon to approach them dialogically such that we leave them unfinished and unfinalized (Frank, 2010).

In my own research, approaching teachers narratively has allowed me to understand more deeply the contexts in which they carry out their work, which almost always implicated relations between general education and special education systems. For instance, a teachers' agonized decision to deliberately use disability labels arrived from the necessity to work with and against a collaborative teaching context where students' learning needs were being obscured (Naraian & Schlessinger, 2018). In another instance, to understand a teacher's decision to allow nondisabled peers to "use" a voice output device assigned to a nonspeaking disabled student, I had to come to learn more deeply her approach to transparent teaching that she sought to enact within her classroom (Naraian, 2011). In each instance, the possibility of a judgmental critique of teachers' practice was immediately available. However, each instance required giving teachers the opportunity to disclose themselves differently, with the expectation that their stories always remained unfinished. Doing thus, allowed me to recognize that as DSE teacher educators, we need to support teachers more adequately to creatively manage the intersecting influences of general and special education on their capability to enact inclusion.

Narrative investigations of teachers' experiences permit the characterization of teachers as more than either heroically resisting ableist practices in schools or as perpetuating those same practices. Such arguably unidimensional characterizations may have historically played an important role in enlisting more educators in the challenge to hegemonic deficit-based discourses in schools. Still, as research has increasingly shown, enacting such commitments is a complex endeavor. In my own coauthored inquiries, it is evident that even "heroic" approaches are not without tensions that still need to be worked through. Such tensions might center on the ways a "race consciousness" can obscure dis/ability during everyday instructional practice or it can mean navigating one's own cultural identity alongside colleagues while serving as a mentor for students of color (Naraian & Schlessinger, 2021). In either case, educators' capability to enact their commitments to equitable opportunities for students remains entangled with their roles and responsibilities, given and assumed, within their school communities. Their inclusive practice emerges from the negotiation of relationships not only with their students, but with their colleagues and professional communities. It may be time, then, for other tropes besides "change agents" to enable us to continue the work of enlarging the community of inclusive educators.

Narratively oriented inquiries into teachers' practice register the complex social, political, and material environments in which teachers' agentive work occurs. In that regard, narrative inquiries not only offer us examples of what "successful" inclusive teaching might mean, they also disclose how "failure" can be indicative of more than just individual capability. For instance, reviewing the findings from a study where I inquired into one novice teacher's increasingly despondent narrative about her experience as a 1st-year teacher, I came to reject explanations of personal incapacity to a recognition of how teacher preparation programs may themselves participate in the production of such "failure." (She had graduated from a DSE-informed teacher preparation program.) This teacher's experiences provoked me to wonder: How do researchers' conceptions of inclusion intra-act with their teacher-participants' understanding of their efficacy? How might a DSE-informed teacher preparation program that draws on *debility* rather than capacity direct my inquiry? What conceptualizations of inclusion does that presume? (Naraian, 2020).

Attending narratively to teachers' becomings, therefore, can permit a more nuanced approach to their preparation as teachers. Teacher education for socially just pedagogy has typically relied on reflective practices such as developing cultural memoirs that allow teacher candidates to trace their emergent selves in relation to their (raced, gendered, classed, abled) experiences, and which predispose them in particular ways to schools and learning (Allen, 2007; Paris, 2012). Such preparatory experiences are vital in raising students' awareness of the conditions in schools that perpetuate inequities. Still, while such experiences do rely on a form of "storying," the teleological orientation of such activity (i.e., some actions/events are inclusive while others are exclusionary) means that the material-discursive arrangements under which inclusion and reflections about inclusion may occur are not prioritized. Said differently, static and abstract goals of equity and justice trump the relationship between teachers' biographies and material contexts in which they are asked to practice inclusion.

Future Inquiries of Inclusion as Open-Ended "Assemblages"

The recognition of teachers' capability to enact inclusion as always entangled within their contexts can permit us to move beyond idealized understandings of inclusion. Even as disability studies scholars have increasingly come to accept that inclusive education is a process that cannot be readily predicted (Danforth & Naraian, 2015), it raises the question of what it can mean, and how it can be recognized.

The unknowable facet of teaching for inclusion arrives from the recognition that teachers are *becoming* alongside other people, places, events, and ideas as they go about their work. Teachers' practices emerge within the multiple overlapping networks within which they are embedded. Understanding networks themselves as dynamic arrangements pulls us away from critique and draws us into a theory of assemblages where constituent elements affect, and are affected by, each other (DeLanda, 2006; MacLure, 2015). Teachers, then, may be understood as coevolving alongside such elements and do not arrive preformed to their intra-actions within such assemblages.

A theory of assemblage, then, eschews a sole reliance on human agency, in this case, teacher intentionality to work toward change. Instead, in recognizing teachers as one of many embedded and embodied actors and actants engaged intra-actively with one another, it allows us to understand how each (teachers, students, schools, families, policies, etc.) coevolve. Tracing the affective force between these agencies can permit a deeper examination of the processes that underlie a phenomenon, in this case, the production of inclusion (Fox & Allred, 2015). A pursuit of affect extends beyond teachers' emotional responses to disability and/or inclusion, although that may well be a part of the assemblage. Instead, tracing the flow of affect between people, places, discourses, and things can disclose how teachers attach themselves to particular forms of practice.

The deflection from human agency to nonhuman entities and forces can be unsettling for DSE teacher educator-scholars who have relied on their ideological demarcation from mainstream special education practices to foster commitments to inclusion. Yet assemblages are not deterministic in their character; on the contrary, they are always open to new formations (DeLanda, 2006). For instance, understanding the entanglements that constitute inclusive practice does not mean that teachers should not recognize the ways that students (and families) are affected by deficit-based discourses. Clearly, a teacher's advocacy for a student to receive an assistive device to promote their increased participation in the classroom can itself produce new assemblages of teaching-learning that allow other entities such as classroom space, peers, digital software, and so on to come to matter. Acknowledging their coevolution allows DSE researchers to pursue lines of inquiry that can open other assemblages of inclusion. Indeed, we may come to understand inclusion as open-ended arrangements of people, practices, and ideas that are continually shifting over time and place (Naraian, 2020). In doing thus, an AP remains principled, while also remaining a process that evolves alongside new and unpredictable influences.

CONCLUSION

At the heart of any theoretically grounded approach to APs lies the requirement to recognize all actors—students, educators, and families—as occupying fluid, often perilous, and always unstable positions within their contexts of practice. The challenge for us as DSE teacher educator-scholars is to remain mindful in this process, of our fundamental commitments to equity as we encounter the myriad attachments brought by multiple competing interests. Who will serve as our "accountability group" in our efforts to disentangle the threads within inclusion (Hurtado, 1996)? In keeping with the fluid orientation of embedded and embodied actors, there may not be a single answer to this question. Said differently and following the work of feminists of color Anzaldua (1987) and Minh-Ha (2001), "home" is never a stable location—it is both "here" *and* "somewhere else" and is almost always on both sides of the fence; a "humanizing pedagogy" for teacher education eschews all forms of binary thought (Carter-Andrews et al., 2019). At a time when teachers are needed more than ever to participate in the global work on addressing inequality, embracing ambiguity and complexifying our own understandings of inclusion in some of the ways described in this chapter can better support their practice.

CHAPTER 12

Curriculum Theorizing, Intersectional Consciousness, and Teacher Education for Disability-Inclusive Practices

Mildred Boveda and Brittany Aronson

As collaborators, we explore the underexamined role of theorizing in inclusive and special education teacher education research, practice, and reform. More specifically, we consider the potential for curriculum theorizing to disrupt the persistent divide between those prepared to offer specialized educational services and those traditionally charged with establishing, enforcing, and implementing the general education curriculum. Informed by our experiences as P–12 teachers and university faculty, we build on our prior examinations of intersectionality and U.S. university-based teacher education to forward two organizing arguments. First, we offer curriculum theorizing's utility for supporting, critiquing, and researching the implementation of teacher education programs that purport to promote inclusive education. Second, we articulate why deeper understandings of asset-based approaches to curricula matter for preservice and in-service teachers who work with disabled students and with students identified as needing specialized services.[1]

Effective collaboration requires intention setting and shared language that leads to mutual understandings. In this chapter, we address the challenge of collaborating across disciplines that have distinct notions of curriculum, curriculum theory, and how to address differences within teacher education programs. Through our self-narrativization, we co-constructed a collaborative framework that we use together and in our respective practice as teacher educators and researchers. More specifically, we turn to curriculum theorizing to elucidate how preparing teachers to understand disability, both as core content and as central to sound pedagogy, can better equip educators to enact asset-based, Culturally Sustaining Pedagogy. We begin by articulating our shared understanding of curriculum theorizing.

UNDERSTANDING CURRICULUM THEORIZING

Just as there are multiple perspectives of what counts as theory in the field of special education or curriculum studies (Clark et al., 2005; Lambert & Tan, 2016; Sullivan & Artiles, 2011), there are varied perspectives of what is meant by curriculum. Eisner (1979) explained that, traditionally, curriculum is framed as "what schools teach" or "a specific educational activity planned for a particular student at a particular point in time" (p. 34). A shift in how those in curriculum studies conceptualized their work, however, allowed for greater explorations of curriculum beyond the consumable content of schooling or lesson plans. Instead, "curriculum is conceived to be an active force having direct impact on the whole fabric of its human and social context" (Eisner & Vallance, 1974, p. 135). Further, Pinar (2004, p. 2) defined curriculum theory as "the interdisciplinary study of educational experience." This broadening of approach made space for theorizing about how curriculum relates to sociocultural identities and power dynamics in schools. That is, a growing group of scholars rejected notions of curriculum studies as apolitical, insisting that curriculum be situated within historical-geographical and sociopolitical contexts (e.g., Mitrano, 1981; Pinar & Miller, 1982; Schubert, 1992; Subedi, 2013).

Recognizing the vastness of what counts as theory and as curriculum, "a major contribution of all curriculum theorizing is that it can expand one's understanding of what is and what could be" (Huenecke, 1982, p. 294). In referencing curriculum theorizing, we examine both the explicit and tacit expectations for what is considered learning, setting our focus beyond *what* is taught through schooling. In doing so, we complicate the notion that inclusive teacher education is an innocuous project and interrogate the emphasis on granting U.S. P–12 students with individualized educational programs "access to the general education curriculum" as articulated in the Individuals with Disabilities Education Act (IDEA, 2004). The standardized, general education curriculum often reinforces ableist concepts about who and what knowledge matters (Boveda et al., 2019).

We thus highlight that curriculum theorizing is not inherently neutral and consider how it is racialized, gendered, classed, and dis/abled. In our collaborative analyses, we join those who critique the "the colonial project of heteropatriarchal White supremacy" (Gaztambide-Fernandez & Murad, 2011, p. 15) and other normative perspectives of curriculum (e.g., Naraian, 2019) to examine how teacher education curricula function. We contribute to the calls for both "browning the curriculum" (Gaztambide-Fernandez, 2006) and "disability as meta curriculum" (Erevelles et al., 2019) as we articulate how intersectional consciousness matters for the preparation of teachers to work with all students, including those requiring specialized educational services.

Drawing on Black curriculum studies (e.g., Baszile et al., 2016; Berry, 2015) and intersectionality as conceptualized by Black feminists (Collins, 2000; Crenshaw, 1993), we explore the diverse tools that curriculum theorizing generates to disrupt how schooling upholds ableism at the intersections of other structural oppressions (e.g., white supremacy, patriarchy, colonial logic, imperialism). We understand that (1) anti-Blackness and white supremacy are transnational, transcontinental projects (Watkins, 1993); (2) embodied knowledges—such as Black people's experiences within their families, communities, and school settings—are sites of curriculum theorizing (Baszile, 2006); and (3) intersectionality underscores the mutual constitutivity of oppressions enacted in P–12 schools (Boveda et al., 2020) and university-based teacher education (Boveda et al., 2019). Denise Baszile (2006), for example, argued that curriculum theorizing can include both stories told and untold and be inclusive of the stories of those who shape and are shaped by normative curriculum. We thus begin with our lived experiences as important starting places for engaging critical analyses of teacher education for inclusive practices. With these perspectives, we explore the curricular implications of collaborative teacher education (e.g., Pugach et al., 2014) as an intervention for inclusive teacher education (Alvarado et al., 2019).

To start, our positionality statements not only situate each author's sociocultural identities and distinct entry points into teacher education communities (Boveda in special education; Aronson in education studies), but also serve as enactments of curriculum theorizing through self-explorations that reveal our embodied (un)learning of ableism and its entanglement with other oppressions (Baszile, 2016). We include a narrative of an anti-Black and ableist event that catalyzed our first co-authored article, before leading into a discussion about how our collaborative scholarship centers asset-based perspectives of curriculum and pedagogy.

POSITIONING OURSELVES AND OUR COLLABORATIONS IN TEACHER EDUCATION

Black feminist epistemologies suggest that those analyzing how intersectionality manifests in society make their own embodied understandings and relationship to marginality explicit (Collins, 2000). Mildred Boveda is a Black Latina whose first learned language was Spanish yet today speaks and writes predominantly in English. She was born and educated in the United States while raised to value her strong familial ties to the Dominican Republic. Her parents did not have access to formal education, and she grew up in a working-class South Florida community. Boveda does not have a disability; she was placed in Miami Dade County Public Schools' gifted and talented program. She thus witnessed, and even benefited from, the stratifying categorization systems enforced by the district's specialized education programming. Motivated to enter education for social justice intentions, Boveda has been professionally socialized within the field of special education since 2002. Prior to pursuing graduate studies, she was a special education teacher who taught in both P–12 resource and general education classroom settings. She currently serves as a special education faculty member within a teacher education program at a research-intensive university. Informed by Black feminist thought, intersectional disability studies (Miles et al., 2017), and DisCrit (Annamma et al., 2013), Boveda works to interrogate and disrupt the ableist and anti-Black implications of her role within special education.

Brittany Aronson is a white Latina who, due primarily to her parents' white streaming aspirations (Urrieta, 2010), never learned Spanish in her household. Her inability to speak Spanish made her feel disconnected from her Latinx roots for much of her upbringing. As she continued to grow in her own critical consciousness about race, she reclaimed her Latinidad and familial ties to Colombia. Her understanding of ableism, however, developed much later. She began her career as a general elementary education teacher in 2006 and felt underprepared to work with disabled students and students identified as needing specialized educational services. The sole class about special education she was required to take as a pre-service teacher taught disability through a medical model, articulating surface definitions of broad disability categories. Aronson never was identified as having a disability during her P–12 schooling experiences, but later received the diagnosis of attention deficit hyperactivity disorder during graduate school; today she uses medication as needed. Given her father's experiences with multiple sclerosis when she was in middle school, however, she grew up near a family member considered disabled and primarily associated disabilities through their physical manifestations. She has since grown to understand the multifaceted ways ableism is enacted in society. She currently serves as a tenured education studies professor in an educational leadership department at a midsized, doctoral-granting, liberal arts university. Further, she has sought to collaborate with colleagues to better address disabilities and specialized education in her current role as an education faculty and principal educator.

COMING TOGETHER

We first established our collaborative partnership after a colleague, who attended high school with Boveda and college with Aronson, introduced us at the 2016 American Educational Research Association Conference. The spring and summer of 2016 were wrought with excessive police violence. Throughout the United States, there were both affirming and negative responses to Black Lives Matter activism and other protests connected to the deaths of Philando Castile, Alton Sterling, and others. For us, the names of Charles Kinsey and Arnaldo Rios Soto were especially significant as their harrowing experience happened in South Florida, near where we each grew up. Unlike others who did not survive their interactions with police, these two men have since recovered. Although their story received less public outcry, we were distressed that yet another Black man, Kinsey, had been shot by police.

Anti-Blackness often intersects with the disproportionate negative encounters disabled people have with law enforcement (Perry & Carter-Long, 2016), but deciphering what happened in the shooting of Kinsey was especially complex as it (1) occurred in a multiethnic community, and (2) the Black man who was shot was a therapist attempting to protect Soto, a disabled, Latino man with autism. Police representatives, all Latinx, used ableist language in their effort to obfuscate the anti-Blackness of what happened. They justified Kinsey's shooting by arguing that it was not racially motivated because the Latino police officer's intended target was actually Soto. While anti-Black racism was clearly taboo, and thus perceived by police officials as worth denying, the blatant ableism and convenient evocation/erasure of Latinidad[2] in the language used to exonerate police frustrated us. Our sense-making about the shooting and the convoluted discourse that followed precipitated the start of our ongoing dialogue about the intersectionality of racism and ableism and the need to disrupt similar anti-Black and ableist logics in our role as teacher educators (Aronson & Boveda, 2017).

COLLABORATIVELY INTERROGATING SPECIALIZED EDUCATION AND TEACHER EDUCATION

Just as Kinsey's racialized identity became a demonstrable point of vulnerability when working with his disabled client, in our second project we examined how the sociocultural identities of pre-service teachers of color, all of whom were enrolled in special education programs, influenced their understanding of intersectionality in P–12 schooling (Boveda & Aronson, 2019). Given Boveda's focus on collaborative general and special education teacher education (e.g., Blanton et al., 2018; Pugach et al., 2014), she was excited to engage a colleague outside of special education to explore issues related to disabilities and the professionals prepared to serve disabled students. Aronson's emphasis on culturally relevant pedagogy and social justice and teacher education (Aronson & Laughter, 2016; Reyes et al., 2021) animated her desire to continue to collaborate with Boveda to gain a greater understanding of how disability advocacy intersects with other teacher education equity concerns.

Collaborating around how racism and ableism were interrelated and manifesting in teacher education seemed almost intuitive for the both of us. When Aronson asked Boveda to use her perspectives to analyze curriculum, however, Boveda hesitated. Beyond the borrowed language of "accessing the general education curriculum" present in IDEA, she found that her preparation within the field of special education left much to be desired in her understanding of curriculum. Like many other special educators of her generation, she was trained to focus on the individualized education program of students and adapting the *existing* curriculum for students (e.g., Sands et al., 1995). Even as someone who was encouraged to advocate for inclusion, the emphasis was on collaborating with "content experts" so that students identified as needing specialized services could conform to the expectations of what already existed in general education. The inclusive education agenda considers a range of student differences (e.g., disability, class, racial/ethnic, gender, and linguistic differences; Waitoller & Artiles, 2013), but as Boveda's equivocation insinuates, inclusive teacher education prioritized disability above all else—a focus partly driven by credentialing requirements that meet local, state, and federal policies for students with disabilities (Alvarado et al., 2019; Blanton et al., 2018).

Since our initial conversations about these topics, we have each collaborated with other colleagues to expand our understandings of intersectionality, asset pedagogies (APs) and curricula, and teacher education. Boveda has continued to analyze the curriculum of specialized education services with collaborators—both outside of (Boveda et al., 2020) and within special education discursive spaces (Pugach et al., 2020). Similarly, Aronson has moved forward to consider how disability matters in critical and social justice agendas. In an upcoming book, she and her collegues argue:

> [T]eaching as an act of resistance rooted in social justice alliance building cannot define inclusion as the end goal, but rather establish a space and praxis where collective work with Disabled students should begin. This paradigm shift in teacher education will happen when we step back from teaching practices centered in atheoretical technicist deliveries to practices rooted in our entangled embodiments, working toward our collective and enmeshed interests." (Coomer et al., forthcoming, p. 25)

Their book chapter emerged from a collaboration among the faculty in the education leadership, teacher education, and educational psychology departments of her college. As part of their collective, they worked to center social justice within courses, including discussions of racism and ableism.

CURRICULUM THEORIZING THROUGH COLLABORATIONS

From our experiences as teachers, and teacher educators, we not only understand curriculum as the content taught in schools but also see ourselves and our students as curriculum-makers operating within and outside of the structure of formal schooling (see Baszile, 2006). For example, Boveda reflected on how she directly benefited from ableist categorization systems in the public school she once attended and later taught in. As someone professionally socialized in special education, moreover, intersectionality as conceptualized by Black feminisms eventually led her to turn to other frameworks that centered the experiences of disabled people (e.g., DisCrit and disability studies in education). In doing so, she was able to see the connections and divergence between her embodied minoritized identities and students receiving specialized education services.

Aronson also reflected on how she is implicated in ableist ideologies. Her engagements with attitudes toward disabilities at home, along with her preparation as a P–12 teacher and as faculty within university-based teacher education programs, fostered an understanding of disability limited by a medical model and hyperfocus on physical manifestations of differences. Additionally, in a review of her course curriculum, she found that just as many education studies scholars in her field, she often left disability out of her course syllabus. Working in collaboration with her colleagues, she found ways to intentionally center disability across the curriculum (Aronson et al., 2020). In coming together, we both realized how much Boveda's hesitation to engage curriculum and Aronson's neglect of disability in her practice are the result of siloed dynamics that assume the general education curriculum is aspirational. We thus created and offer this framework to help other university-based teacher educators avoid some of pitfalls we encountered as we engaged curriculum theory to disrupt ableism.

Given the siloed nature of the academy, it is too easy to move about independently of each other and to miss opportunities to share resources, understandings, and background knowledge that can strengthen pedagogy and curriculum, as our narratives set to demonstrate. Our experiences and sense-making as researchers and teacher educators in general and special education informed the framework we offer below. This framework is intended for teacher educators and researchers seeking to collaborate through asset-based approaches and provides a tool to interrogate the ways university-based teacher education programs advance, sustain, or prevent disability as AP. It includes prompts for those preparing educators to offer specialized education services to leverage their understanding of curriculum and to better disrupt ableist ideologies in their praxis.

FRAMING AN APPROACH TO CURRICULUM AND INCLUSIVE TEACHER EDUCATION RESEARCH AND PRACTICE

By centering disability, both in general education and in offering specialized educational services, we can begin to disrupt how teacher education upholds discriminatory perspectives on disabled people. Thinking through the framework presented in Figure 12.1 may help faculty working to redesign

Curriculum Theorizing, Intersectional Consciousness

Figure 12.1. A Framework for Curriculum Theorizing in Teacher Education Programming

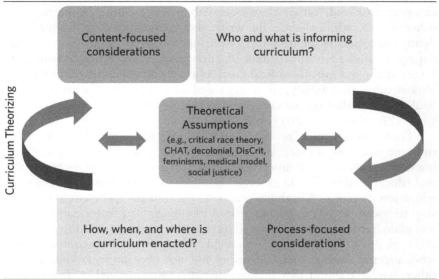

teacher education programs to evaluate how programs are making connections between schools and community-embedded perspectives about disabilities and how curriculum theorizing can inform teacher education research and praxis. Below are some overarching questions to complement traditional asset-pedagogical approaches and that draw on the literature within disability studies, inclusive education, and special education that centers how disability and ableism shape curriculum. The framework addresses theoretical assumptions, content-focused considerations, and process-focused considerations of teacher education programs with a disability-affirming and AP emphasis.

Theoretical Assumptions

A heightened awareness of the absence of discussions around disability in fields outside of special education or disability studies has animated dialogues about how disabled people are framed in education discourse. Interdisciplinary spaces such as curriculum or education studies, which have typically "prided themselves" for their social justice commitments across social identities, are no exception. Erevelles (2005) has been an early voice to connect disability studies and curriculum theory. Loutzenheiser and Erevelles (2019, p. 376) found that even in critical discussions about curriculum and education studies, the sociohistorical and political implications of disability as a social identity continues to be "an outlier . . . usually regarded as the social identity or biologic category to avoid, rather than one with which to build solidarity." In other words, while those who write about education for disabled students and students identified as requiring specialized education services engage in limited examinations of curriculum, "disability continues to linger at the margins of radical curriculum studies—sometimes taken up almost opportunistically, often regarded as synonymous with deviance/brokenness/pathology, or conceived as the inevitable outcome of oppression" (Erevelles et al., 2019, p. 357).

Loutzenheiser and Erevelles (2019, p. 357) also noted how the structural intersections of race, class, gender, sexuality, are "rarely engaged during discussions of social difference within curriculum studies, in particular, and educational studies, in general." Similarly, when examining the teacher education literature, "disability remains an intractable problem in relationship to social justice, requiring a need to engage far greater complexity—and plain hard work—to transcend its precarious status quo" (Pugach et al., 2021, p. 257). There are multiple fields of educational research engaging work around various social identities but not necessarily talking to each other; we have found that this problematic pattern is reflected in teacher education (Boveda et al., 2019).

The first set of questions that anchor our framework thus focus on the purpose of teacher education programs. That is, what are the theoretical assumptions centered in the curriculum and how do they shape attitudes about disability?

- What are the driving forces or intentions that are motivating the education of disabled people and students in need of specialized educational services?
- Why is the inclusive education or special education teacher education program organized and structured in the way that it is?
- What theories about disability and about the purpose of education are used to center disabled students, including students at the intersection of other minoritized or marginalized identities?

For example, Boveda is familiar with "inclusive models" that prioritize individualism and disabled students conforming and fitting into the general education curriculum (e.g., medical model, character education). Aronson and her colleagues are working toward social justice models in which decolonial, community-focused attitudes about differences shape curriculum (Aronson et al., 2021; Reyes et al., 2021). DisCrit offers yet another set of tenets and assumptions that prioritize the intersections between disability and racism (e.g., Annamma & Morrison, 2018). In other words, our framework prompts teacher educators to think through the implicit and explicit theoretical impulses of their teacher education programming decisions.

Content-Focused Considerations

As scholars within disability studies and inclusive education are making headway toward interrupting the limited ways curriculum studies and teacher education address disability, some voices have interrogated how curriculum is taken up—or neglected—by those in special and inclusive education. For example, a group of scholars explored trends in the discipline-based (general education) curriculum (e.g., mathematics, social studies, science) and considered how they affected students receiving specialized education services (Pugach & Warger, 1996). Ten years later, Brantlinger (2006b) and colleagues questioned who benefits from the field of special education, explicitly looking at curriculum that teaches about specialized education, including numerous critiques about how texts about special education sustain the medical model and other deficit perspectives regarding meeting the needs of minoritized students.

Traditional notions of curriculum revolve around what is taught in schools, who is teaching it, and who is learning the content. Inclusive education for disabled students and students requiring specialized education services is often frame as granting access to the existing general education curriculum. However, in applying disability through an asset-based lens, we offer the following considerations:

- Does the content presented in the teacher education program center disabled people's experiences from their own perspectives?
- Are disabled scholars, community members, and students positioned as experts who inform teacher education? Are these disabled experts' intersecting identities also seen as a source of expertise (e.g., Black disabled scholars)?
- Do educators consider how their own relationship to disability shape their understanding of specialized education services?
- Do the assigned readings and activities include diverse perspectives about disabilities and the need for specialized education support (e.g., intersectional, neurodivergent, nonbinary, queering of disability)?

Aronson, for example, discussed how her relationship with her father and his disability shaped her attitude toward ableism and its intersections with other systemic oppressions. Relatedly, most people with disabilities are not only taught by nondisabled educators, but also raised within families where they may be the only ones with a disability. Understanding who is positioned as having valuable experiences and expertise within teacher education thus compels us to consider how disability is accounted for in embodiments and lived experiences. These questions encourage teacher educators to disrupt normative expectations of who best understands what specialized educational services should prioritize and what aspects of curriculum matter in relationship to disabled people.

Process-Centered Considerations

More recently, there are those calling for special and inclusive education to turn to curriculum theory to better prepare teachers to understand how to best meet the needs of students receiving specialized education services (Pugach et al., 2020). For example, collaborative teacher education for inclusive practices has largely prioritized bringing special and general education teacher candidates together (e.g., Pugach & Blanton, 2009; Weinberg et al., 2020). These efforts have helped to disrupt the siloed dynamics of university-based teacher preparation (e.g., Waitoller & Kozleski, 2013). Reviews of this literature, however, reveal the tendency to focus on program components, assessments of candidates' pedagogical skills, organizing of general and special education candidates to work together, and partnerships between faculty members across different departments within schools of education (Blanton et al., 2018; Pugach et al., 2014). While the focus on structures and pedagogical practices are important, scholars have paid insufficient attention to the role that theory and theorizing have in shaping these processes (Boveda et al., 2019, 2020; Pugach et al., 2020). Neglecting to attend to the theoretical underpinnings driving practices such as coteaching, curriculum development, and culturally sustaining pedagogies limits the potential teacher education has in meeting the needs of students at the intersection of disabilities and other(ed) sociocultural markers of identities.

In addition to thinking about what curriculum is taught and by whom, we also must consider *how, where, and when curriculum is enacted*. The following questions are starting points for considering the distinctive ways that teacher education engages a disability affirming approach:

- Is the curriculum taught and enacted with an anti-ableist, asset-based approach or are educators prepared to offer specialized education services to operate within existing normative structures?
- How is the structure of the teacher program either obstructing or supporting ableist ideologies?
- How are the knowledges generated from disabled people informing the structure, focus, and efforts of teacher education?
- How are university faculty bringing students together across and working together across programs?

- How are multiple of ways of being and knowing affirmed within the teacher education program?
- Where are connections between the lived experiences of disabled people and what occurs in schools acknowledged?
- When are educators encouraged to understand the multiple spaces that educators learn about disability?

These process-centered considerations are not intended to be exhaustive, but reminders of how curriculum is explicit and hidden, informed by and informing of individuals' behavior, and not "constructed and understood through a neutral, distant, and objective process independent and decontextualized from the full range of human experience" (Pugach et al., 2020, p. 87).

CONCLUSION

In this chapter, we considered how explicitly examining the role of theorizing teacher education—and more specifically, curriculum theorizing in special, inclusive, and collaborative teacher education—could potentially support Culturally Sustaining Pedagogy that disrupts ableist ideologies. For example, a heavy emphasis on whether students with disabilities are accessing the general education curriculum does not sufficiently address whether general education is affirming of student differences (Boveda et al., 2019).

In revisiting how discourse and praxis around curriculum, disabilities, and specialized education manifested throughout our educational and professional trajectory, we have named ways that our preparation has either failed or left much more to be desired in offering tools to understand disability and ableist structures. We have consistently advocated for elevating the intersectional consciousness of those examining social issues and the social identities of students and teachers. We also understand, however, that there are some identities that have been grossly neglected, such as disability, and thus require more scaffolding in teacher preparation. Thus, we considered how curriculum theory (e.g., Erevelles et al., 2019), Black curriculum studies and Black feminisms (e.g., Boveda et al., 2019), and existing entry points into theorizing about disability studies (Annamma et al., 2013; Erevelles, 2011) and special education (Clark et al, 2005; Sullivan & Artiles, 2011) elucidated our own understandings of how theoretical perspectives can help transform inclusive teacher education and APs.

To help our colleagues who also may be collaborating across teacher education communities to meet the needs of diverse learners (e.g., bilingual education, special education, social justice, urban education), and those who are examining how disabled students and specialized education services can inform disciplined-based education (e.g., language arts, mathematics, and science), we offered a framework for curriculum theorizing centering disability. Our embodied experiences, as well as our engagement with the literature about curriculum and collaboration between special and general education, informed this framework intended as a tool to enact more inclusive teacher education research and practice.

CHAPTER 13

Leveraging Asset Pedagogies at Race/Disability Intersections in Equity-Expansive Technical Assistance

Kathleen A. King Thorius[1]

As a white nondisabled woman and a school psychologist from 1998 to 2005, many crucial moments shaped my path toward an interdisciplinary PhD program focused on preparing culturally responsive special education faculty, during which I was a graduate assistant in the *National Center for Culturally Responsive Educational Systems*. In 2005, when I began my doctoral work and apprenticeship in this national technical assistance center that aimed to eliminate racial disproportionality in special education, I did not have the tools or experiences to adequately interpret what I had encountered and perpetuated in my practice as a school psychologist. I continue to en/counter my reproduction of racial and ability hierarchies in my professional and personal life, while coming to learn more about how my individual and collective actions can contribute to systemic transformation toward equitable, just schools for students at the intersection of race, disability, and other minoritized identities.

As a scholar, I have focused much of my work on designing and coleading national and regional technical assistance (TA) centers with the express goal of equitable, inclusive, just, and responsive education for all students and with particular emphasis for students of color with disabilities. Broadly, TA is a term used in government, education, and industry to refer to professional consultation and specific nonfinancial supports to build organizational capacity for addressing issues and/or needs (UNESCO, 2017). Although TA traditionally has not been recognized nor ratified as scholarly activity within the higher education academy, I have come to recognize TA as praxis: scholarly activity "explicitly committed to critiquing the status quo and building a more just society" (Lather, 2017, p. 72). I offer this chapter to build understanding about the potential of TA as praxis toward eliminating educational inequities at the intersection of race and disability, and specifically, how educators' engagement with asset pedagogies (APs) as an element of TA can mediate these processes.

In this chapter, I detail how TA has contributed to educational justice for students at the intersection of race and disability, and then extend existing work toward this goal through leveraging APs as mediating artifacts within equity-expansive TA. To begin, I offer a brief history of how TA as a federal strategy has shepherded federal disability and race-related policy to local implementation. Next, I present challenges associated with TA responses that rely on medical models of disability, focus on intervening with students over systems, and fail to account for the historical and mutually constitutive nature of racism and ableism (Annamma et al., 2013; Artiles, 2011; Erevelles, 2011; Waitoller & Thorius, 2016). In doing so, I provide examples of national and regional TA centers with which I have worked to address race- and disability-related educational inequities. Then, I describe the application of theoretical and practical features of equity-expansive TA toward disrupting inequities in the education of youth of color with disabilities by expressly drawing from APs that account for the intersection of student race and disability. I close with a brief discussion of what these approaches offer for mediating teacher and leadership preparation and professional development.

THEORIZING EQUITY-EXPANSIVE TA

For me and my mentors and colleagues in this work (e.g., Kozleski & Thorius, 2014; Skelton, 2019; Thorius & Artiles, in press), TA is an activity system (González & Artiles, 2020; Kozleski & Artiles, 2015) that can be examined holistically (Jonassen & Rohrer-Murphy, 1999) through historical and sociocultural lenses. TA services aimed at professional and organizational capacity development are carried out in myriad forms including sharing information and working knowledge, instruction, consulting services, as well as program and policy review.

The USDOE funds several types of TA centers to work with state and local education agencies toward policy and practice implementation and improvement. Among these are four regional Equity Assistance Centers (EACs); I have coled three different EACs with colleagues since 2008. EACs are funded by the USDOE's Office of Elementary and Secondary Programs to "address special educational problems as a result of the racial desegregation of public schools" (Civil Rights Act of 1964, Title IV, Section 403). Legislated under the Civil Rights Act, EACs are the longest-standing type of TA centers in the United States. Over time, federal regulations have changed to add national origin, sex, and religion desegregation to the policy and practice arenas they are charged to address. EACs often provide TA to address disability and language desegregation at these intersections, as well.

Unique to our EAC, however, we draw from cultural historical activity theory (CHAT; Engeström, 1987) to frame TA. CHAT is an interdisciplinary approach for studying human learning and development grounded in the work of Soviet psychologists L. S. Vygotsky, A. R. Luria, and A. N. Leontiev. Although there are some differences in the central units of analysis across these three individuals' contributions, CHAT analyses attend to human cognition and behavior as mediated by cultural artifacts (Vygotsky, 1978). CHAT-informed research is typically concerned with participants' mediated actions within a given cultural context, or *activity system* (Engeström, 1987). A CHAT frame attends to the interactions of educators and TA providers within the activity system(s) of a TA partnership and in relation to interacting activity systems of local school/district/state agency settings. Therefore, our TA and associated research (e.g., Thorius, 2016) are concerned with the individuals involved and the elements of joint TA activity, such as the object and outcomes of the activity, mediating artifacts, community members, division of labor, and the rules that guide how people work toward the activity outcome (Engeström, 1987). Just as these elements interact and influence each other, they also are shaped by cultural and historical factors; these may include socialization into education professions, personal racial and disability biases, and experiences with privilege and oppression connected with identity and role: all of which account for the cultural-historical aspects of CHAT (Koszalka & Wu, 2005). Thus, CHAT holds potential for "new ways of theorizing phenomena that emphasize relations and histories" (Roth, 2012, p. 101) and rests on the notion that systemic change—in this case, toward the object of dismantling race/ability hierarchies—occurs through goal-oriented, tool-mediated cultural practices (Engeström & Sannino, 2010). CHAT has informed our approach to the study and indeed, the design of TA as a mediating structure (González & Artiles, 2021) with the purpose of facilitating educational organizations' development toward equity-related goals.

Equity-expansive TA—the term for the specific approach to TA that we have developed over the past 16 years—aims to mediate partners' learning toward innovative action and equity-driven systemic goals. A theory of *expansive learning*, which emerged from CHAT (Engeström, 1987), informs this term because within the expansive learning cycles (Engeström & Sannino, 2010) that are characteristic of equity-expansive TA (Tan & Thorius, 2018), TA providers develop and/or introduce artifacts (Cole, 1996) to (1) mediate educators' examination of local conditions for in/equities; (2) stimulate contradictions between this status quo and partners' desired outcome of the partnership; and (3) support partners' development and refinement of innovations toward equity-focused systemic changes in policy, practice, and belief systems (Thorius, 2019).

Cycles of expansive learning inform the *process* of equity-expansive TA. Expansive learning identifies seven steps in cycles undertaken by participants to develop and enact capacities to address local problems of practice (Engeström & Sannino, 2010). In step one, participants analyze their current activity system, examining problematic situations and contributing forces. Step two is geared toward discovering and evoking contradictions and tensions in the status quo. In step three, participants work on transforming the problematic systemic structure toward an expansive way of resolving the contradictions within it. Step four is about expanding the purpose, or object of the activity system through determining a new model of activity. In step five, participants implement the new model of activity while shoring up and testing out innovations, putting initial steps into action, and developing and implementing new tools for change. Finally, steps six and seven involve reflecting on the implementation of this new model of activity, building into it processes and efficiencies, and then disseminating the new model throughout connected activity systems (Engeström, 1987). Equity-expansive TA has the potential to remediate educators' socialization, schools' cultural patterns, and collective goals toward equity and justice that lead to systemic change through the dismantling of racist and ableist educational contexts (Thorius, 2016; Thorius & Kyser, 2021). For example, Tan and Thorius (2018) aimed to remediate special and general educators' approaches to teaching mathematics to students with significant disabilities by engaging them with tools in which they analyzed their beliefs about their students' mathematical capacities and how their teaching accounted for student assets and preferences, rather than a more typical focus of special education: students' deficits and teaching as a set of prescriptive interventions (Johnson & Pugach, 1990).

TA AS A SHEPHERD FOR RACE AND DISABILITY-FOCUSED FEDERAL LAW AND ACCOUNTABILITY STRUCTURES: LEGISLATIVE FOUNDATIONS AND CENTER'S HISTORY

Over time, injustices faced by students at the intersection of race and disability have ranged from exclusion from school all together (Ferguson, 2008), institutionalization and disproportionate incarceration (Stanford et al., 2017), physical segregation (U.S. Department of Education, 2019), and lower expectations and opportunities connected with lower academic achievement and tracking (U.S. Department of Education, 2018). Federal responses to these injustices have generally fallen into two categories, accountability structures and TA, often with the latter geared toward supporting educational agencies to meet requirements of the former. Spurred by attention to racial disproportionality in special education (the prominent framing of educational injustice for students at the intersection of race and disability) (Donovan & Cross, 2002; Heller et al., 1982), systems were built into federal legislation to increase accountability requirements for public education agencies. For example, 2004 amendments to the Individuals with Disabilities Education Act (IDEA) required that states submit state performance plans (SPPs) every 6 years, along with annual performance reports

(APRs) related to their SPPs. SPP/APRs include indicators that measure compliance with monitoring priority areas that include disproportionate representation of racial and ethnic groups in special education and related services, to the extent the representation is the result of inappropriate identification.

Such legal and related accountability requirements were tied to the emergence of the first TA Centers that addressed race and disability inequities. Two years prior to IDEA's 2004 reauthorization, the USDOE's Office of Special Education Programs (OSEP) sought applicants for a national center that would work with states to prevent and address instances of significant disproportionality identified through federal accountability systems. NCCRESt was funded by OSEP to "provide technical assistance and professional development to close the achievement gap between students from culturally and linguistically diverse backgrounds and their peers, and reduce inappropriate referrals to special education" (NCCRESt, 2009, p. 4). As the only TA center explicitly funded to address race/disability intersections in education, much of NCCRESt's work reconceptualized racial disproportionality as a special *and* general education problem indicative of social and cultural issues manifested in school systems, and thus engaged in examination of systemic policies, practices, and personal domains. Upon IDEA's 2004 reauthorization, NCCRESt partnered with states to establish a procedure for determining significant disproportionality as part of the SPP/APR process. Broadly, NCCRESt TA aimed to "increase the use of prevention and early intervening strategies," "decrease inappropriate referrals to special education," and increase use of "effective literacy and behavioral interventions for students who are culturally and linguistically diverse . . . by expand(ing) the field's understanding of disproportionality and its impact on students and their families" (NCCRESt, 2009, p. 5). NCCRESt was funded from 2002 to 2009 during the politically conservative years of the Bush (43) administration in which educational equity was framed within the context of the No Child Left Behind Act (Artiles, 2011). Remarkably, NCCRESt forwarded a critical and systemic approach to addressing educational inequities like disproportionality, laying this foundation for future generations of TA centers to adopt and expand (Skelton et al., 2020).

CONTRIBUTIONS AND CHALLENGES WITH TA RESPONSES TO RACE/DISABILITY INEQUITIES

NCCRESt and the National Institute for Urban School Improvement (NIUSI; housed with NCCRESt in the Equity Alliance at Arizona State University) were among the first TA Centers to assert that *systemic* solutions to racial and disability injustices such as disproportionality were necessary considering federal policies tended to focus only on improvements in quantitative outcome data (e.g., office discipline referrals). Accordingly, as NCCRESt TA endeavored to focus on "social structures, institutional contexts, and decision-making processes" (Artiles, 2011, p. 432) shaping disproportionality, both NCCRESt's and NIUSI's efforts drew from Ferguson et al.'s (2001) framework for systemic change, rather than supporting LEAs and SEAs with the discrete and technical intervention-based approaches that prevailed in existing TA. Moreover, Kozleski, Artiles, and NCCRESt and NIUSI colleagues contributed a theoretical and practical roadmap for the intentional design of TA to center concerns with equity and to interrogate culture, history, and power in inclusive (and special) education (Artiles & Kozleski, 2007; Artiles, 2011. Accordingly, Kozleski and Artiles (2012) asserted that TA must stimulate development of complex solutions to historical issues undergirded by systemic oppressions and seek to remediate how systems facilitate equity in student opportunities rather than simply consult on technical improvements to operations.

Moreover, just as Artiles (2011, p. 432) argued that reliance on distributive justice models to craft equity policies for racial minoritized students tended to emphasize outcomes (e.g., academic achievement scores), thus erasing "social structures, institutional contexts, and decision-making processes that shape" the outcomes targeted in accountability policies, scholars of race and disability asserted the need to emphasize relations and histories of inequitable policies and practices with regard to race and disability hierarchies. That is, the heavy structural influence of race and racism (Ross, 1990) as well as of disability and ableism (Baglieri & Lalvani, 2019) in U.S. history and schools also must be examined and transformed in relation to policy and practice improvements.

LEVERAGING ASSET PEDAGOGIES TO REMEDIATE UNDERPINNINGS OF RACE/DISABILITY INJUSTICES

The rest of this chapter picks up where NCCRESt left off (although the PIs have continued to contribute to theory and practice of TA). That is, within NCCRESt's (2009) stated goals of increasing early intervening and effective opportunities to learn for racially minoritized students with and without disabilities, there is reference to understanding the underpinnings of race/disability inequities as crucial to the development of related policy and practice. Relatedly, TA must account explicitly for the mediating roles and interlocking nature of racist and ableist education contexts in tandem: discriminatory structures and influences that hinder students' affirmation, access, participation, and outcomes, and that on the surface may even appear to be benevolent (Thorius, 2019). Yet some of these structures and influences have been perpetuated in the field of special education and associated TA: reliance on or failure to challenge medical models of disability and a focus on interventions to either prevent disability labels in the first place or remediate students to whom they have been applied. With relevance for solutions to both, some disabled[2] scholars and activists of color have detailed their own and others' experiences of stigma and trauma associated with labeling processes and special education (Hernández-Saca, 2019; Hernández-Saca & Cannon, 2019). Others have discussed school and societal failure to account for disability identity formation and associated cultural practices of disabled communities and assets and opportunities for learning and innovation in educational settings (Forber-Pratt et al., 2017).

Existing TA approaches have accounted for some structural aspects of racism through identifying disproportionate patterns and examining with organizational partners root causes of disproportionality in policies, practices, and interpersonal dynamics such as racial bias in referrals to special education (Kozleski & Zion, 2006; Waitoller et al., 2010). However, mixed messages remain about the value of disability as social location, culture, and lived experience at the intersection of race, given that disproportionality continues to be framed as *inappropriate* identification (Thorius et al., 2021).

Missed opportunities remain for the examination of how structural failures to integrate and educate disabled students of color are as much underpinned by ableism as by racism (Thorius & Waitoller, 2017). Moreover, as much as APs work toward justice for students belonging to minoritized racial, ethnic, and linguistic groups, a failure to account for disability beyond prevailing (deficit-based) medical models has meant the erasure of disability and disabled people as worthy of sustaining through curriculum (Nusbaum & Steinborn, 2019; Waitoller & Thorius, 2016). Andrews et al. (2019, p. 111) provide us with strong rationale to end this erasure: "the disability movement is moving toward the status of a diverse cultural group with a social justice agenda parallel to those of other marginalized communities." The cycles of equity-expansive learning characteristic of our TA approach provide opportunities for leveraging APs that account for students at race/disability intersections to develop locally relevant and innovative solutions.

EQUITY-EXPANSIVE TA TO DISRUPT INTERLOCKING ABLEISM AND RACISM

Part 1: Stimulating Contradictions in the Status Quo Through Race/Disability Asset Pedagogies

The overarching goal of equity-expansive TA is to evoke, counter, and remediate prevailing medical and deficit notions of competence and intelligence in schools in relation to students' race, disability, religion, sex, national origin, language, and other intersectional forms of difference (Thorius et al., under review). Equity-expansive TA aims to create broader "strategic coalitions toward inclusive education and against exclusion" at the intersections of disability and race (Thorius & Waitoller, 2017, p. 252) and as part of "longer and much broader movements of cultural and educational justice" (Paris & Alim, 2017, p. 11).

Equity-expansive TA that disrupts intersectional race/disability oppression requires that the TA facilitator introduce certain tools into cycles of expansive learning to mediate partners' development toward accomplishing the object. In the first steps of such cycles, such tools mediate educators' examination of and encounters with equity tensions in historical and current policies, practices, relationships, and belief systems that reproduce and reify race/ability hierarchies. In this way, equity-expansive TA is a formative intervention (Engeström, 2011), which requires that participants encounter "a problematic and contradictory object, embedded in their vital life activity." Unlike the construct of intervention typical in special education research (e.g., Haager et al., 2007) and in traditional TA approaches (Blase, 2009), formative intervention refers to "purposeful action by a human agent to create change" (Engeström, 2011, p. 606).

Contradictions are instrumental in expansive learning cycles; they remediate the object and motive of activity "to embrace a radically wider horizon of possibilities" (Engeström, 1987, p. 137). This means that new qualitative stages and forms of activity emerge as solutions to the contradictions of the preceding stage or form. This takes place in the form of "invisible breakthroughs" (Engeström, 1987, p. 45). Engeström drew from Bateson's (1972) notion of inner contradictions as a social "double-bind" (Engeström, 1987, p. 4): a dilemma that is imperative to resolve. Accordingly, within TA theorized and designed as a formative intervention, equity-expansive learning occurs as partners collectively generate new models of activity to resolve contradictions between desires for equity and an inequitable status quo.

Asset pedagogies that account for students at the intersection of race/disability provide powerful guidance for selecting and designing tools for resolving such contradictions. Drawing from Universal Design for Learning's (UDL) curricular framework—goals, methods, materials, and assessment (Rose & Meyer, 2002)—and features of Culturally Sustaining Pedagogy (Paris, 2012), Waitoller and I (2016, 2017) posed a cross-pollination and loving critique of these APs as an intersectional approach to curriculum and instruction with promise for abolishing ableism/racism in tandem by sustaining and affirming disabled youth of color.

Instead of fully rearticulating this framework here, I provide a brief overview of the curricular cycle within this cross-pollination. I apply the first two of these elements, *goals* and *materials*, to the initial steps of equity-expansive learning cycles in which TA facilitators introduce tools to mediate educators' encountering and examination of equity tensions in historical and current policies, practices, relationships, and belief systems that reproduce and reify race/ability hierarchies. I apply the elements of *methods* and *assessment* to later steps of equity-expansive learning cycles in which partners expand their object of activity toward applying APs with students at minoritized race/disability intersections.

A primary goal of a cross-pollinated UDL/CSP curriculum is to debunk and provide alternatives to sorting and tracking people along racial and ability hierarchies within schools and communities (Waitoller & Thorius, 2016). In a CSP/UDL cross-pollination, curriculum goals incorporate the strengths of both frameworks. Waitoller and I emphasized how UDL goals diverge from uniform context mastery in standardized curricula toward becoming an expert learner through educators' development of goals that account for variability in who students are and how they learn (Rose, Gravel, & Domings, 2010). Along with CSP's goals for contributing to students' academic achievement and developing students who can critique and work toward eliminating intersecting oppressions in schools and society, UDL/CSP cross-pollination goals are to create expert learners "who can interrogate and change complex forms of exclusion" and to sustain "the cultural repertoires and abilities of those students who have been marginalized in curricula informed by whiteness and smartness," (i.e., white and nondisabled hierarchies; Waitoller & Thorius, 2016, p. 380). In equity-expansive TA informed by APs, this goal can be applied to educators who interrogate and change the status quo of race/disability inequities.

One of the most prominent contradictions experienced by educators within equity-expansive TA partnerships focused on addressing disability/race inequities is related to the goals—the purpose—of education for students at these intersections. Artifacts that account for these intersections can mediate educators' encounters with (special) education's history of racist and ableist practices and belief systems that are cloaked by overarching beliefs about its benevolence. Elsewhere (Tan & Thorius, 2019; Thorius, 2016; 2019), I have written about these initial TA steps, providing examples of artifacts that engage educators with historical and current aspects of educational exclusion, discrimination, and dehumanization of people with disabilities, people of color, and at these intersections. Such artifacts include psychometric resources still used in special education eligibility determination processes such as diagrams of bell curves upon which standardized scores are distributed, partnered with historical artifacts that show how such standardizations have been applied to sort children by race, disability, and sex (Dudley-Marling & Gurn, 2010). For example, I was invited to engage with a group of about 100 school psychologists from one state's professional association about equity imperatives within special education. The title of the conversation I planned to facilitate was *Countering Problematic Legacies of the Practice of Psychology in Schools: From "Gatekeeper" to "Inclusive Education Activist"* (Thorius, 2017).

Simply by chance, upon entering the meeting room these participants had received a laminated copy of a bell curve plotted with the standardized scores for a popularly used intelligence test from an educational testing company representative. Our subsequent discussion with these psychologists about the origins of intelligence tests and the ways in which notions of human intelligence, and its measurement, have contributed to violence toward and segregation of women, people of color, and disabled people created palpable tensions, particularly as they faced the contradictions between our discussions and their laminated souvenir. Following the daylong discussion, one participant approached me in tears, sharing her discomfort but also her commitment to reevaluating her own belief systems in relation to the goal of her profession. We talked at length about her reflections on the profession as one mainly concerned with locating student deficits, and her emerging reorientation toward locating systemic deficits and student assets with the overarching goal of inclusive education. This was the beginning of ongoing engagement with a set of participants from this state's professional agency.

In this and other instances, we have introduced and engaged with mediating artifacts that have stimulated contradictions between educators' socialization into professional roles as special, patient, and even as practitioners of "magic" (Thorius, 2016, p. 8), which in turn reify white, nondisabled educators' ability and racial hierarchies in relation to their students. As another example, in a multiyear partnership with one school district with ongoing racial disproportionality in the suspension and expulsion of students of color, with disabilities, and at these intersections, we studied research transcripts of "child study team" and IEP meetings within the special education process wherein educators and parents/families interact and children of color with disabilities are the subject of discussion fraught with educators' deficit descriptions (e.g., Klingner & Harry, 2006; Mehan, 1993; Rogers, 2000; Thorius, et al., 2014). After analyzing these transcripts and excavating the oppressive systemic and individual practices and belief systems that positioned students and families in these ways, we examined local protocols for facilitating such meetings including referral forms and forms where student interventions are documented (Thorius, 2016), along with local audio-recordings of such meetings. In doing so, our partners reflected on their own practices including their own deficit-framings of student learning and capacity and moved toward new processes and protocols for designing asset-based instruction (e.g., Thorius, 2015).

Over the past 16 years of engaging in TA, I have found that two thematic contradictions emerge for educators as they en/counter historical legacies and status of race/disability inequities in their own settings and reflect on their own practices and beliefs:

1. Educators experience contradictions when they gain understandings of how racial and ability hierarchies are socially, politically, and culturally constructed to perpetuate educational and social benefit for some and marginalization for others.

2. That is, they develop and deepen understandings that one racial (Kendi, 2019) or dis/ability group (Lalvani & Bacon, 2019) is not inherently superior to another. Educators have been socialized into deficit-thinking about students based on race and disability that manifests in oppressive practices that place students along racial and ability hierarchies. These practices include classifying students in relation to perceived risk and qualifying disability along fixed gradients of student capacities (e.g., low or high functioning, severe or mild, for example, or recent-past special education labels that define the "educability" of students with disabilities), all of which are grounded in special education's reliance on a medical model of disability (Triano, 2000). Educators also experience contradictions when they learn that many practices utilized in special education and with students of color are fraught with the residue of eugenics: segregated settings, labeling, and the use of intellectual and achievement testing to justify exclusion. (Special) education has a history of racist and ableist practices and belief systems cloaked by overarching beliefs about its benevolence (Thorius, 2019). Teachers' socialization into deficit thinking about their students at the intersection of race and disability is underpinned by the racial and disability hierarchies of the eugenics era. Yet most educators have come to believe that special education's past and present, as well as their own roles, are purely benevolent. As educators en/counter how beliefs about students at raced/disabled intersections are mediated by beliefs about educators' roles as students' saviors, helpers, and fixers, they also come to examine how these beliefs position themselves as superior to their students and perpetuate racial and ability hierarchies.

As educators experience and struggle with these tensions, equity-expansive TA facilitators introduce additional artifacts that also remediate educators' understanding of disability/race intersections as rich with cultural repertoires and capabilities, rather than sources of deficit. Such artifacts are aimed at remediating the object of activity from fixing students at race/disability intersections to developing and sustaining their identities, and include protocols for instructional coaching conversations within which educators examine curricular material that present student disability as an identity "claimed by people bound by shared socio-political experience, rather than the mental or physical 'abnormality' it is positioned to be via the structure of 'special' education (Dudley-Marling & Gurn, 2010)" (Waitoller & Thorius, 2016, p. 382).

Over my time engaging educators with these types of artifacts, another contradiction often emerges, and relates to the previous example. That is, disability and race are socially and culturally relevant to students, families, and educators' identities and cultural practices. As much as the current U.S. sociopolitical context has renewed tensions about the relevance of students' racial identities for curriculum and instruction in schools, because disability has most often been constructed by nondisabled people as a deficit, and by educators as something to be remediated or mitigated, educators experience contradictions when they encounter cultural and social models of disability, and disability pride and visibility movements, led by disabled people at racial and other minoritized identity intersections.

I offer examples of these artifacts that illustrate the second curricular element of a cross-pollinated UDL/CSP framework: materials. Materials are the primary way curriculum is represented and through which people engage with content; however, materials privilege some students' identities and cultural practices and deny or erase others. In response, APs at the intersection of disability/race must be flexible in format and grounded in the cultural repertoires of youth, particularly youth of color with disabilities. TA artifacts that remediate educators' encounters with the social and cultural relevance of disability and race and other intersections include blogs, social media posts, videos, books, and other artistic and scholarly works such as song lyrics and poems within which disabled people of color describe their experiences of marginalization and trauma in special education systems. Here, as well, TA artifacts include scholarly and creative works by disabled people of color, such as those included in *Disability Visibility: First Person Stories from the 21st Century*, edited by Alice Wong (2020). Educators also explore the work of fellows under the *Disability Futures* initiative: a partnership between the Ford Foundation and Andrew W. Mellon Foundation and administered by United States Artists, which "spotlights the work of disabled creatives across disciplines and geography and amplify their voices individually and collectively (https://www.fordfoundation.org/work/investing-in-individuals/disability-futures-fellows/). Finally, other artifacts introduced into TA at this stage include assertions of disabled scholars of color that disability should not be euphemized or avoided. Rather, it is an important aspect of (student) identity at other intersections and on its own (see Skelton, this volume). For example, Forber-Pratt asserts, "[D]isabled people are reclaiming our identities, our community, and our pride. We will no longer accept euphemisms that fracture our sense of unity as a culture" (in Brasher, 2019). Their work, and the work of other disabled activists and scholars of color has contributed to the #SAYTHEWORD movement: a social media campaign to embrace disabled identity. These remediating artifacts stand in sharp contradiction to others we introduce in equity-expansive learning cycles at this point to stimulate more disruptions in the status quo, such as a recruitment video from the USDOE in which children with disabilities are described as "hot-house flowers" and special education teachers are described as "special people" who "have the highest highs of almost any other work" and whose professional roles are to "figure out the puzzle" that is the disabled child (USDOE, 2011).

Part 2: Remediating the Object Toward Sustaining Students Through Asset Pedagogies

In the next steps of equity-expansive learning cycles, partners and TA providers engage with more tools that mediate the development of local solutions to resolve the contradictions that emerged earlier in these cycles, try out these solutions, and build them into systemic approaches. Accordingly, equity-expansive TA deliberately responds to partners' generation of ideas that may be enacted via their agency "in other settings as frames for the design of locally appropriate new solutions" (Engeström 2011, p. 606).

More specifically, as educators connect the racism and ableism of historical policy and practices to the current, TA facilitators introduce a second round of artifacts to facilitate partners' development of locally relevant innovations to resolve contradictions identified in earlier steps of the learning cycle. Here, I draw from UDL/CSP cross-pollinated *methods* and *assessments* as resources educators encounter to expand their object of activity toward applying APs with students at race/disability intersections. Methods refer to instruction, including design. Key methodological features are that (1) all students are positioned by the teacher as capable of learning and experts of their own experiences and learning practices, thus redistributing power from the teacher to the students; and (2) methods include flexible participation structures with varying levels of supports to support learning within students "zone of proximal development" (Vygotsky, 1978). And, in contrast to the ways in which assessments have been used to exclude, sort, pathologize, and stigmatize students of color/disabled students, assessments in this context mediate teachers' exploration of student understanding and empower students to demonstrate their knowledge and learning in flexible, relevant ways (Thorius, 2021).

Artifacts introduced in this stage of expansive learning cycles take on several formats. First, we introduce and examine with our partners cross-pollinations of APs that account for students race AND disability. As we do so, educators have opportunities to examine videos and vignettes that demonstrate aspects of these methods and assessments. Then, TA facilitators provide additional information and examples for educators as they write their own pedagogical vignettes, extending existing lesson plans they have brought from their own practice. In some instances, educators use lesson-planning templates we provide as resources for them to revise existing lessons and unit plans.

As a result of ongoing cycles of equity-expansive learning, we have observed systemic shifts from the deficit-based language historically used to describe students toward identity-affirming language. In one example, a state department of education and a group of about 100 educators we worked with over about a year shifted from talking about "IEP students" to "students of color with disabilities" or "Black students with disabilities." Another expanded object of activity has manifested as changes in state-designed professional development curricula from intervention-based purposes, forms of literacy instruction, and supports for students at the intersection of disability and other marginalized identities toward those that affirm identity and ways of engaging in relevant literacy practices and materials. Within other partnerships, we have observed new practices become codified in the development of new forms to guide discussion of student capabilities and design of asset-based instruction, moving away from documenting "weaknesses" and "interventions." Across these and other examples, we have observed how leveraging cross-pollinated APs in TA design and facilitation have contributed to shifts in policy, practice, and belief systems toward sustaining youth of color with disabilities. Beyond observations within specific TA partner professional learning sessions, the systemic nature of these impacts has been further observed through annual partner interviews, post-session questionnaires, an annual Library of Congress survey administered by the USDOE, and through annual in-depth case studies of selected TA partnerships, all part of our center's approach to program evaluation and continuous improvement.

IMPLICATIONS

There is not a one-size-fits all approach to the remediation of racism/ableism in educational policies, practices, and belief systems. However, the theory and practice of equity-expansive TA, when paired with artifacts informed by APs at the intersection of race and disability, moves us forward on the roadmap originally charted by NCCRESt and other national TA Centers offering systemic solutions to addressing racial disproportionality in special education. Central to this approach is the development of systemic solutions to race/disability-related educational injustices, which requires that educators en/counter histories and status quo of racism and ableism in schools. Also central is the development of new understandings of disability as a cultural and social location at the intersection of race, and that can be a source of students' affiliation and pride when understood and positioned this way through APs. Finally, TA theorized and practiced as described in this chapter provides educators with opportunities to expand their goals from fixing students, toward sustaining students at their race and disability intersections: a key endeavor in a pluralistic, democratic society.

Notes

Chapter 3

1. Roscigno, 2020; Savarese, 2017; Williams, 2018; Klaar & Wolfond, 2020; Srinivasan, 2021.

2. In Deleuze and Guattari's philosophy, lines of flight are "bolts of pent-up energy that break through the cracks in a system of control and shoot off on the diagonal. By the light of their passage, they reveal the open spaces beyond the limits of what exists" (Rayner, 2013, para. 7).

Chapter 6

1. As we have previously asserted (Annamma et al., 2013), tracing the lineage of DisCrit merits a whole chapter and would include scholars across multiple disciplines.

2. We acknowledge that there is dissention in the field of special education research about overrepresentation of children of color in various disability labels, and guide readers seeking to know more to Collins et al. (2016).

Chapter 8

1. The word disability is written as dis/ability in two instances in this chapter to accentuate the existing human variance within disability and ability, as well as to indicate the continuum across these two categories (Annamma et al., 2013).

2. Cantonese differs from Mandarin Chinese particularly when communicating orally as speakers of the two languages cannot mutually understand.

Chapter 11

1. Although the term "inclusion" has, in practice, largely come to signify placement of disabled students in general education classrooms, for most disability studies informed educators "inclusive education" is about producing the conditions of learning that can support all children and youth, particularly those who experience inequity in multiple overlapping ways through their affinities with historically marginalized communities (Slee, 2011; Valle & Connor, 2019). While I subscribe to the latter orientation, I have deliberately used these terms interchangeably in this chapter, to signal a recognition of the complexities of enacting inclusive education within the material contexts of schools. This approach expresses a suspicion of any universal understanding of the term while also assuming the distinction from practices that have a deficit orientation.

Chapter 12

1. Scholars such as María Cioè-Peña (2021) note that although disability is a sociocultural identity, not all P–12 students with individualized educational programs or who are receiving specialized education services realize that they are identified as having disabilities. Consequently, in this chapter we use both language recognizing disability as social identity (e.g., disabled students) and the phrase "students identified as needing specialized services."

2. Latinidad is itself a contested term referring to the shared experiences of those with familial ties to Latin America. Critiques of Latinidad refer to problematic moves that essentialize differences across continents, often through denials of Indigenous and African heritages. Though imperfect, in the Kinsey example Latinidad was both brought up (on behalf of the police) and ignored (in Soto, a disabled man) in attempts to deny the anti-Blackness of the shooting.

Chapter 13

1. I am grateful to Seena Skelton, my ongoing partner in this work, who pushes and supports me to grow in my own understandings of how identity, history, and socialization contribute to TA provision. Much of this chapter is informed by ideas we have developed together over the years.

2. Throughout the chapter, I use both people-first, and identity-first language (i.e., person with a disability, disabled person/communities) under the guidance of Lydia X. Z. Brown: "Different communities of actually-disabled people or people with disabilities have different preferences, but as with any group, especially any group of marginalized people, it's the people who we're talking about who should be dictating what they're called. The same word that's empowering for some people might be retraumatizing for others" (Brown, 2018).

References

Acevedo, S. M. (2020). "Effective schooling" in the age of capital: Critical insights from advocacy anthropology, anthropology of education, and critical disability studies. *Canadian Journal of Disability Studies*, 9(5), 265–301. https://doi.org/10.15353/cjds.v9i5.698

Acevedo, S. M. (2021). Lifelines: A neuroqueer politics of non-arrival in an undergraduate disability studies classroom. *International Journal of Qualitative Studies in Education*. https://doi.org/10.1080/09518398.2021.2017505

Acevedo, S. M., & Nusbaum, E. A. (2020). Autism, neurodiversity, and inclusive education. In G. Noblit (Ed.), *The Oxford research encyclopedia of education* (pp. 1–25). Oxford University Press. https://doi.org/10.1093/acrefore/9780190264093.013.1260

Adjapong, E. S., & Emdin, C. (2015). Rethinking pedagogy in urban spaces: Implementing hip-hop pedagogy in the urban science classroom. *Journal of Urban Learning, Teaching, and Research*, 11, 66–77.

Ahmed, S. (2006). Orientations: Toward a queer phenomenology. *GLQ: A Journal of Lesbian and Gay Studies*, 12(4), 543–574.

Alarcon, N. (1991). The theoretical subjects of this bridge called my back and Anglo-American feminism. In H. Calderon, & J. D. Saldivar (Eds.), *Studies in Chicano literature, culture and ideology* (pp. 140–152). Duke.

Albrecht, G. L. (1992). *The disability business: Rehabilitation in America*. SAGE Pulications.

Aldana, A., & Byrd, C. M. (2015). School ethnic–racial socialization: Learning about race and ethnicity among African American students. *The Urban Review*, 47(3), 563–576.

Alim, H. S., Baglieri, S., Ladson-Billings, G., Paris, D., Rose, D. H., & Valente, J. M. (2017). Responding to "Cross-pollinating Culturally Sustaining Pedagogy and Universal Design for Learning: Toward an inclusive pedagogy that accounts for dis/ability." *Harvard Educational Review*, 87(1), 4–25.

Allen, J. (2007). *Creating welcoming schools: A practical guide to home-school partnerships with diverse families*. Teachers College Press.

Alston, R. J., Bell, T. J., & Feist-Price, S. (1996). Racial identity and African Americans with disabilities: Theoretical and practical considerations. *Journal of Rehabilitation*, 62, 11–15.

Altman, B. M. (2001). Disability definitions, models, classification schemes, and applications. In G. Albrecht, K. Seelman, & M. Bury (Eds.), *Handbook of disability studies* (97–122). SAGE Publicaions.

Alvarado, S. L., Salinas, S. M., & Artiles, A. J. (2019). Teacher education and inclusivity. *Oxford Research Encyclopedia of Education.* https://doi.org/10.1093/acrefore/9780190264093.013.278

American Baby & Child Law Centers. (2018). *Involuntary sterilization of disabled Americans: A historical overview.* https://www.abclawcenters.com/blog/2018/11/06/involuntary-sterilization-of-%09disabled-americans-an-historical-overview/

Americans with Disabilities Act Amendments Act of 2008, Pub. L. No. 110-325 (2008, September 25).

Americans with Disabilities Act of 1990, Pub. L. No. 101-336, §2, 104 Stat. 328 (1991).

Andrews, E. E. (2019). *Disability as diversity: Developing cultural competence.* Oxford University Press.

Andrews, E. E., & Forber-Pratt, A. J. (2021). Disability and group of seven. In A. Kassan & R. Moodley (Eds.), *Diversity & social justice in counseling psychology & psychotherapy: A case study approach* (pp. 245–260). Cognella Press.

Andrews, E. E., & Forber-Pratt, A. J. (2022). Disability language and identity. In D. Dunn, & M. Wehmeyer (Eds.), *The positive psychology of personal factors: Implications for understanding disability* (pp. 27–40). Lexington Books.

Andrews, E. E., Forber-Pratt, A. J., Mona, L. R., Lund, E. M., Pilarski, C. R., & Balter, R. (2019). #SaytheWord: A disability culture commentary on the erasure of "disability." *Rehabilitation Psychology, 64*(2), 111–118.

Annamma, S. A. (2015). Innocence, ability, and whiteness as property: Teacher education and the school-to-prison pipeline. *Urban Review. 47*(2), 293–316.

Annamma, S. A. (2015). Whiteness as property: Innocence and ability in teacher education. *Urban Review, 47*(2), 293–316.

Annamma, S. A. (2018a). *The pedagogy of pathologization.* Routledge.

Annamma, S. A. (2018b). Mapping consequential geographies in the carceral state: Education journey mapping as a qualitative method with girls of color with dis/abilities. *Qualitative Inquiry, 24*(1), 20–34.

Annamma, S. A., Anyon, Y., Joseph, N. M., Farrar, J., Greer, E., Downing, B., & Simmons, J. (2016). Black girls and school discipline: The complexities of being overrepresented and understudied. *Urban Education, 54*(2), 211–242. https://doi.org/10.1177/0042085916646610

Annamma, S. A., Connor, D., & Ferri, B. (2013). Dis/Ability critical race studies (Discrit): Theorizing at the intersections of race and dis/ability. *Race Ethnicity and Education 16*(1), 1–31. https://doi.org/10.1080/13613324.2012.730511

Annamma, S. A., & Handy, T. (2021). Sharpening justice through DisCrit: A contrapuntal analysis of education. *Educational Researcher, 50*(1), 41–50.

Annamma, S. A., Jackson, D. D., & Morrison, D. (2017). Conceptualizing color-evasiveness: Using dis/ability critical race theory to expand a color-blind racial ideology in education and society. *Race Ethnicity and Education, 20*(2), 147–162. https://doi.org/10.1080/13613324.2016.1248837A

Annamma, S. A., & Morrison, D. (2018). DisCrit classroom ecology: Using praxis to dismantle dysfunctional education ecologies. *Teaching and Teacher Education, 73,* 70–80.

Anzaldua, G. (1987). *Borderlands, La Frontera: The new mestiza* (3rd ed.). Aunt Lute Books.

References

Aronowitz, S. (2002, February). *What is worth knowing and why*. Lecture presented at Occasional Seminars, International Cultural Studies Certificate Program, University of Hawaii, Manoa.

Aronson, B., & Boveda, M. (2017). The intersection of white supremacy and the education industrial complex: An analysis of #BlackLivesMatter and the criminalization of people with disabilities. *Journal of Educational Controversy, 12*(1), article 6. https://cedar.wwu.edu/jec/vol12/iss1/6

Aronson, B., & Laughter, J. (2016). The theory and practice of culturally relevant education: A synthesis of research across content areas. *Review of Educational Research, 86*(1), 163–206.

Aronson, B. A., Banda, R., Johnson, A., Kelly, M., Radina, R., Reyes, G., . . . & Wronowski, M. (2020). The social justice teaching collaborative: A collective turn towards critical teacher education. *Journal of Curriculum Studies Research, 2*(2), 21–39.

Artiles, A. J. (1998). The dilemma of difference: Enriching the disproportionality discourse with theory and context. *The Journal of Special Education, 32*(1), 32–36.

Artiles, A. J. (2003). Special education's changing identity: Paradox and dilemmas in views of culture and space. *Harvard Educational Review, 73*, 164–202.

Artiles, A. J. (2011). Toward an interdisciplinary understanding of educational equity and difference: The case of the racialization of ability. *Educational Researcher, 40*, 431–445.

Artiles, A. J., Dorn, S., & Bal, A. (2016). Objects of protection, enduring nodes of difference: Disability intersections with "other" differences, 1916–2016. *Review of Research in Education, 40*(1), 777–820.

Artiles, A. J., & Kozleski, E. B. (2007). Beyond convictions: Interrogating culture, history, and power in inclusive education. *Language Arts, 84*, 357–364.

Artiles, A. J., Rose, D., Gonzalez, T., & Bal, A. (2020). Culture and biology in learning disabilities research. In N. S. Nasir, C. D. Lee, R. Pea, & M. Mckinney de Royston (Eds.), *Handbook of the cultural foundations of learning* (pp. 160–177). Routledge.

Artiles, A., & Trent, S. C. (1994). Overrepresentation of minority students in special education: A continuing debate. *Journal of Special Education, 27*, 410–437.

Asch, A. (2017). Critical race theory, feminism, and disability: Reflections on social justice and personal identity. In E. F. Emens, & M. A. Stein (Eds.), *Disability and equality law* (pp. 143–176). Routledge.

Ashby, C. (2012). Disability studies and inclusive teacher preparation: A socially just path for teacher education. *Research and Practice for Persons with Severe Disabilities, 37*(2), 89–99. https://doi.org/10.1177/154079691203700204

Ashby, C., & Kasa, C. (2013). Pointing forward: Typing for academic access. *Perspective on Augmentative and Alternative Communication, 22*(3), 143–156.

Athanasiou, A., & Butler, J. (2013). *Dispossession: The performative in the political*. Polity Press.

Austin, J. L., Jeffries, B. S., Winston, W., & Brady, S. S. (2021). Race-related stressors and resources for resilience: Associations with emotional health, conduct problems, and academic investment among African American early adolescents. *Journal of the American Academy of Child and Adolescent Psychiatry*, online first.

Autism Self-Advocacy Network (ASAN). (2020). *Awareness and lobbying*. Autistic Advocacy. https://autisticadvocacy.org/wp-content/uploads/2018/03/AutismSpeaksFlyer2020.pdf

Autism Self-Advocacy Network (ASAN). (2021). *2021 Anti-filicide toolkit.* https://autisticadvocacy.org/projects/community/mourning/anti-filicide/

Baglieri, S. (2016). Toward unity in school reform: What DisCrit contributes to multicultural and inclusive education. In D. Connor, B. Ferri, & S. Annamma (Eds.), *DisCrit: Disability studies and critical race theory in education* (pp. 167–179). Teachers College Press.

Baglieri, S., Bejoian, L. M., Broderick, A. A., Connor, D. J., & Valle, J. (2011). [Re]Claiming "inclusive education" toward cohesion in educational reform: Disability studies unravels the myth of the normal child. *Teachers College Record, 113*(10), 2122–2154.

Baglieri, S., & Lalvani, P. (2019). *Undoing ableism: Teaching about disability in K-12 classrooms.* Routledge.

Baglieri, S., Valle, J., Connor, D. J., & Gallagher, D. (2011). Disability studies and special education: The need for plurality of perspectives on disability. *Remedial and Special Education, 32*(4), 267–278.

Baker, B. (2002). The hunt for disability: The new eugenics and the normalization of school children. *Teacher College Record, 104*(4), 663–703.

Bal, A., Waitoller, F. R., Mawene, D., & Gorham, A. (2020). Culture, context, and disability: A systematic literature review of cultural-historical activity theory-based studies on the teaching and learning of students with disabilities. *Review of Education, Pedagogy and Cultural Studies.* https://doi.org/0.1080/10714413.2020.1829312

Bandura, A. (1989). Human agency in social cognitive theory. *American Psychologist, 44*(9), 1175–1184. https://doi.org/10.1037/0003-066X.44.9.1175

Banks, J. (2017). "These people are never going to stop labeling me": Educational experiences of African American male students labeled with learning disabilities. *Equity & Excellence in Education, 50*(1), 96–107.

Banks, J., & Hughes, M. S. (2013). Double consciousness: Postsecondary experiences of African American males with disabilities. *The Journal of Negro Education, 82*(4), 368–381.

Banks, J., Smith, P. S., & Neal, D. C. (2022). Expanding the emancipatory possibilities of DisCrit by exploring the cultural experiences of disability within contextualized communities. In S. A. Annamma, B. Ferri, & D. Connor (Eds.), *DisCrit expanded: Reverberations, ruptures, and inquiries* (pp. 96–111). Teachers College Press.

Barad, K. (2007). *Meeting the universe halfway: Quantum physics and the entanglement of matter and meaning.* Duke University Press.

Barclay, J. (2021). *The mark of slavery: Disability, race, and gender in antebellum America.* University of Illinois Press.

Barnes, C., & Mercer, G. (2001). Disability culture: Assimilation or inclusion? In L. Albrecht, K. Seelman, & M. Bury (Eds.), *Handbook of disability studies* (pp. 515–534). SAGE Publication. https://doi.org/10.4135/9781412976251.n22

Barnes, C., Oliver, M., & Barton, L. (2002). Disability and the academy. *Disability Studies Today.* https://disability-studies.leeds.ac.uk/wp-content/uploads/sites/40/library/Barnes-paris-presentation.pdf

Baszile, D. T. (2006). Rage in the interest of Black self: Curriculum theorizing as dangerous knowledge. *Journal of Curriculum Theorizing, 22*(1), 89–98.

Baszile, D. T., Edwards, K. T., & Guillory, N. A. (2016). *Race, gender, and curriculum theorizing: Working in womanish ways.* Lexington Books.

References

Bat-Chava, Y. (2000). Diversity of deaf identities. *American Annals of the Deaf, 5*, 420–428.
Bateson, G. (1972). *Steps to an ecology of mind.* Chandler.
Bauman, H. D. L., & Murray, J. J. (2014). *Deaf gain: Raising the stakes for human diversity.* University of Minnesota Press.
Bell, C. M. (Ed.). (2011). *Blackness and disability: Critical examinations and cultural interventions.* Michigan State University Press.
Ben Moshe, L. (2020). *Decarcerating disability.* University of Minnesota Press.
Beneke, M. R., Siuty, M. B., & Handy, T. (2022). Emotional Geographies of Exclusion: Whiteness and Ability in Teacher Education Research. *Teachers College Record, 124*(7), 105–130. https://doi.org/10.1177/01614681221111431
Bennett A., & Robards B. (2014). Introduction: Youth, cultural practice and media technologies. In A. Bennett, & B. Robards (Eds.), *Mediated youth cultures* (pp. 1–7). Palgrave Macmillan. https://doi.org/10.1057/9781137287021_1
Berlant, L., & Edelman, L. (2013). *Sex, or the unbearable.* Duke University Press.
Berne, P., Morales, A. L., Langstaff, D., & Invalid, S. (2018). Ten principles of disability justice. *WSQ: Women's Studies Quarterly, 46*(1–2), 227–230. https://doi.org/10.1353/wsq.2018.0003
Berry, T. (2015). Me and Bill: Connecting Black curriculum orientations to critical race feminism. *Educational Studies: Journal of the American Educational Studies Association, 51*(1), 423–433.
Bertrand, M., Durand, E. B., & González, T. (2017). "We're trying to take action": Transformative agency, role re-mediation, and the complexities of youth participatory action. *Equity & Excellence in Education, 50*(2), 142–154. https://doi.org/10.1080/10665684.2017.1301837
Bhabha, H. K. (1994). *The location of culture.* Routledge.
Bhattacharya, K. (2017). *Fundamentals of qualitative research: A practical guide.* Taylor & Francis.
Biklen, D. (1992). *Schooling without labels: Parents, educators, and inclusive education.* Temple University Press.
Biklen, D., & Burke, J. (2006). Presuming competence. *Equity & Excellence in Education, 39*(2), 166–175.
Blanchett, W. (2006). Disproportionate representation of African American students in special education: Acknowledging the role of White Privilege and Racism. *Educational Researcher, 35*(6), 24–28.
Blanton, L. P., Pugach, M. C., & Boveda, M. (2018). Interrogating the intersections between general and special education in the history of teacher education reform. *Journal of Teacher Education, 69*(4), 354–366.
Blase, K. A. (2009). *Technical Assistance to Promote Service and System Change. Roadmap to Effective Intervention Practices #4.* Technical Assistance Center on Social Emotional Intervention for Young Children.
Blustein, J. (2012). Philosophical and ethical issues in disability. *Journal of Moral Philosophy, 9*(4), 573–587. https://doi.org/10.1163/17455243-00904002
Bogard, W. (2000). Smoothing machines and the constitution of society. *Cultural Studies, 14*(2), 269–294. https://doi.org/10.1080/095023800334887
Bogart, K. R., & Dunn, D. S. (2019). Ableism special issue introduction. *Journal of Social Issues, 75*(3), 650–664.
Bogart, K. R., Lund, E. M., & Rottenstein, A. (2018). Disability pride protects self-esteem through the rejection-identification model. *Rehabilitation Psychology, 63*(1), 155–159.

Bogdan, B., & Taylor, S. (1989). Relationships with severely disabled people: The social construction of humanness. *Social Problems, 36*(2), 135–148.

Bogdan, R., & Biklen, D. (1977). Handicapism. *Social Policy, 7*(5), 14–19.

Bøttcher, L. (2012). Culture and the learning and cognitive development of children with severe disabilities: Continuities and discontinuities with children without disabilities. *Mind, Culture, and Activity, 19*(2), 89–106. https://doi.org/10.1080/10749039.2011.632050

Bøttcher, L., & Dammeyer, J. (2012). Disability as a dialectical concept: Building on Vygotsky's defectology. *European Journal of Special Needs Education, 27*(4), 433–446.

Bourdieu, P. (1993). *The field of cultural production.* Columbia University Press.

Boveda, M., & Aronson, B. A. (2019). Special education preservice teachers, intersectional diversity, and the privileging of emerging professional identities. *Remedial and Special Education, 40*(4), 248–260.

Boveda, M., Jackson, J., & Clement, V. (2020). Rappers' (special) education revelations: A Black feminist decolonial analysis. *Curriculum Inquiry, 51,* 98–117. DOI.org/10.1080/03626784.2020.1819146

Boveda, M., Reyes, G., & Aronson, B. A. (2019). Disciplined to access the general education curriculum: Girls of color, disabilities, and specialized education programming. *Curriculum Inquiry 4*(4), 405–425.

Braidotti, R. (2019a). A theoretical framework for the critical posthumanities. *Theory, Culture and Society, 36*(6), 31–61.

Braidotti, R. (2019b). *Posthuman knowledge.* Polity Press.

Brantlinger, E. A. (1997). Using ideology: Cases of non-recognition of the politics of research and practice in special education. *Review of Educational Research, 67,* 425–459.

Brantlinger, E. A. (2006a). The big glossies: How textbooks structure (special) education. In E. A. Brantlinger (Ed.), *Who benefits from special education?* (pp. 59–90). Routledge.

Brantlinger, E. A. (Ed.). (2006b). *Who benefits from special education? Remediating (fixing) other people's children.* Routledge.

Brasher, J. (2019, April 23). Disability is not a dirty word; 'Handi-capable' should be retired. *Vanderbilt University Research News.* https://news.vanderbilt.edu/2019/04/23/disability-is-not-a-dirty-word-handi-capable-should-be-retired/

Braun, V., & Clarke, V. (2006). Using thematic analysis in psychology. *Qualitative Research in Psychology, 3*(2), 77–101.

Brewer, E., Brueggemann, B., Hetrick, N., & Yergeau, M. (2012). Introduction, background, and history. In B. Brueggemann, & G. L. Albrecht (Eds.), *Disability key issues and future directions: Arts and humanities* (pp. 1–62). SAGE Publication.

Broderick, A., & Lalvani, P. (2017). Dysconscious ableism: Toward a liberatory praxis in teacher education. *International Journal of Inclusive Education, 21*(9), 894–905.

Broderick, A., & Leonard, Z. (2016). What is a good boy? The deployment and distribution of "goodness" as ideological property in schools. In D. Connor, B. Ferri, & S. A. Annamma (Eds.), *DisCrit: Critical conversations across race, class, & dis/ability* (pp. 55–69). Teachers College Press.

References

Brown, L. X. Z. (2018). *Autistic person or person with Autism: Is there a right way to identify people?* https://news.northeastern.edu/2018/07/12/unpacking-the-debate-over-person-first-vs-identity-first-language-in-the-autism-community/

Brown, S. (2003). *Movie stars and sensuous scars: Essays on the journey from disability shame to disability pride.* Universe, Inc.

Brown, S. E. (2002). What is disability culture? *Disability Studies Quarterly, 22*(2), 34–50.

Buck v. Bell, 274 U.S. 200, 47 S. Ct. 584, 71 L. Ed. 1000 (1927).

Bumiller, K. (2009). The geneticization of autism: From new reproductive technologies to the conception of genetic normalcy. *Signs: Journal of Women in Culture and Society, 34*(4), 875–899. https://doi.org/10.1086/597130

Burke, M. (2014). *Ableism in the deaf community and the field of deaf studies through the eyes of a deafdisabled person.* (Unpublished master thesis). Gallaudet University.

Butler, J. (2004). *Precarious life: The power of mourning and violence.* Verso.

Cabral, B., Annamma, S. A., Le, A., Harvey, B., Wilmot, J., & Morgan, J. (in press). Solidarity incarcerated: Building authentic relationships with girls of color in youth prisons. *Teachers College Record.*

Cammarota, J. (2011). From hopelessness to hope: Social justice pedagogy in urban education and youth development. *Urban Education, 46*(4), 828–844.

Campbell, F. A. K. (2008). Exploring internalized ableism using critical race theory. *Disability & Society, 23*(2), 151–162.

Campbell, F. K. (2009). *Contours of ableism: The production of disability and abledness.* Palgrave Macmillan.

Cannon, M. A. (2019). *"Because I Am Human": Centering Black women with dis/abilities in transition planning from high school to college.* Doctoral dissertation, ProQuest LLC.

Cannon, M. A., & Hernández-Saca, D. I. (2021). The gift of disruption: Feeling and communicating subverted truths at the intersection of racist and ableist practices. In C. A. Mullen (Ed.), *Handbook of social justice interventions in education* (pp. 1057–1080). Cham: Springer International Publishing.

Carman, T. (1999). The body in Husserl and Merleau-Ponty. *Philosophical Topics Intersection of Analytic and Continental Philosophy 27*(2), 205–226. https://doi.org/10.5840/philtopics199927210

Carson, L. R. (2009). "I am because we are": Collectivism as a foundational characteristic of African American college student identity and academic achievement. *Social Psychology of Education: An International Journal, 12*(3), 327–344. https://doi.org/10.1007/s11218-009-9090-6

Carter-Andrews, D. J., Brown, T., Castillo, B. M., Jackson, D., & Vellanki, V. (2019). Beyond damage-centered teacher education: Humanizing pedagogy for teacher educators and preservice teachers. *Teachers College Record, 121,* 060305.

CAST. (2018). *Universal Design for Learning Guidelines Version 2.2.* http://udlguidelines.cast.org

Center for Disease Control and Prevention (CDC). (2021, March 29). *Certain medical conditions and risk for severe COVID-19 illness.* https://www.cdc.gov/coronavirus/2019-ncov/need-extra-precautions/people-with-medical-conditions.html

Centers for Disease Control and Prevention. (2020). *Disability impacts all of us infographic*. https://www.cdc.gov/ncbddd/disabilityandhealth/infographic-disability-impacts-all.html

Cepeda, M. E. (2021). Thrice unseen, forever and borrowed time: Latina feminist reflections on mental disability and the neoliberal academy. *South Atlantic Quarterly, 120*(2), 301–320.

Chapple, R. L. (2019). Toward a theory of Black deaf feminism: The quiet invisibility of a population. *Journal of Women and Social Work, 34*(2), 186–198.

Charlton, J. I. (2006). The dimensions of disability oppression: An overview. In L. J. Davis (Ed.), *The disability studies reader* (pp. 217–227). Routledge.

Charmaraman L., & Grossman J. M. (2010). Importance of race and ethnicity: An exploration of Asian, Black, Latino, and multiracial adolescent identity. *Culture Diverse Ethnic Minor Psychology, 16*(2), 144–151.

Charmaz, K. (1995). The body, identity, and self: Adapting to impairment. *Sociological Quarterly, 36*(4), 657–680.

Chavous, T. M., Rivas-Drake D., Smalls C., Griffin, T., & Cogburn C. (2008). Gender matters, too: The influences of school racial discrimination and racial identity on academic engagement outcomes among African American adolescents. *Developmental Psychology, 44*(3), 637–654.

Chen, M. Y., & Puar, J. K. (2021). *ANIMA: Critical race studies otherwise*. Duke University Press. https://www.dukeupress.edu/books/browse/by-series/series-detail?IdNumber=2880459

Cherryholmes, C. H. (1988). *Power and criticism: Poststructural investigations in education*. (Advances in contemporary educational thought, Vol. 2.) Teachers College Press.

Christensen, C., & Rizvi, F. (Eds.). (1996). *Disability and the Dilemmas of Education and Justice*. Open University Press.

Chrysostomou, M., & Symeonidou, S. (2017). Education for disability equality through disabled people's life stories and narratives: Working and learning together in a school-based professional development programme for inclusion. *European Journal of Special Needs Education, 32*(4), 572–585.

Cioè-Peña, M. (2021). *(M)othering labeled children: Bilingualism and disability in the lives of Latinx mothers*. Multilingual Matters.

Clandinin, D. J. (2013). *Engaging in narrative inquiry*. Left Coast Press.

Clandinin, D. J., & Connelly, F. M. (1996). Teachers' professional knowledge landscapes: Teacher stories. Stories of teachers. School stories. Stories of schools. *Educational Researcher, 25*(3), 24–30.

Clandinin, D. J., & Connelly, F. M. (2000). *Narrative inquiry: Story and experience in qualitative research*. Wiley.

Clare, E. (1999). *Exile and pride: Disability, queerness, and liberation*. South End Press.

Clark, C., Dyson, A., & Millward, A. (Eds.). (2005). *Theorising special education*. Routledge.

Clark, N. M., D'Ardenne, C., Erickson, K. A., Koppenhaver, D. A., & Noblit, G. W. (in press). Unveiling the intersections of race and severe disability. In S. Annamma, B. Ferri, & D. Connor (Eds), *DisCrit expanded: Reverberations, ruptures, and inquiries*. Teachers College Press.

Cochran-Smith, M., Piazza, P., & Power, C. (2013). The politics of accountability: Assessing teacher education in the United States. *The Educational Forum, 77*, 6–27.

Cole, M. (1996). *Cultural psychology: A once and future discipline.* Harvard University Press.
Cole, M. (2005). Cultural-historical activity theory in the family of socio-cultural approaches. *International Society for the Study of Behavioral Development Newsletter, 1,* 1–4.
Cole, M., & Packer, M. (2016). Design-based intervention research as the science of the doubly artificial. *Journal of the Learning Sciences, 25*(4), 503–530.
Coles, J. A. (2019). The Black literacies of urban high school youth countering antiblackness in the context of neoliberal multiculturalism. *Journal of Language and Literacy Education, 15*(2), n2.
Collins, K., Connor, D. J., Ferri, B. A., Gallagher, D., & Samson, J. (2016). Dangerous assumptions and unspoken limitations: A disability studies in education response to Morgan, Farkas, Hillemeir, Mattison, Maczuga, Li, and Cook (2015). *Multiple Voices, 16*(1), 4–16
Collins, P. H. (2000). *Black feminist thought: Knowledge, consciousness, and the politics of empowerment.* Routledge.
Connor, D. J., & Bejoian, L. (2007). Cripping school curricula: 20 ways to reteach disability. *Review of Disability Studies, 3*(3), 3–13.
Connor, D. J., & Cavendish, W. (2018). Sharing power with parents: Improving educational decision making for students with learning disabilities. *Learning Disability Quarterly, 41*(2), 79–84.
Connor, D. J., & Ferri, B. A. (2013). Historicizing dis/ability: Creating normalcy, containing difference. In M. Wappat, & K. Arnt (Eds.), *Foundations of disability studies* (pp. 29–67). Palgrave.
Connor, D. J., & Ferri, B. A. (Eds.). (2019). *How teaching shapes our thinking about disabilities: Stories from the field.* Peter Lang.
Connor, D. J., Ferri, B., & Annamma, S. A. (Eds.). (2016). *DisCrit: Disability studies and critical race theory in education.* Teachers College Press.
Connor, D. J., Gabel, S. L., Gallagher, D. J., & Morton, M. (2008). Disability studies and inclusive education—implications for theory, research, and practice. *International Journal of Inclusive Education, 12*(5–6), 441–457. https://doi.org/10.1080/13603110802377482
Connor, D. J., & Valle, J. (2019). *Rethinking disability* (2nd ed.). Routledge.
Coole, D., & Frost, S. (Eds). (2010). Introducing the new materialisms. *New materialisms: Ontology, agency and politics.* Duke University Press.
Coomer, M. N., Johnson, A., Reyes, G., & Aronson, B. (in press). Critical coalition with/in the boundaries: A radical love response to neoliberal debilitation in special education. In D. I. Hernández-Saca, H. Pearson, & C. Kramarczuk Voulgarides (Eds.), *Understanding the boundaries between disability studies and special education through consilience, self-study, and radical love.* Lexington Books.
Cooper, A. J. (1892/1988). *A voice from the South.* Oxford University Press.
Corker, M., & Shakespeare, T. (2002). *Disability, postmodernity: Embodying disability theory.* Continuum Intl Pub Group.
Crenshaw, K. W. (1989). Demarginalizing the intersection of race and sex: A Black feminist critique of anti-discrimination doctrine, feminist theory and antiracist politics. *University of Chicago Legal Forum, 8,* 139–167.

Crenshaw, K. W. (1991). Mapping the margins: Intersectionality, identity politics, & violence against women of color. *Stanford Law Review, 43*(6), 1241–1299. https://doi.org/10.2307/1229039

Crenshaw, K. W. (1993). Beyond racism and misogyny: Black feminism and 2 Live Crew. In M. J. Matsuda, C. R. Lawrence III, R. Delgado, & K. W. Crenshaw (Eds.), *Words that wound: Critical race theory, assaultive speech and the first amendment* (pp. 111–132). Westview Press.

Crenshaw, K. W., Gotanda, N., Peller, G., & Thomas, K. (1996). *Critical race theory: The key writing that formed the movement*. The New Press.

Creswell, J. W., & Poth, C. N. (2016). *Qualitative inquiry and research design: Choosing among five approaches*. SAGE publications.

Crosman, C. (2019). Good autistic advocacy organizations vs. bad autism "Charities." *In the Loop About Neurodiversity*. https://intheloopaboutneurodiversity.wordpress.com/2019/11/28/good-autistic-advocacy-organizations-vs-bad-autism-charities/

Cushner, K. (2003). *Human diversity in action: Developing multicultural competencies for the classroom*. McGraw-Hill.

Danforth, S., & Naraian, S. (2015). This new field of inclusive education: Beginning a dialogue on conceptual foundations. *Intellectual and Developmental Disabilities, 53*(1), 70–85.

Darden, J., Rahbar, M., Jezierski, L., Li, M., & Velie, E. (2010). The measurement of neighborhood socioeconomic characteristics and black and white residential segregation in metropolitan Detroit: Implications for the study of social disparities in health, *Annals of the Association of American Geographers, 100*(1), 137–158.

Darling, R. B. (2019). *Disability and identity: Negotiating self in a changing society*. Lynne Rienner.

Davidson, J., & Orsini, M. (2013). *Worlds of autism: Across the spectrum of neurological difference*. University of Minnesota Press.

Dávila, B. (2015). Critical race theory, disability microaggressions and Latina/o student experiences in special education. *Race Ethnicity and Education, 18*(4), 443–468.

Davis, L. J. (1997a). Introduction. In L. J. Davis (Ed.), *The disability studies reader* (pp. 1–6). Routledge.

Davis, L. J. (1997b). Constructing normalcy: The bell curve, the novel, and the invention of the disabled body in the nineteenth century. In L. J. Davis (Ed.), *The disability studies reader* (pp. 9–28). Routledge.

Davis, L. J. (2013). The end of identity politics: On disability as an unstable category. In L. J. Davis (Ed.), *The disability studies reader* (pp. 263–277). Routledge.

Davis, L. J. (2017). The ghettoization of disability: Paradoxes of visibility and invisibility in cinema. In A. Waldschmid, H. Berressem, & M. Ingwersen (Eds.), *Culture—theory—disability* (pp. 63–81). Transcript.

De Lissovoy, N. (2014). *Education and emancipation in the neoliberal era: Being, teaching, and power*. Palgrave Macmillan.

Deacon, R. (2006). Michel Foucault on education: A preliminary theoretical overview. *South African Journal of Education, 26*(2), 177–187.

Delanda, M. (2006). *New philosophy of society: Assemblage theory and social complexity*. Bloomsbury Academy.

References

Deleuze, G., & Guattari, F. (1983). *Anti-Oedipus: Capitalism and schizophrenia.* University of Minnesota Press.
Deleuze, G., & Guattari, F. (1986). *Nomadology: The war machine.* Semiotext(e).
Detroiturbex.com. (n.d.). Dr. Charles Oakman Orthopedic School. http://www.detroiturbex.com/content/schools/oakman/index.html
Devlieger, P. J. (2000). Rejoinder: The culture and disability perspective on disability. *Disability and Rehabilitation, 22*(11), 526–527.
Dind, J. (2021). Neurodiversity studies. *Disability Studies Quarterly, 41*(1). https://doi.org/10.4324/9780429322297
Disabled Parenting Project. (2021). https://disabledparenting.com
Dixson, A. D., & Rousseau, C. K. (2006). And we are still not saved: Critical race theory in education ten years later. In A. D. Dixson, & C. K. Rousseau (Eds.), *Critical race theory in education: All god's children got a song* (pp. 31–54). Taylor & Francis Group.
Donovan, S., & Cross, C. I. (2002). *Minority students in special and gifted education.* The National Academies Press.
Douglas, P., Rice, C., Runswick-Cole, K., Easton, A., Gibson, M. F., Gruson-Wood, J., . . . Shields, R. (2019). Re-storying autism: A body becoming disability studies in education approach. *International Journal of Inclusive Education, 25*(5), 605–622. https://doi.org/10.1080/13603116.2018.1563835
DuBois, W. E. B. (1920). Race intelligence. *The Crisis, 20*(3). Reprinted: 60th Anniversary Issue of *The Crisis, 77*(9), 326.
Dudley-Marling, C., & Gurn, A. (Eds.). (2010). *The myth of the normal curve.* Peter Lang.
Dumas, M. J., & ross k. m. (2016). "Be real Black for me": Imagining BlackCrit in education. *Urban Education, 51*(4), 415–442.
Dunn, D. S., & Burcaw, S. (2013). Disability identity: Exploring narrative accounts of disability. *Rehabilitation Psychology, 58*(2), 148–157. DOI:10.1037/a0031691
Dunn, L. (2005). A dream deferred: Deaf people of African heritage and the struggle of equality and opportunity. In J. Fuller, B. Hollrah, J. G. Lewis, & C. McCaskill-Henry (Eds.), *Black perspectives on the deaf community* (pp. 163–172). Gallaudet University.
Durr, P. (1999). Deconstructing the forced assimilation of deaf people via De'VIA resistance and affirmation art. *Visual Anthropology Review, Society for Visual Anthropology, 15*(2), 47–68.
Dyer Arts Center. (n.d.). Black is Black: Blackity AF. https://dyerartscenter.omeka.net/exhibits/show/blackisblack/intro
Eisner, E. W. (1979). *The educational imagination.* Macmillan.
Eisner, E. W., & Vallance, E. (Eds.). (1974). *Conflicting conceptions of curriculum.* McCutchan.
Ellis-Robinson, T. (2021). Bringing DisCrit theory to practice in the development of an action for equity collaborative network: Passion projects. *Journal of Race, Ethnicity & Education, 24*(5), 703–719.
Emdin, C. (2010). Affiliation and alienation: Hip-hop, rap, and urban science education. *Journal of Curriculum Studies, 42*(1), 1–25.
Engeström, Y. (1987). *Learning by expanding: An activity-theoretical approach to developmental research.* Orienta-Konsultit Oy.
Engeström, Y. (2016). *Studies in expansive learning: Learning what is not yet there.* Cambridge University Press.

Engeström, Y., & Sannino, A. (2010). Studies of expansive learning. *Educational Research Review, 5*(1), 1–24.

Erevelles, N. (2000). Educating unruly bodies: Critical pedagogy, disability studies, and the politics of schooling. *Educational Theory, 50*(1), 25–47. https://doi.org/10.1111/j.1741-5446.2000.00025.x

Erevelles, N. (2005). Understanding curriculum as normalizing text: Disability studies meet curriculum theory. *Journal of Curriculum Studies, 37*(4), 421–439.

Erevelles, N. (2011). "Coming out crip" in inclusive education. *Teachers College Record, 113*(10), 2155–2185.

Erevelles, N. (2011). *Disability and difference in global contexts: Enabling a transformative body politic* (1st ed.). Palgrave MacMillan.

Erevelles, N. (2014). "What . . . [thought] cannot bear to know": Crippin' the limits of "Thinkability." *Review of Disability Studies an International Journal, 8*(3). https://www.rdsjournal.org/index.php/journal/article/view/90

Erevelles, N. (2016). *Disability and difference in global contexts: Enabling a transformative body politic* (2nd ed.). Palgrave Macmillan.

Erevelles, N., Grace, E. J., & Parekh, G. (2019). Disability as meta curriculum: Ontologies, epistemologies, and transformative praxis. *Curriculum Inquiry, 49,* 357–372.

Erevelles, N., & Minear, A. (2010). Unspeakable offenses: Untangling race and disability in the discourses of intersectionality. *Journal of Literary and Cultural Disability Studies, 4*(2), 127–145.

Esteva, G., & Prakash, M. S. (1998). *Grassroots post-modernism: Remaking the soil of cultures* (1st ed.). Zed Books.

Fairchild, S. (2015, November 3). Native American oral storytelling & history | Seth Fairchild TEDxSMU. https://www.youtube.com/watch?v=6JcKbN_GjCE

Farlie, R. W. (2002). Drug dealing and legitimate self-employment. *Journal of Labor Economics, 20*(3), 538–537.

Fereday, J., & Muir-Cochrane, E. (2006). Demonstrating rigor using thematic analysis: A hybrid approach of inductive and deductive coding and theme development. *International Journal of Qualitative Methods, 5*(1), 80–92.

Ferguson, D., Kozleski, E. B., & Smith, A. (2001). *On . . . transformed, inclusive schools: A framework to guide fundamental change in urban schools.* National Institute for Urban School Improvement.

Ferguson, P. M. (2008). The doubting dance: Contributions to a history of parent/professional interactions in early 20th century America. *Research and Practice for Persons with Severe Disabilities, 33*(1–2), 48–58.

Ferri, B. A. (2008). Changing the script: Race and disability in Lynn Manning's Weights. *International Journal of Inclusive Education, 12*(5–6), 497–509. https://doi.org/10.1080/13603110802377524

Ferri, B. A. (2016). Response to intervention: Persisting concerns. In B. Amrhein (Ed.), *Diagnostics in the context of inclusive education: Theories, ambivalences, operators, concepts* (pp. 7–21). Verlag.

Ferri, B., & Connor, D. J. (2006). *Reading resistance: Discourses of desegregation & inclusion debates.* Peter Lang.

Ferri, B. A., Connor, D. J., Solis, S., Valle, J., & Volpitta, D. (2005). Teachers with LD: Ongoing negotiations with discourses of disability. *Journal of Learning Disabilities, 38*(1), 62–78. https://doi.org/10.1177/00222194050380010501

References

Ferri, B. A., Keefe, C., & Gregg, N. (2001). Teachers with learning disabilities: A view from both sides of the desk. *Journal of Learning Disabilities, 34*(1), 22–32. https://doi.org/10.1177/002221940103400103

Ferrigon, P., & Tucker, K. (2019). Person-first language vs. identity-first language: An examination of the gains and drawbacks of Disability Language in society. *Journal of Teaching Disability Studies.* https://jtds.commons.gc.cuny.edu/person-first-language-vs-identity-first-language-an-examination-of-the-gains-and-drawbacks-of-disability-language-in-society/

Finkelstein, V. (1980). *Attitudes and disabled people.* World Rehabilitation Fund.

Fitch, E. F. (2002). Disability and inclusion: From labeling deviance to social valuing. *Educational Theory, 52*(4), 463–477.

Flynn, S. (2021). Corporeality and critical disability studies: Toward an informed epistemology of embodiment. *Disability & Society, 36*(4), 636–655.

Forber-Pratt, A. J. (2016). "It's not like you're going to college anyway!" A performative autoethnography. In R. J. Berger & L. S. Lorenz (Eds.), *Disability and qualitative inquiry: methods for rethinking an ableist world* (pp. 175–207). Ashgate.

Forber-Pratt, A. J. (July 26, 2017). Finding ourselves: What we know about disability identity development. *Vanderbilt Kennedy Center Notables.* https://notables.vkcsites.org/2017/07/finding-ourselves-what-we-know-about-disability-identity-development/

Forber-Pratt, A. J. (2019). (Re)defining disability culture: perspectives from the Americans with Disabilities Act generation. *Culture & Psychology, 25*(2), 241–256. doi:10.1177/1354067x18799714

Forber-Pratt, A. J., Lyew, D. A., Mueller, C., & Samples, L. B. (2017). Disability identity development: A systematic review of the literature. *Rehabilitation Psychology, 62*(2), 198–207. https://doi.org/10.1037/rep0000134

Forber-Pratt, A. J., Mueller, C. O., & Andrews, E. E. (2019). Disability identity and allyship in rehabilitation psychology: Sit, stand, sign, and show up. *Rehabilitation Psychology, 64*(2), 119–129. https://doi.org/10.1037/rep0000256

Forber-Pratt, A. J., & Zape, M. P. (2017). Disability identity development model: Voices from the ADA-generation, *Disability and Health Journal. 10*(2), 350–355. https://doi.org/10.1016/j.dhjo.2016.12.013

Ford, D. Y. (2010). *Reversing underachievement among gifted black students.* Prufrock.

Ford, D. Y. (2013). *Recruiting and retaining culturally different students in gifted education.* Routledge.

Fornauf, B. S., & Mascio, B. (2021). Extending DisCrit: A case of universal design for learning and equity in a rural teacher residency. *Journal of Race, Ethnicity & Education, 24*(5), 671–686.

Foucault, M. (1982). The subject and power. *Critical Inquiry, 8*(4), 777–795.

Foucault, M. (1995). *Discipline and punish: The birth of the prison.* Vintage Books.

Foucault. M. (2009). *History of madness.* Routledge.

Fox, N. J., & Allred, P. (2015). New materialist social inquiry: Designs, method and the research-assemblage. *International Journal of Social Research Methodology, 18*(4), 339–414.

Frank, A. W. (2012). *Letting stories breathe: A socio-narratology.* University of Illinois.

Freire, P. (1970/2010). *Pedagogy of the oppressed: 30th anniversary edition.* Continuum.

Freire, P. (1972). *Pedagogy of the oppressed.* Penguin.

Freire, P. (1993). *Pedagogy of the oppressed*. Seabury Press.
Fricker, M. (2007). *Epistemic injustice: Power and the ethics of knowing* (1st ed.). Oxford University Press.
Friedman, J., Applebaum, A., Woodfield, C., & Ashby, C. (2019). Integrating disability studies pedagogy in teacher education. *Journal of Teaching Disability Studies*, 1(1). https://jtds.commons.gc.cuny.edu/integrating-disability-studies-pedagogy-in-teacher-education/
Friedman, T., Hallaran, A., & Locke, M. (2020). Rubberbanding in a liminal space: Teachers contemplate the intersection of race and dis/ability and race in inclusive classrooms. *Journal of Race, Ethnicity, & Education*, 1–21. https://doi.org/10.1080/13613324.2020.1753677
Fuligni, A. J., Witkow, M., & Garcia, C. (2005). Ethnic identity and the academic adjustment of adolescents from Mexican, Chinese, and European backgrounds. *Developmental Psychology*, 41(5), 799–811.
Gallagher, D. (2004). Entering the conversation: The debate behind the debates in special education. In D. J. Gallagher, L. Heshusius, R. P. Iano, & T. M. Skrtic (Eds.), *Challenging orthodoxy in special education: Dissenting voices* (pp. 3–26). Love Publishing.
Gallagher, D. J., Connor, D. J., & Ferri, B. A. (2014). Beyond the far too incessant schism: Special education and the social model of disability. *International Journal of Inclusive Education*, 18(11), 1120–1142.
Gallaudet University. (n.d.). Center for Black deaf studies. https://www.gallaudet.edu/center-for-black-deaf-studies/
Gallego, M. A., Cole, M., & Laboratory of Comparative Human Cognition. (2001). Classroom cultures and cultures in the classroom. In V. Richardson (Ed.), *Handbook of research on teaching* (4th ed., pp. 951–997). Washington, DC: American Educational Research Association.
Galvin, R. (2003). The paradox of disability culture: The need to combine versus the imperative to let go. *Disability & Society*, 18(5), 675–690.
García-Fernández, C. M. (2014). *Deaf Latina/Latino critical theory in education: The lived experiences and multiple intersecting identities of deaf-Latina/o high school students*. (Unpublished doctoral dissertation). University of Texas, Austin.
García-Fernández, C. M. (2020). Intersectionality and autoethnography: DeafBlind, DeafDisabled, Deaf and Hard of Hearing-Latinx children are the future. Special Issue: *Disability Justice, Race, and Education*, 6(1), 40–67.
Garland-Thomson, R. (2002). Integrating disability, transforming feminist theory. *NWSA Journal*, 14(3), 1–32. http://www.jstor.org/stable/4316922
Garland-Thomson, R. (2017). Eugenic world building and disability: The strange world of Kazuo Ishiguro's "Never Let Me Go." *Journal of Medical Humanities*, 38(2), 133–145.
Garland-Thomson, R., & Bailey, M. (2010). Never fixed: Modernity and disability identities. In M. Wetherell, & C. T. Mohanty (Eds.), *The SAGE handbook of identities* (pp. 403–418). SAGE Publication.
Gay, G. (2002). Preparing for culturally responsive teaching. *Journal of Teacher Education*, 53(2), 106–116.
Gaztambide-Fernandez, R. A. (2006). Regarding race: The necessary browning of our curriculum and pedagogy public project. *Journal of Curriculum and Pedagogy*, 3(1), 60–65. https://doi.org/10.1080/15505170.2006.10411576

Gaztambide-Fernandez, R. A., & Murad, Z. (2011). Out of line: Perspectives on the "browning" of curriculum and pedagogy. *Journal of Curriculum and Pedagogy, 8*(1), 14–16. https://doi.org/10.1080/15505170.2011.571538

Gee, J. P. (2000). Identity as an analytic lens for research in education. *Review of Research in Education, 25,* 99–125. https://doi.org/10.2307/1167322

Gershwin, G., Heyward, D., Gershwin, I., White, W., Haymon, C., Evans, D., . . . & Rattle, S. (1935). *Porgy and Bess.* Decca.

Gertz, E. N. (2003). *Dysconscious audism and critical deaf studies: Deafcrit's analysis of unconscious internalization of hegemony within the deaf community.* (Unpublished doctoral dissertation). University of California Los Angeles.

Giangreco, M. F., & Taylor, S. J. (2003). "Scientifically based research" and qualitative inquiry. *Research and Practices for Persons with Disabilities, 28*(3), 133–137.

Gill, C. J. (1995). A psychological view of disability culture. *Disability Studies Quarterly, 15,* 16–19.

Gill, C. J. (1997). Four types of integration in disability identity development. *Journal of Vocational Rehabilitation, 9*(1), 39–46. https://doi.org/10.1016/S1052-2263(97)00020-2

Gillborn, D. (2015). Intersectionality, critical race theory, and the primacy of racism: Race, class, gender, and disability in education. *Qualitative Inquiry, 21*(3), 277–287.

Gilman, A. (2021, February 12). *Stimulus funds help, but will they be enough for schools?* The Hechinger Report. https://hechingerreport.org/how-much-will-it-take-to-reopen-catch-up-kids-and-save-public-schooling-long-term/

Gindis, B. (1995). The social/cultural implication of disability: Vygotsky's paradigm for special education. *Educational Psychologist, 30*(2), 77–81. doi:10.1207/s15326985ep3002_4

Gindis, B. (2003). Remediation through education. In A. Kozulin, B. Gindis, V. Ageyev, & S. Miller (Eds.), *Vygotsky's educational theory in cultural context* (pp. 200–222). Cambridge University Press.

Gipps, C. (1999). Socio-cultural aspects of assessment. *Review of Educational Research, 24*(1), 355–392.

Giwa Onaiwu, M. (2020). "They Don't Know, Don't Show, or Don't Care": Autism's White privilege problem. *Autism in Adulthood, 2*(4), 270–272. https://doi.org/10.1089/aut.2020.0077

Goffman, E. (1963). *Stigma; notes on the management of spoiled identity.* Prentice-Hall.

González, N., & Moll, L. (2002). Cruzando el puente: Building bridges to funds of knowledge. *Educational Policy, 16*(4), 623–641. https://doi.org/10.1177/0895904802016004009

Gonzalez, N., Moll, L., & Amanti, C. (2005). *Funds of knowledge: Theorizing practice in households, communities, and practices.* Routledge.

González, T., & Artiles, A. J. (2020). Wrestling with the paradoxes of equity: A cultural-historical reframing of technical assistance interventions. *Multiple voices: Disability, race, and language intersections in special education, 20*(1), 5–15.

González, T., McCabe, K. M., & Lobo de Castro, C. (2017, September). *An equity toolkit for inclusive schools: Centering youth voice in school change.* Great Lake Equity Center. https://glec.education.iupui.edu/Images/equity_tools/Gonzalez_centeringyouthvoiceinschoolchangetoolkit.pdf

Goodley, D., Lawthom, R., Liddiard, K., & Runswick-Cole, K. (2019). Provocations for critical disability studies. *Disability & Society, 34*(6), 972–997.

Goodley, D., Runswick-Cole, K., & Liddiard, K. (2015). The DisHuman child. *Discourse: Studies in the Cultural Politics of Education, 37*(5), 770–784.

Goodman, N., Morris, M., & Boston, K. (n.d.). Financial inequality: Disability, race and poverty in America, National Disability Institute. https://www.nationaldisabilityinstitute.org/wp content/uploads/2019/02/disability-race-poverty-in-america.pdf

Green, A. L., Cohen, D. R., & Stormont, M. (2019). Addressing and preventing disproportionality in exclusionary discipline practices for students of color with disabilities. *Intervention in School and Clinic, 54*(4), 241–245.

Green, E. L. (2020, April 28). DeVos decides against special education waivers during the pandemic. *New York Times.* https://www.nytimes.com/2020/04/28/us/politics/coronavirus-devos-special-education.html

Greenfield, R. (2013). Perceptions of elementary teachers who educate linguistically diverse student. *The Qualitative Report, 18*(47), 1–26.

Greenstein, A. (2014). Is this inclusion? Lessons from a very "special" unit. *International Journal of Inclusive Education, 18*(4), 379–391. https://doi.org/10.1080/13603116.2013.777130

Greenstein, A. (2016). *Radical inclusive education: Disability, teaching and struggles for liberation.* Routledge. https://doi.org/10.4324/9781315690483

Grove, D., & Longnecker, E. (2021, January 15). *U.S. Department of Education investigating Indiana's handling of special education during pandemic.* https://www.wthr.com/article/news/local/indiana/us-department-of-education-investigating-indianas-handling-of-special-education-during-pandemic/531-8735473f-c9b6-4d52-bd18-167c4bf53eb5

Grue, J. (2016). The problem with inspiration porn: A tentative definition and a provisional critique. *Disability & Society, 31*(6), 838–849.

Gustavsson, A. (2004). The role of theory in disability research-springboard or strait jacket? *Scandinavian Journal of Disability Research, 6*(1), 55–70. https://doi.org/10.1080/15017410409512639

Gutiérrez, K. D. (2008). Developing a sociocritical literacy in the third space. *Reading Research Quarterly, 43*(2), 148–164.

Gutiérrez, K. D., Baquedano-López, P., & Tejeda, C. (1999). Rethinking diversity: Hybridity and hybrid language practices in the third space. *Mind, Culture, and Activity, 6*(4), 286–303.

Gutiérrez, K. D., Becker, B. L. C., Espinoza, M. L., Cortes, K. L., Cortez, A., Lizárraga, J. R., Rivero, E., Villegas, K., & Yin, P. (2019). Youth as historical actors in the production of possible futures. *Mind, Culture, and Activity, 26*(4), 291–308. https://doi.org/10.1080/10749039.2019.1652327

Gutiérrez, K. D., & Rogoff, B. (2003). Cultural ways of learning: Individual traits or repertoires of practice. *Educational Researcher, 32*(5), 19–25.

Gutiérrez, K. D., & Stone, L. D. (1997). A cultural-historical view of learning and learning disabilities: Participating in a community of learners. *Learning Disabilities Research and Practice, 12*(2), 123–131.

Haager, D. E., Klingner, J. E., & Vaughn, S. E. (2007). *Evidence-based reading practices for response to intervention.* Paul H Brookes Publishing.

Haapasaari, A., Engeström, Y., & Kerosuo, H. (2014). The emergence of learners' transformative agency in a Change Laboratory intervention. *Journal of Education and Work, 29*(2), 232–262. https://doi.org/10.1080/13639080.2014.900168

References

Hadley, B., & McDonald, D. (2018). *Handbook of disability arts, culture, and media*. Routledge.

Haegele, J. A., & Hodge, S. (2016). Disability discourse: Overview and critiques of the medical and social models. *Quest, 68*(2), 193–206.

Hahn, H. (1988). The politics of physical differences: Disability and discrimination. *Journal of Social Issues, 44*(1), 39–47. https://doi.org/10.1111/j.1540-4560.1988.tb02047.xJohn-

Hahn, H. D., & Belt, T. L. (2004). Disability identity and attitudes toward cure in a sample of disabled activists. *Journal of Health and Social Behavior, 45*(4), 453–464.

Hairston, E., & Smith, L. (1983). *Black and deaf in America*. T. J. Publishers.

Hall, W. C. (2017). What you don't know can hurt you: The risk of language deprivation by impairing sign language development in deaf children. *Maternal and Child Health Journal, 21*(5), 961–965.

Halstead M., & Xiao J. (2010). Values education and the hidden curriculum. In T. Lovat, R. Toomery, & N. Clement (Eds.), *International research handbook on values education and student wellbeing* (pp. 303–317). Springer. https://doi.org/10.1007/978-90-481-8675-4_19

Hames-Garcia, M. (2000). "Who are our own people?": Challenges for a theory of social identity. In P. M. L. Moya, & M. R. Hames-Garcia (Eds.), *Reclaiming identity: Realist theory and the predicament of postmodernism* (pp. 102–129). University of California Press.

Hanley, M. S., & Noblit, G. W. (2009). *Cultural responsiveness, racial identity and academic success: A review of literature*. The Heinz Endowments. http://www.heinz.org/userfiles/library/culture-report_final.pdf

Hanson, M. (2020, December 22). *COVID relief deal includes billions for schools to improve entilation, address learning loss*. https://www.masslive.com/coronavirus/2020/12/covid-relief-deal-includes-billions-for-schools-to-improve-ventilation-address-learning-loss-during-the-pandemic.html

Haraway, D. (1988). Situated knowledges: The science question in feminism and the privilege of partial perspective. *Feminist Studies, 14*(3), 575–599. https://doi.org/10.2307/3178066

Harrell, E. (2017). *Crime against persons with disabilities, 2009-2015-Statistical tables*. Bureau of Justice Statistics. https://bjs.ojp.gov/library/publications/crime-against-persons-disabilities-2009-2015-statistical-tables

Hartman, S. (2006). *Lose your mother: A journey along the Atlantic slave route*. Macmillan.

Haslam, S. A., Jetten, J., Postmes, T., & Haslam, C. (2009). Social identity, health, and well-being: An emerging agenda for applied psychology. *Applied Psychology, 58*(1), 1–23. https://doi.org/10.1111/j.1464-0597.2008.00379.x

Hehir, T. (2002). Eliminating ableism in education. *Harvard Educational Review, 72*(1), 1–33.

Heller, K. A., Holtzman, W. H., & Messick, S. (Eds.). (1982). *Placing children in special education: A strategy for equity*. National Academy Press.

Heller, R., & McKlindon, D. (1996). Families as "faculty": Parents educating caregivers about family-centered care. *Pediatric Nursing, 22*(5), 428–431.

Hernández-Saca, D., & Cannon, M. A. (2019). Interrogating disability epistemologies: Towards collective dis/ability intersectional emotional, affective and spiritual autoethnographies for healing. *International Journal of Qualitative Studies in Education, 32*(3), 243–262.

Hernández-Saca, D. I. (2019). Re-framing master narratives of dis/ability through an affective lens: Sophia Cruz's LD story at her intersections. *Anthropology & Education Quarterly, 50*(4), 424–447.

Heumann, J. (2020). *Being Heumann: An unrepentant memoir of a disability rights activist.* Beacon Press.

Hill, J. C. (2012). *Language attitudes in the American deaf community.* Gallaudet University Press.

Hipolito-Delgado, C. P. (2014, March 27). Beyond cultural competence. *Counseling Today, 56*, 50–55. https://ct.counseling.org/ 2014/03/beyond-cultural-competence/

Holcomb, T. K. (2012). *Introduction to American deaf culture.* Oxford University Press.

hooks, b. (1994). *Teaching to transgress: Education as the practice of freedom.* Routledge.

Howard, T. C. (2003). A tug of war for our minds: African American high school students' perceptions of their academic identities and college aspirations. *High School Journal, 87*(1), 4–17. https://doi:10.1353/hsj.2003.0017

Huenecke, D. (1982). What is curriculum theorizing? What are its implications for practice? *Educational Leadership, 39*(4), 290–294.

Humphries, T. (1975). *Audism: The making of a word.* Unpublished essay.

Hunt, P. (2017). A critical condition. In J. Boys (Ed.), *Disability, space, architecture: A reader* (n. p). Routledge. https://doi.org/10.4324/9781315560076

Hurd, N. M., Sánchez, B., Zimmerman, M. A., & Caldwell, C. H. (2012). Natural mentors, racial identity, and educational attainment among African American adolescents: Exploring pathways to success. *Child Development, 83*(4), 1196–1212. https://doi.org/10.1111/j.1467-8624.2012.01769.x

Hurtado, A. (1996). *The color of privilege: Three blasphemies on race and feminism.* University of Michigan Press.

Husserl, E. (1912). *Phenomenology.* Stanford.

Hypoxic-Ischemic Encephalopathy (HIE) Help Center. (2017). *Disability terminology: Choosing the right words when talking about disability.* https://hiehelpcenter.org/

Individuals with Disabilities Education Improvement Act (2004), 20 U.S.C. § 614 *et seq.*

Iseke, J. (2013). Indigenous storytelling as research. *International Review of Qualitative Research, 6*(4), 559–577.

Jensen, B. (2004). A nonhumanist disposition. *Configurations, 2*, 229–261.

Johnson, A. M., Yoder, J., & Richardson-Nassif, K. (2006). Using families as faculty in teaching medical students family-centered care: What are students learning? *Teaching & Learning in Medicine, 18*(3), 222–225.

Johnson, L. J., & Pugach, M. C. (1990). Classroom teachers' views of intervention strategies for learning and behavior problems: Which are reasonable and how frequently are they used? *The Journal of Special Education, 24*(1), 69–84.

John-Steiner, V., & Mahn, H. (1996). Sociocultural approaches to learning and development: A Vygotskian framework. *Educational Psychologist, 31*(3–4), 191–206.

Jonassen, D. H., & Rohrer-Murphy, L. (1999). Activity theory as a framework for designing constructivist learning environments. *Educational Technology Research and Development, 47*(1), 61–79.

References

Jones, K. (2018, November 4). *Keith Jones: American hip hop artist with cerebral palsy.* https://ukdhm.org/keith-jones-american-hip-hop-artist-with-cerebral-palsy/

Jones, L., Bellis, M. A., Wood, S., Hughes, K., McCoy, E., Eckley, L., . . . & Officer, A. (2012). Prevalence and risk of violence against children with disabilities: A systematic review and meta-analysis of observational studies. *The Lancet, 380*(9845), 899–907.

Kafer, A. (2013). *Feminist queer crip.* Indiana University Press.

Kamenetz, A. (2020, July 23). *Families of children with special needs are suing in several states. here's why.* NPR. https://www.npr.org/2020/07/23/893450709/families-of-children-with-special-needs-are-suing-in-several-states-heres-why

Kapp, S. (Ed.). (2020). *Autistic community and the neurodiversity movement: Stories from the Frontline.* Springer Nature. https://library.oapen.org/handle/20.500.12657/23177

Keightley, E. (2010). Remembering research: memory and methodology in the social sciences. *International Journal of Social Research Methodology, 13*(1), 55–70.

Kendi, I. X. (2019). *How to be an antiracist.* One World.

Kim, E. (2011). Asexuality in disability narratives. *Sexualities, 14*(4), 479–493.

Kincheloe, J. (1993). Toward a critical politics of teacher thinking: Mapping the postmodern. Bergin and Garvey.

Kirk, G., & Okazawa-Rey, M. (2010). Identities and social locations: Who am I? Who are my people? In M. Adams, W. J. Blumenfeld, C. Castaneda, H. W. Hackman, M. L. Peters, & X. Zuniga (Eds.), *Readings for diversity and social justice* (pp. 8–14). Routledge.

Klar, E., & Wolfond, A. (2020). S/pace: Neurodiversity in relation. *Ought: The Journal of Autistic Culture, 2*(1). https://scholarworks.gvsu.edu/ought/vol2/iss1/7/

Klingner, J. K., & Harry, B. (2006). The special education referral and decision-making process for English language learners: Child study team meetings and staffing. *Teachers College Record, 108,* 2247–2281.

Kolářová, K. (2014). The inarticulate post-socialist crip. On the cruel optimism of neoliberal transformations in the Czech Republic. *Cripistemologies: The Journal of Literary and Cultural Disability Studies, 8*(3), 245–256.

Kooy, M., & de Freitas, E. (2007). The diaspora sensibility in teacher identity: Locating self through story. *Canadian Journal of Education, 30*(3), 865–880.

Koss, M. D., & Pacgia, K. A. (2020). Diversity in Newberry medal-winning titles: A content analysis. *Journal of Language & Literacy Education, 16*(2), 1–28.

Koszalka, T. A., & Wu, C. P. (2005). *A cultural historical activity theory [CHAT] analysis of technology integration: Case study of two teachers.* Presented at the Association for Educational Communications and Technology Annual Meeting 2005. https://www.learntechlib.org/p/76944/

Kozleski, E. B., & Artiles, A. J. (2012). Technical assistance as inquiry: Using activity theory methods to engage equity in educational practice communities. In S. Steinberg, & G. Canella (Eds.), *Handbook on critical qualitative research* (pp. 431–445). Peter Lang.

Kozleski, E. B., Thorius, K. A. K., & Smith, A. (2013). Theorizing systemic reform in urban schools. In E. B. Kozleski, & K. A. K. Thorius (Eds.), *Ability, equity, and culture: Sustaining inclusive urban education reform* (pp. 11–31). Teachers College Press.

Kozleski, E. B., & Zion, S. (2006). *Preventing disproportionality by strengthening district policies and procedures: An assessment and strategic planning process*. National Center for Culturally Responsive Education Systems.

Kozyra, K. L. (2021). Beyond inclusion: Meaningfully engaging visitors with disabilities. In B. Bobick, & C. DiCindio (Eds.), *Engaging communities through civic engagement in art museum education* (pp. 78–95). IGI Global. http://doi:10.4018/978-1-7998-7426-3.ch004

Kulkarni, S., Nussbaum, E., & Boda, P. (2021). DisCrit at the margins of teacher education: Informing curriculum, visibilization, and disciplinary integration. *Journal of Race, Ethnicity & Education, 24*(5), 654–670.

Kulkarni, S. S. (2021). Special education teachers of color and their beliefs about dis/ability and race: Counter-stories of smartness and goodness. *Curriculum Inquiry, 51*(5), 496521. doi:10.1080/03626784.2021.1938973

Ladau, E. (2015, July 15). Why Person-First Language Doesn't Always Put the Person First. Retrieved May 1, 2017, from Think Inclusive: https://www.thinkinclusive.us/why-person-first-language-doesnt-always-put-the-person-first/

Ladd, P. (2008). Colonialism and resistance: A brief history of Deafhood. In H. L. Bauman (Ed.), *Open your eyes: Deaf studies talking* (pp. 42–59). University of Minnesota Press.

Ladson-Billings, G. (1994). *The dreamkeepers: Successful teachers of African American children*. Jossey-Bass.

Ladson-Billings, G. (1995). Toward a theory of culturally relevant pedagogy. *American Educational Research Journal, 32*(3), 465–491.

Ladson-Billings, G., & Tate, W. F. (1995). Toward a critical race theory of education. *Teachers College Record, 97*(1), 47–68.

Lagemann, E. C. (2000). *An elusive science: The troubling history of educational research*. University of Chicago.

Lalor, M. (2020). 3 steps to developing an asset-based approach to teaching. http://www.edutopia.org/article/3-steps-developing-asset-based-approach-teaching

Lalvani, P., & Bacon, J. K. (2019). Rethinking "We are all special": Anti-ableism curricula in early childhood classrooms. *Young Exceptional Children, 22*(2), 87–100.

Lambert, R., & Tan, P. (2016b). Theorizing the research divide between special education and mathematics. In M. B. Wood, E. E. Turner, M. Civil, & J. A. Eli (Eds.), *Proceedings of the 38th annual meeting of the North American chapter of the international group for the psychology of mathematics education* (pp. 1057–1063). North American Chapter of the Psychology of Mathematics Education.

Landson-Billings, G., & Tate, William F. Iv (1995). Toward a critical race theory of education. *The Teachers College Record, 97*(1), 47–68.

Langer-Osuna, J. M., & Nasir, N. i. S. (2016). Rehumanizing the "other": Race, culture, and identity in education research. *Review of Research in Education, 40*(1), 723–743. doi:10.3102/0091732x16676468

Lane, H., Hoffmeister, R., & Bahan, B. (1996). *A journey into the deaf world*. DawnSignPress.

Lawyer, G. (2018). *Removing the colonizer's coat in deaf education: Exploring the curriculum of colonization and the field of Deaf Education*. (Unpublished doctoral dissertation). University of Tennessee-Knoxville.

Lawyer, G. (in press). I still have joy: Disability Justice as praxis, theory, and research in a special education teacher preparation program. In D. I. Hernández-Saca,

H. Pearson, & C. K. Voulgarides (Eds.), *Understanding the boundaries between disability studies and special education through consilience, self-study, and radical love*. Lexington Press

Lawyer. G. (in press). Theorizing the curriculum of colonization in the U.S. deaf context: Situating DisCrit within a framework of decolonization. In S. A. Annamma, B. Ferri, & D. Connor (Eds.), *DisCrit expanded: Inquiries, reverberations & ruptures*. Teachers College Press.

Leary, J. D. (2005). *Post traumatic slave syndrome: America's legacy of enduring injury and healing*. Uptone Press.

Lee, C. D. (2006). "Every good-bye ain't gone": Analyzing the cultural underpinnings of classroom talk. *International Journal of Qualitative Studies in Education, 19*(3), 305–327. https://doi.org/10.1080/09518390600696729

Lee, C. D. (2007). *Culture, literacy and learning: Blooming in the midst of the whirlwind*. Teachers College Press.

Lee, C. D. (2017). An ecological framework for enacting culturally sustaining pedagogy. In H. S. Alim, & D. Paris (Eds.), *Culturally sustaining pedagogies: Teaching and learning for justice in a changing world* (pp. 261–274). Teachers College Press.

Lee, E., Menkart, D., & Okazwa-Rey, M. (1997). *Beyond heroes and holidays: A practical guide to K-12 anti-racist, multicultural education and staff development*. Network of Educators on the Americas.

Lester, J., & Nusbaum, E. (2021). *Centering diverse bodyminds in critical qualitative inquiry*. Routledge.

Lewis, K. E. (2016). Beyond error patterns: A sociocultural view of fraction comparison errors in students with mathematical learning disabilities. *Learning Disability Quarterly, 39*(4) 199–212.

Lewis, K. E., & Lynn, D. L. (2018). Access through compensation: Emancipatory view of a mathematics learning disability. *Cognition & Instruction 36*(4), 424–459. DOI: 10.1080/07370008.2018.1491581.

Lewis, T. L. (2016). *Honoring arnaldo rios-soto and Charles Kinsey: Achieving liberation through disability solidarity*. https://www.talilalewis.com/blog/emmett-till-disability-erasure

Lewis, T. L. (2017, February 28). *Disability ain't for ya dozens (or demons): 10 ableist phrases Black folks should retire immediately*. https://www.talilalewis.com/blog/february-28th-2017

Lewis, T. L. (2021, January 1). *Working definition of ableism*. https://www.talilalewis.com/blog/january-2021-working-definition-of-ableism

Li, S. C. (2003). Biocultural orchestration of developmental plasticity across levels: The interplay of biology and culture in shaping the mind and behavior across the life span. *Psychological Bulletin, 129*(2), 171–194.

Liasidou, A. (2014). The cross-fertilization of critical race theory and disability studies: Points of convergence/ divergence and some education policy implications. *Disability & Society, 29*(5) 724–737.

Liebowitz, C. (2015, March 20). I am disabled: On identity-first versus people-first language. Retrieved April 28, 2017, from the body is not an apology: Radical self love for everybody and every body. https://thebodyisnotanapology.com/magazine/i-am-disabled-on-identity-first-versus-people-first-language/

Lindholm-Leary, K. (2001). *Dual language education*. Multilingual Matters.

Linton, S. (1998). *Claiming disability: Knowledge and identity*. NYU Press.
Lipsky, D., & Gartner, A. 2008. *Inclusion, a service not a place: A whole school approach*. Dude Publishing.
Locke, M., Guzman, V., Hallaran, A., Arciniegas, M., Friedman, T., & Brito, A. (2022). Counternarratives as DisCrit praxis: Disrupting classroom master narratives through imagined composite stories. *Teachers College Record*. https://www.tcrecord.org/Content.asp?ContentID=24071
Longmore, P. K. (2003). *Why I burned my book and other essays on disability*. Temple University Press.
López, F. A. (2017). Altering the trajectory of the self-fulfilling prophecy: Asset-based pedagogy and classroom dynamics. *Journal of Teacher Education, 68*(2), 193–212.
Lorde, A. (1984). *Sister outsider*. Crossing Press.
Lorde, A. (2000). *The collected poems of Audre Lorde*. W. W. Norton & Company.
Losen, D. J. (2015). *Closing the school discipline gap: Equitable remedies for excessive exclusion*. Teachers College Press.
Losen, D. J., Hodson, C. L., Keith II, M. A., Morrison, K., & Belway, S. (2015). *Are we closing the school discipline gap?* University of California, Los Angeles. https://escholarship.org/uc/item/2t36g571
Loutzenheiser, L. W., & Erevelles, N. (2019). "What's disability got to do with it?": Crippin' educational studies at the intersections. *Educational Studies, 55*(4), 375–386.
Love, H. R., & Beneke, M. (2021). Pursuing justice-driven inclusive education research: Disability critical race theory (DisCrit) in early childhood. *Topics in Early Childhood Special Education*. https://doi.org/10.1177/0271121421990833
Lugones, M. (1987). Playfulness, "world"-traveling, and loving perception. *Hypatia, 2*(2), 3–19.
Maag, J. W., & Katsiyannis, A. (2012). Bullying and students with disabilities: Legal and practice considerations. *Behavioral Disorders, 37*(2), 78–86.
Mackelprang, R. W., & Salsgiver, R. O. (2016). *Disability: A diversity model approach in human service practice* (3rd ed.). Oxford University Press.
MacLure, M. (2013). Classification or wonder? Coding as an analytic practice in qualitative research. In R. Coleman, & J. Ringrose (Eds.), *Deleuze and research methodologies* (pp. 164–184). Edinburgh University Press.
MacLure, M. (2015). The 'new materialisms': A thorn in the flesh of critical qualitative inquiry? In G. Cannella, M. S. Perez, & P. Pasque (Eds.), *Critical qualitative inquiry: Foundations and futures* (pp. 93–112). Left Coast Press.
MacNay, L. (1994). *Foucault: A critical introduction*. Continuum Intl Pub Group.
Macy, M., & Squires, J. (2009). L'arte D'arrangiarsi: Evaluation of an innovative practice in a preservice practicum. *Journal of Early Intervention, 31*(4), 308–325.
Majors, R., & Billson, J. M. (1993). *Cool pose: The dilemma of Black manhood in America*. Simon and Schuster.
Manning, E. (2016). *The minor gesture*. Duke University Press.
Manning, E., & Massumi, B. (2014). *Thought in the act: Passages in the ecology of experience*. University of Minnesota Press.
Mantler, G. K. (2013). *Power to the poor: Black-Brown coalition and the fight for economic justice*. University of North Carolina Press.
Margolis, E. (2001). *The hidden curriculum in higher education*. Routledge.

References

Martineau, H. (1845). *Life in the sick room*. William Crosby.
Martínez-Álvarez, P. (2020). Dis/ability as mediator: Opportunity encounters in hybrid learning spaces for emergent bilinguals with dis/abilities. *Teachers College Record, 122*(5), 1–44.
Martínez-Álvarez, P., Son, M., & Arana, B. (2020). Pre-service teachers' efforts to mediate learning with bilingual children with disabilities. *Teaching and Teacher Education, 91*. https://doi.org/10.1016/j.tate.2020.103044
Massey, D. (1993). Politics and space/time. In M. Keith, & S. Pile (Eds.) *Place and politics of identity*. Routledge.
Matsuda, M. J. (1987). Looking to the bottom: Critical legal studies and reparations. *Harvard Civil Rights-Civil Liberties Law Review, 22*, 323.
Mayer, C. (2010). The demands of writing and the deaf writer. In M. Marschark, & P. Spencer (Eds.), *Oxford handbook of deaf studies, language, and education* (2nd ed., pp. 144–155). Oxford University Press.
McCaskill, C. (2005). *The education of Black Deaf Americans in the 20th century: Policy implications for administrators in residential schools for the Deaf* (Unpublished doctoral dissertation). Gallaudet University.
McCaskill, C., Lucas, C., Bayley, R., & Hill, J. C. (2011). *The hidden treasure of Black ASL: Its history and structures*. Gallaudet University Press.
McClain, D. (2016). The Black Lives Matter Movement Is Most Visible on Twitter. Its True Home Is Elsewhere. *The Nation*, April 19.
McGuire, A. (2018). *War on autism on the cultural logic of normative violence*. University of Michigan Press.
McInerey, M., & Hamilton, J. L. (2007). Elementary and middle schools' technical assistance center: An approach to support the effective implementation of scientifically based practices in special education. *Exceptional Children, 73*(2), 242–255.
McLaren, P. (2002). *Critical pedagogy: A look at the major concepts*. Routledge/Falmer Press.
McRuer, R. (2016). Compulsory able-bodiedness and queer/disabled existence. In L. J. Davis (Ed.), *The disability studies reader* (4th ed., pp. 412–421). Routledge. https://doi.org/10.4324/9781315680668-37
Meekosha, H., Shuttleworth, R., & Soldatic, K. (2013). Disability and critical sociology: Expanding the boundaries of critical social inquiry. *Critical Sociology, 39*(3), 319–323. https://doi.org/10.1177/0896920512471220
Mehan, H. (1996). The construction of an LD student: A case study in the politics of representation. In M. Silverstein, & G. Urban (Eds.), *Natural histories of discourse* (pp. 253–276). University of Chicago Press.
Merleau-Ponty, M. (2002). *Phenomenology of perception*. Routledge. (Original work published 1945)
Merriam-Webster. (n.d.). Volition. https://www.merriam-webster.com/dictionary/volition
Michalko, R. (2002). *The difference that disability makes*. Temple University Press.
Michalko, R. (2002). Estranged-familiarity. In M. Corker, & T. Shakespeare (Eds.), *Disability/Postmodernity: Embodying Disability Theory*. (pp. 175–183). Continuum.
Michals, T., & McTiernan, C. (2018). "Oh, why can't you remain like this forever!": Children's literature, growth, and disability. *Disability Studies Quarterly, 38*(2). https://dsq-sds.org/article/view/6107/4914#endnote15

Michigan State Board of Education. (1987, July). *Revised administrative rules for special education and rules for school social worker and school psychological services*. Michigan State Board of Education.

Migliarini, V., & Annamma, S. (2019). Applying disability critical race theory in the practice of teacher education in the United States. *Oxford Research Encyclopedia*. Oxford University Press. https://doi.org/10.1093/acrefore/9780190264093.013.783

Migliarini, V., Stinson, C., Hernández-Saca, D. (2022). "It feels like living in a limbo": Exploring the limits of inclusion for Italian and U.S. children living at the intersections of disability, citizenship and migration. In S. Annamma, B. Ferri, and D. Connor (Eds.), *DisCrit expanded: Inquiries, reverberations & ruptures* (pp. 62–80). Teachers College Press.

Miles, A. L., Nishida, A., & Forber-Pratt, A. J. (2017). An open letter to white disability studies and ableist institutions of higher education. *Disability Studies Quarterly, 37*(3). https://dsq-sds.org/article/view/5997/4686

Miller, A. L., Wilt, C. L., Allcock, H. C., Kurth, J. A., Morningstar, M. E., & Ruppar, A. L. (2020). Teacher agency for inclusive education: An international scoping review. *International Journal of Inclusive Education*. https://doi.org/10.1080/13603116.2020.1789766

Mindess, A. (2000). *Reading between the signs: Intercultural communication for sign language interpreters*. Intercultural Press.

Minear, A. (2011). Unspeakable offenses: Disability Studies at the intersections of multiple differences. In N. Erevelles (Ed.), *Disability and difference in global contexts: Enabling a transformative body politic* (pp. 95–120). Palgrave Macmillan.

Mingus, M. (2009/2012). Leaving evidence. http://leavingevidence.wordpress.com

Mingus, M. (2017, April 12). *Access intimacy, interdependence and disability justice*. Leaving evidence. https://leavingevidence.wordpress.com/2017/04/12/access-intimacy-interdependence-and-disability-justice/

Minh-Ha, T. T. (2011). *Elsewhere, within here: Immigration, refugeeism and the boundary event*. Routledge.

Mitchell, D., Snyder, S., & Ware, L. (2014). [Every] child left behind: Curricular cripistemologies and the crip/queer art of failure. *Journal of Literary & Cultural Disability Studies, 8*, 295–313.

Mitchell, D. T., & Snyder, S. L. (2015). *The biopolitics of disability: Neoliberalism, ablenationalism, and peripheral embodiment*. University of Michigan Press.

Mitrano, B. S. (1981). Feminism and curriculum theory: Implications for teacher education. *Journal of Curriculum Theorizing, 3*(2), 5–85.

Moges, R. (2017). Cripping deaf studies and deaf literature: Deaf queer ontologies and intersectionality. In A. Kusters, M. De Meulder, & D. O'Brien (Eds.), *Innovations of deaf scholars* (pp. 330–364). Oxford University Press.

Moges, R. T. (2020). "From White Deaf People's Adversity to Black Deaf Gain": A proposal for a new lens of Black deaf educational history. *JCSCORE, 6*(1), 68–99.

Mohanty, C. T. (2003). *Feminism without borders: Decolonizing theory, practicing solidarity*. Duke University Press.

Mohanty, C. T. (2013). Transnational feminist crossings: On neoliberalism and radical critique. *Signs, 38*(4), 967–991.

Moll, L., & Ruíz, R. (2002). The schooling of Latino children. In M. M. Súarez-Orozco, & M. M. Páez (Eds.), *Latinos: Remaking America* (pp. 362–374). University of California Press/David Rockefeller Center for Latin American Studies.

Moll, L. C. (1992). Funds of knowledge for teaching: Using a qualitative approach to connect homes and classrooms. *Theory into Practice, 31*(2): 132–141.

Moll, L. C. (2014). *L. S. Vygotsky and education*. Routledge.

Moll, L. C., & Gonzalez, N. (1994). Lessons from research with language minority children. *Journal of Reading Behavior, 26*(4), 23–41.

Moore, L. (2017). *Black disabled art history 101*. Xóchitl Justice Press.

Moore, L. (2019). *Krip hop graphic novel vol 1*. Poor Press.

Morgan, J. (in press). Towards a DisCrit approach to American law. In S. Annamma, B. Ferri, & D. Connor (Eds.), *DisCrit expanded: Reverberations, ruptures, and inquiries*. Teachers College Press.

Morrell, E., & Duncan-Andrade, J. (2002). Toward a critical classroom discourse: Promoting academic literacy through engaging hip-hop culture with urban youth. *English Journal, 91*(6), 88–94.

Morris, J. (1993). Feminism and disability. *Feminist Review, 43*(1), 57–70.

Morrison, S., & Johnson, N. (2020). Pilot study: Understanding how Deaf Blind people make meaning of their avowed and ascribed identities. *Deaf Studies Digital Journal, 5*. https://quod.lib.umich.edu/d/dsdj/images/15499139.0005.004-transcript.pdf

Mpofu, E., & Harley, D. A. (2006). Racial and disability identity: Implications for the career counseling of African Americans with disabilities. *Rehabilitation Counseling Bulletin, 50*(1), 14–23.

Mueller, C. (2019). Adolescent understandings of disability labels and social stigma in school. *International Journal of Qualitative Studies in Education, 32*(3), 263–281. https://doi.org/10.1080/09518398.2019.1576940

Muhammad, G. (2020). *Cultivating genius: An equity framework for culturally and historically responsive teaching*. Scholastic.

Mukopadhyay, T. R. (2015). *Plankton dreams: What I learned in special ed*. Open Humanities Press.

Munguia, B. (2018, February 2). *Solange Knowles: Role model for African American performers with disabilities*. https://www.respectability.org/2018/02/solange-knowles-role-model-african-american-performers-disabilities/

Nadesan, M. H. (2013). *Constructing autism: Unravelling the 'truth' and understanding the social* (1st ed.). Routledge.

Naraian, S. (2008). Institutional and self-stories: Investigating peer interpretations of significant disability. *International Journal of Inclusive Education, 12*(5), 525–542.

Naraian, S. (2011). Seeking transparency: The production of an inclusive classroom community. *International Journal of Inclusive Education, 15*(9), 955–973.

Naraian, S. (2014). Agency in real time? Situating teachers' efforts towards inclusion in the context of local and enduring struggles. *Teachers College Record, 116*(6), 1–38.

Naraian, S. (2016a). Inclusive education complexly defined for teacher preparation: The significance and uses of error. *International Journal of Inclusive Education, 20*(9), 946–961.

Naraian, S. (2016b). Spatializing student learning to re-imagine the "place" of inclusion. *Teachers College Record, 118*(12), 1–46.

Naraian, S. (2017). *Teaching for inclusion: Eight principles for effective and equitable practice*. Teachers College Press.

Naraian, S. (2019). Precarious, debilitated, and ordinary: Rethinking (in) capacity for inclusion. *Curriculum Inquiry, 49*(4), 464–484.

Naraian, S. (2019). "Real" reading: Reconciling explicit instruction with inclusive pedagogy in a fourth-grade classroom. *Urban Education. 54*(10), 1581–1607.

Naraian, S. (2020). Diffractively narrating teacher agency within entanglements of inclusion. *Teaching Education.* https://doi.org/10.1080/10476210.2020.1796957

Naraian, S., & Schlessinger, S. (2018). Becoming an inclusive educator: Agentive maneuverings in collaboratively taught classrooms. *Teaching and Teacher Education, 71*, 179–189.

Naraian, S., & Schlessinger, S. (2021). *Narratives of inclusive teaching: Stories of "becoming" in the field.* Peter Lang.

Nario-Redmond, M. R. (2019). *Ableism: The causes and consequences of disability prejudice.* Wiley Blackwell.

Nario-Redmond, M. R., Kemerling, A. A., & Silverman, A. (2019). Hostile, benevolent, and ambivalent ableism: Contemporary manifestations. *Journal of Social Issues, 75*(3), 726–756.

National Center for Culturally Responsive Education Systems. (2009). *Final report: How the disproportionality center changed the nature of the conversation about disproportionality in special education.* Author.

National Center for Education Statistics (NCES). (2020). *Table 219.90. Number and percentage distribution of 14-through 21-year-old students served under Individuals with Disabilities Education Act (IDEA), Part B, who exited school, by exit reason, sex, race/ethnicity, age, and type of disability: 2016–17 and 2017–18.* https://nces.ed.gov/programs/digest/d19/table/dt19_219.90.asp

National Center for Education Statistics. (2020, May). *The Condition of Education—Preprimary, Elementary, and Secondary Education—High School Completion Public High School Graduation Rates—Indicator May (2020).* https://nces.ed.gov/programs/coe/indicator_coi.asp

National Center for Educational Statistics. (2020). The conditions of education at a glance: Students with disabilities. https://nces.ed.gov/programs/coe/indicator_cgg.asp

Nelson, R. (Director). (1977). *A hero ain't nothin' but a sandwich* [Film]. Radnitz/Mattel Productions.

Nicholas, J. G., & Geers, A. E. (2006). Effects of early auditory experience on the spoken language of deaf children at 3 years of age. *Ear and Hearing, 27*(3), 286–298.

Nijs, G., & Heylighen, A. (2015). Turning disability experience into expertise in assessing building accessibility: A contribution to articulating disability epistemology. *Alter, 9*(2), 144–156. https://doi.org/10.1016/j.alter.2014.12.001

Noguera, P., & Alicia, J. A. (2020). Structural racism and the urban geography of education. *Phi Delta Kappan, 102*(3), 51–56.

Nomikoudis, M., & Starr, M. (2016). Cultural humility in education and work: A valuable approach for teachers, learners and professionals. In J. Arvanitakis, & D. J. Hornsby (Eds.), *Universities, the citizen scholar, and the future of higher education* (pp. 54–68). Palgrave Macmillan.

References

Nowicki, J. M. (2020). *K-12 Education: School districts need better information to help improve access for people with disabilities*. Report to Congressional Requesters. GAO-20-448.

Nusbaum, E. A., & Steinborn, M. L. (2019). A "visibilizing" project: "Seeing" the ontological erasure of disability in teacher education and social studies curricula. *Journal of Curriculum Theorizing, 34*(1), 24–35.

Okilwa, N. (2017). *The school to prison pipeline: The role of culture and discipline in school*. Emerald.

Okun, T. (1999). *White supremacy culture*. www.dismantlingracism.org

Oliver, M. (1983). *Social work with disabled people*. Macmillan.

Oliver, M. (2013). The social model of disability: Thirty years on. *Disability & Society 28*(7), 1024–1026.

Oliver, M., & Barnes, C. (2012). *The new politics of disablement* (2nd ed.). Palgrave MacMillan.

Olkin, R. (2017). *Disability-affirmative therapy*. Oxford University Press.

Orsini, M. (2012). Autism, neurodiversity and the welfare state: The challenges of accommodating neurological difference. *Canadian Journal of Political Science, 45*(4), 805–827. https://doi.org/10.1017/s000842391200100x

Ortiz, A. A., Robertson, P. M., Wilkinson, C. Y., Liu, J., McGhee, B. D., & Kushner, M. (2011). The role of bilingual education teachers in preventing inappropriate referrals of ELLs to special education: Implications for response to intervention. *Bilingual Research Journal, 34*(3), 316–333. https://doi.org/10.1080/15235882.2011.628608

Padilla, A. (in press). LatDisCrit: Exploring latinx global south DisCrit reverberations as spaces toward emancipatory learning and radical solidarity. In S. Annamma, B. Ferri, & D. Connor (Eds.), *DisCrit expanded: Reverberations, ruptures, and inquiries*. Teachers College Press.

Parasnis, I. (2012). Diversity and Deaf identity: Implications for personal epistemologies in Deaf education. In P. Paul, & D. Moores (Eds.), *Deaf epistemologies: Multiple perspectives on the acquisition of knowledge* (pp. 63–80). Gallaudet University Press.

Paradise, R. (2002). Finding ways to study culture in context. *Human Development, 45*, 229–236.

Parekh, G. (2017). The tyranny of "ability." *Curriculum Inquiry, 47*(4), 337–343. doi:10.1080/03626784.2017.1383755

Paris, D. (2012). Culturally sustaining pedagogy: A needed change in stance, terminology, and practice. *Educational Researcher, 41*(3), 93–97. https://doi.org/10.3102/0013189X12441244

Paris, D., & Alim, H. S. (2014). What are we seeking to sustain through Culturally Sustaining Pedagogy? A loving critique forward. *Harvard Educational Review, 84*(1) 85–100.

Paris, D., & Alim, H. S. (2017). *Culturally sustaining pedagogies: Teaching and Learning for Justice in a Changing World*. Teachers College Press.

Paterson, K. B., & Hughes, B. (1999). Disability studies and phenomenology: The carnal politics of everyday life. *Disability & Society, 14*(5), 597.

Patterson, K. B., Webb, K. W., & Krudwig, K. M. (2009). Family as faculty parents: Influence on teachers' beliefs about family partnerships. *Preventing School Failure, 54*(1), 41–50.

Paul, P. (1998). *Literacy and deafness: The development of reading, writing, and literate thought.* Allyn & Bacon.

Payne-Tsoupros, C., & Johnson, N. (in press). A DisCrit call for police free schools. In S. Annamma, B. Ferri, & D. Connor (Eds), *DisCrit expanded: Reverberations, ruptures, and inquiries.* Teachers College Press.

Pearse, N. (2019). *An illustration of deductive analysis in qualitative research.* Kidmore End: Academic Conferences International Limited. http//dx.doi.org.proxy.ulib.uits.us.edu/10.34190/RM.19.006

Pearson, H., & Dickens B. (2021). (Re)framing qualitative research as a prickly artichoke. In J. Lester, & E. A. Nusbaum (Eds.), *Centering diverse bodyminds in critical qualitative inquiry* (pp. 81–94). Routledge.

Perry, D. M., & Carter-Long, L. (2016). The Ruderman white paper on media coverage of law enforcement use of force and disability. *Ruderman Family Foundation.*

Perry, D. M., Kopić, K., Thompson, V., & Seidel, K. (2017). *On media coverage of the murder of people with disabilities by their caregivers.* https://rudermanfoundation.org/white_papers/media-coverage-of-the-murder-ofpeople-with-disabilities-by-their-caregivers/

Peters, S. J. (2015, December 21). Disability culture. Encyclopedia Britannica. https://www.britannica.com/topic/disability-culture

Pfeiffer, D. (2004). An essay on the beginnings of disability culture and its study. *Review of Disability Studies: An International Journal, 1*(1), 14–15.

Piepzna-Samarasinha, L. L. (2018). *Care work.* Arsenal Pulp Press.

Pinar, W. F. (2004). *What is curriculum theory?* (2nd ed.). Lawrence Erlbaum Associates.

Pinar, W. F., & Miller, J. L. (1982). Feminist curriculum theory: Notes on the American field 1982. *The Journal of Educational Thought (JET)/Revue de la Pensée Educative, 16*(3), 217–224.

Priestly, M., Biesta, G., & Robinson, S. (2015). *Teacher agency: An ecological approach.* Bloomsbury.

Protopapas, A., & Parrila, R. (2018). Is dyslexia a brain disorder? *Brain Sciences, 8*(4), 61.

Pugach, M. C., & Blanton, L. P. (2009). A framework for conducting research on collaborative teacher education. *Teaching and Teacher Education, 25*(4), 575–582.

Pugach, M. C., Blanton, L. P., & Boveda, M. (2014). Working together: Research on the preparation of general education and special education teachers for inclusion and collaboration. In P. T. Sindelar, E. D. McCray, M. T. Brownell, B. Lignugaris/Kraft (Eds), *Handbook of research on special education teacher preparation* (pp. 143–160). Taylor and Francis.

Pugach, M. C., Blanton, L. P., Mickelson, A. M., & Boveda, M. (2020). Curriculum theory: The missing perspective in teacher education for inclusion. *Teacher Education and Special Education, 43*(1), 85–103.

Pugach, M. C., Matewos, A. M., & Gomez-Najarro, J. (2021). Disability and the meaning of social justice in teacher education research: A precarious guest at the table? *Journal of Teacher Education, 72*(2), 237–250.

Pugach, M. C., & Warger, C. L. (1996). *Curriculum trends, special education, and reform: Refocusing the conversation* (Special Education Series). Teachers College Press.

References

Qadri, D., & MacFarlane, L. (2018). Disability pride is back. Paper presented at the Public Pedagogies Institute Conference, Victoria University, Melbourne, Australia, pp. 1–62.

Quick Statistics About Hearing. (2020, October 2). NIDCD. https://www.nidcd.nih.gov/health/statistics/quick-statistics-he

Rabaka, R. (2010). *Against epistemic apartheid: WEB DuBois and the disciplinary decadence of sociology*. Lexington Books.

Ray, C. E. (2017). "On your feet!": Addressing ableism in theatre of the oppressed facilitation. *Pedagogy and Theatre of the Oppressed Journal*, 2. https://scholarworks.uni.edu/ptoj/vol2/iss1/6

Rayner, T. (2013, June 18). Lines of flight: Deleuze and nomadic creativity. *Philosophy for change*. https://philosophyforchange.wordpress.com/2013/06/18/lines-of-flight-deleuze-and-nomadic-creativity/

Reyes, G., Aronson, B., Batchelor, K. E., Ross, G., & Radina, R. (2021). Working in solidarity: An intersectional self-study methodology as a means to inform social justice teacher education. *Action in Teacher Education*, 43(3), 353–369.

Robertson, S. M. (2009). Neurodiversity, quality of life, and autistic adults: Shifting research and professional focuses onto real-life challenges. *Disability Studies Quarterly*, 30(1). https://doi.org/10.18061/dsq.v30i1.1069

Robinson, O. (2010). We are of a different class: Ableist rhetoric in deaf America, 1880–1920. *Deaf and disability studies: Interdisciplinary perspectives* (5–21). Gallaudet University Press.

Rodas, J. M. (2018). *Autistic disturbances: Theorizing autism poetics from the DSM to Robinson Crusoe*. University of Michigan Press.

Rogers, R. (2002). Through the eyes of the institution: A critical discourse analysis of decision making in two special education meetings. *Anthropology & Education Quarterly*, 33(2), 213–237.

Rogoff, B. (2003). *The cultural nature of human development*. Oxford University Press.

Roscigno, R. (2020). Semiotic stalemate: Resisting restraint and seclusion through Guattari's micropolitics of desire. *Canadian Journal of Disability Studies*, 9(5), 156–184. https://doi.org/10.15353/cjds.v9i5.694

Rose, C. A., & Gage, N. A. (2017). Exploring the involvement of bullying among students with disabilities over time. *Exceptional Children*, 83(3), 298–314. DOI: 10.1177/0014402916667587

Rose, D. H., & Meyer, A. (2002). *Teaching every student in the digital age: Universal design for learning*. Association for Supervision and Curriculum Development.

Ross, T. (1990). The rhetorical tapestry of race: White innocence and Black abstraction. *William & Mary Law Review*, 32, 1.

Roth, W. M. (2012). Cultural-historical activity theory: Vygotsky's forgotten and suppressed legacy and its implication for mathematics education. *Mathematics Education Research Journal*, 24, 87–104.

Ruiz-Williams, E., Burke, M., Chong, V. Y., & Chainarong, N. (2015) My deaf is not your deaf: Realizing intersectional realities at Gallaudet University. In M. Friedner, & A. Kusters (Eds.), *It's a small world: International deaf spaces and encounters* (pp. 262–274). Gallaudet University Press.

Samuels, E., & Elizabeth, F. (2021). Introduction: Crip temporalities. *Atlantic Quarterly*, 120(2), 245–254.

Sánchez, L. (2010). Positionality. In B. Warf (Ed.), *Encyclopedia of geography* (pp. 2258–2258). SAGE Publication. https://www.doi.org/10.4135/9781412939591.n913

Sandoval, C. (2000). *Methodology of the oppressed*. University of Minnesota Press.

Sandoval, C. (2003). US third-world feminism: The theory and method of oppositional consciousness in the postmodern world. In R. Lewes, & S. Mills (Eds.), *Feminist postcolonial theory* (pp. 75–99). Edinburgh University Press.

Sands, D. J., Adams, L., & Stout, D. M. (1995). A statewide exploration of the nature and use of curriculum in special education. *Exceptional Children, 62*(1), 68–83.

Saner, E. (2020, September 28). "There is a fear that this will eradicate dwarfism": The controversy over a new growth drug. *The Guardian*. https://www.theguardian.com/science/2020/sep/28/there-is-a-fear-that-this-will-eradicate-dwarfism-the-controversy-over-a-new-growth-drug

Sannino, A. (2015). The principle of double stimulation: A path to volitional action. *Learning, Culture and Social Interaction, 6*, 1–15. https://doi.org/10.1016/j.lcsi.2015.01.001

Sannino, A. (2020). Enacting the utopia of eradicating homelessness: Toward a new generation of activity-theoretical studies of learning. *Studies in Continuing Education, 42*(2), 163–179. https://doi.org/10.1080/0158037x.2020.1725459

Santamaría Graff, C. (2021). Co-investigation and -education in family as faculty approaches: A (re)positioning of power. *Theory Into Practice, 60*(1), 39–50.

Santamaría Graff, C. (in press). Family as faculty: An approach to centering families' expertise for the benefit of youth with disabilities. T. Aceves, & B. Talbott (Eds.), *Handbook of research on special education*. Routledge.

Santamaría Graff, C., Manlove, J., Stuckey, S., & Foley, M. (2020). Examining preservice special education teachers' biases and evolving understandings about families through a Family as Faculty approach. *Preventing School Failure, 65*(1), 20–37. https://doi.org/10.1080/1045988X.2020.1811626

Santamaría Graff, C., & Vázquez, S. L. (2014). Family resistance as a tool in urban school reform. In E. B. Kozleski, & K. A. K. Thorius (Eds.), *Ability, equity, and culture: Sustaining inclusive urban education reform* (pp. 80–106). Teachers College Press.

Sauer, S. J., & Jorgensen, C. M. (2016). Still caught in the continuum. In S. J. Taylor (Ed.), *Studies in inclusive education* (pp. 36–64). Brill.

Savarese, D., & Rooy, R. (Directors). (2017, October 17). *Deej* [Video file]. Retrieved April 14, 2021, https://www.deejmovie.com

Schubert, W. H. (1992). Personal theorizing about teacher personal theorizing. *Teacher personal theorizing: Connecting curriculum practice, theory, and research*, 257–272. https://jhiblog.org/2019/03/11/time-travelers-part-iii-nomadic-thought-and-the-creation-of-new-utopias/

Schult, A. (2019, March 11). Nomadic thought and the creation of new utopias. *JHI Blog*. https://jhiblog.org/2019/03/11/time-travelers-part-iii-nomadic-thought-and-the-creation-of-new-utopias/

Schweik, S. (2009). *The ugly laws: Disability in public*. NYU Press.

Sedgwick, E. K. (1990). *Epistemology of the closet*. University of California Press.

Sellman, E., Cremin, H., & McCluskey, G. (2013). *Restorative approaches to conflict in schools: Interdisciplinary perspectives on whole school approaches to managing relationships*. Routledge.

References

Sequenzia, A. (2014). Is autism speaks a hate group? *Autistic Women & Nonbinary Network (AWN)*. https://awnnetwork.org/is-autism-speaks-a-hate-group/

Sequenzia, A. (2016). *Person First Langauge and Ableism*. Ollibean. Retrieved https://ollibean.com/person-first-language-and-ableism/

Settles, S. Y., & Pratt-Hyatt, J. I. (2011). Mediators of the relationship between racial identity and life satisfaction in a community sample of African American women and men. *Cultural Diversity & Ethnic Minority Psychology, 17*, 89–97.

Shakespeare, T. (1994). Cultural representations of disability: Dustbins for disavowal? *Disability & Society, 9*(3), 283–299.

Shakespeare, T. (2014). *Disability rights and wrongs revisited* (2nd ed.). Routledge. DOI: https://doi.org/10.4324/9781315887456

Shakespeare, T., & Watson, N. (2002). The social model of disability: An outdated ideology? *Research in Social Science and Disability, 2*, 9–28.

Shallish, L., Smith, M. D., & Taylor, A. (in press). Disabled whiteness as property: A DisCrit analysis of higher education. In S. Annamma, B. Ferri, & D. Connor (Eds.), *DisCrit expanded: Reverberations, ruptures, and inquiries*. Teachers College Press.

Shapiro, J. P. (1994). *No pity: People with disabilities forging a new civil rights movement*. Broadway Books.

Shartrand, A. M., Weiss, H. B., Kreider, H. M., & Lopez, M. E. (1997). *New skills for new schools: Preparing teachers in family involvement*. Harvard Family Research Project, ED414254. http://www.ed.gov/pubs/NewSkills/

Sheppard, A. (2019, February 27). Opinion: I dance because I can. *New York Times*. https://www.nytimes.com/2019/02/27/opinion/disability-dance-alice-sheppard.html

Sherry, M. (2016). *Disability hate crimes: Does anyone really hate disabled people?* Routledge.

Shifrer, D. (2013). Stigma of a label: Educational expectations for high school students labeled with learning disabilities. *Journal of Health and Social Behavior, 54*(4), 462–480.

Siebers, T. (2010). Disability and the theory of complex embodiment—for identity politics in a new register. In L. J. Davis, (Ed.), *The disability studies reader* (3rd ed.), (pp. 316–335). Routledge.

Silberman, S. (2015). *Neurotribes: The legacy of autism and the future of neurodiversity*. Penguin.

Simms, L., Rusher, M., Andrews, J., & Coryell, J. (2008). Apartheid in deaf education: Examining workforce diversity. *American Annals of the Deaf, 153*(4), 384–395.

Simon, R., & Campano, G. (2013). Activist literacies: Teacher research as resistance to the "normal curve." *Journal of Language and Literacy Education, 9*(1), 21–39.

Simpson, H. (2019). Disability, neurodiversity, and feminism. *Journal of Feminist Scholarship, 16*(16), 81–83. https://doi.org/10.23860/jfs.2019.16.10

Sins Invalid. (2015). 10 Principles of disability justice. https://www.sinsinvalid.org/blog/10-principles-of-disability-justice

Skelton, S. M. (2019). Situating my positionality as a Black woman with a dis/ability in the provision of equity-focused technical assistance: A personal reflection. *International Journal of Qualitative Studies in Education, 32*(3), 225–242. DOI: 10.1080/09518398.2019.1576942

Skelton, S. M., Santamaría Graff, C., & Thorius, K. A. K. (2020). NCCRESt's legacy and impact on disproportionality: Where are we today? *Multiple Voices: Disability, Race, and Language Intersections in Special Education, 20*(1), 1–4.

Skelton, S. M. (Director). (1984). *Our side of the story* [Film]. Charles R. Drew Middle School.

Skiba, R., Poloni-Stardinger, L., Gallini, S., Simmons, A. B., & Feggins-Azziz, R. (2006). The disproportionality of African American students with disabilities across educational environments. *Exceptional Children, 72*(4), 411–424.

Skrtic, T. M. (1987). An organizational analysis of special education reform. *Counterpoint, 8*(2), 15–19.

Skrtic, T. M. (1992). The special education paradox: Equity as the way to excellence. In T. Heir, & T. Latus (Eds.), *Special education at the century's end: Evolution of theory and practice since 1970* (pp. 203–272). Harvard Education Press.

Skrtic, T. M. (1995). *Disability and democracy: Reconstructing (special) education for postmodernity*. Teachers College Press.

Skutnabb-Kangas, T. (1988). Multilingualism and the education of minority children. In T. Skutnabb-Kangas, & J. Cummins (Eds.), *Minority education: From shame to struggle*, (pp. 9–44). Multilingual Matters.

Slee, R. (2011). *The irregular school: Exclusion, schooling, and inclusive education*. Routledge.

Slee, R. (2019). Belonging in an age of exclusion. *International Journal of Inclusive Education, 23*(9), 909–922.

Sleeter, C. E. (1986). Learning disabilities: The social construction of a special education category. *Exceptional Children 53*, 46–54. https://doi.org/10.1177/001440298605300105

Sleeter, C. E. (2011). The academic and social value of ethnic studies: A research review. National Education Association Research Department. https://files.eric.ed.gov/fulltext/ED521869.pdf

Smagorinsky, P. (2012). Vygotsky, "defectology," and the inclusion of people of difference in the broader cultural stream. *Journal of Language and Literacy Education, 8*(1), 1–25.

Smith, P. (Ed.). (2009). *Whatever happened to inclusion? The place of students with intellectual disabilities in education*. Peter Lang.

Smitherman, G. (1977). *Talkin' and testifyin': The language of Black America*. Houghton Mifflin.

Soja, E. W. (1996). *Thirdspace: Journeys to Los Angeles and other real-and-imagined places*. Blackwell.

Spivak, G. C. (1999). *A critique of postcolonial reason: Toward a history of the vanishing past*. Harvard University Press.

Srinivasan, H. (2021, February 26). A boy like me. *Disability Visibility Project*. https://disabilityvisibilityproject.com/2021/02/06/a-boy-like-me/

Stapleton, L. (2015). When being deaf is centered: d/Deaf women of color's experiences with racial/ethnic and d/Deaf identities in college. *Journal of College Student Development, 56*(6), 570–586.

Stapleton, L. D. (2016). Audism and racism: The hidden curriculum impacting Black d/Deaf college students in the classroom. *The Negro Educational Review, 67*(1–4), 150–168.

Stiker, H. (1999). *A history of disability*. University of Michigan Press.

References

Stillman, J. (2011). Teacher learning in an era of high-stakes accountability: Productive tension and critical professional practice. *Teachers College Record, 113*(1), 133–180.

Stillman, J., & Anderson, L. (2015). From accommodation to appropriation: Teaching, identity, and authorship in a tightly coupled policy context. *Teachers and Teaching, 21*(6), 720–744.

Stolz, S. (2010). Disability trajectories: Disabled youths' identity development, negotiation of experience and expectation, and sense of agency during transition. UC San Diego. ProQuest ID: Stolz_ucsd_0033D_10890. Merritt ID: ark:/20775/bb6315283f. Retrieved from https://escholarship.org/uc/item/7zg9w5ht

Stornaioulo, A., & Whitney, E. (2018). Reenvisioining writing pedagogy and learning disabilities through a black girl's literacies framework. *International Literacy Association, 62*(6), 1–9.

Stovall, D. (2006). We can relate: Hip-hop culture, critical pedagogy, and the secondary classroom. *Urban Education, 41*(6), 585–602.

Subedi, B. (2013). Decolonizing the curriculum for global perspectives. *Educational Theory, 63*(6), 621–638.

Sullivan, A. L., & Artiles, A. J. (2011). Theorizing racial inequity in special education: Applying structural inequity theory to disproportionality. *Urban Education, 46*(6), 1526–1552.

Sullivan, P. M. (2009). Violence exposure among children with disabilities. *Clinical Child and Family Psychology Review, 12*(2), 196–216.

Sutton, X. R. (2020). *"How did you get here?": Using counter-narratives and Critical Race Theory to explore the placement experiences of Black males in self-contained special education settings.* (Doctoral dissertation). https://scholarcommons.sc.edu/etd/5751

Symeonidou, S., & Damianidou, E. (2013). Enriching the subject of Greek Literature with the experience of the 'Other': An approach that fosters citizenship education in Cyprus. *International Journal of Inclusive Education, 17*(7), 732–752.

Tan, P., & Thorius, K. A. K. (2019). Toward equity in education for students with dis/abilities: A case study of professional learning. *American Educational Research Journal, 56*, 995–1032.

Tan, P., & Thorius, K. K. (2018). En/countering inclusive mathematics education: A case of professional learning. *Mathematics Teacher Educator, 6*(2), 52–67.

Taylor, S. (1988). Caught in the continuum: A critical analysis of the principle of the least restrictive environment. *Journal of the Association for the Intellectually Handicapped, 13*(1), 41–53.

Taylor, S. J. (2006). Before it had a name: Exploring the historical roots of disability studies in education. In S. Danforth, & S. L. Gabel (Eds.), *Vital questions facing Disability Studies in Education* (pp. xiii–xxiii). Peter Lang.

Tefera, A. A., & Fischman, G. E. (2020). How and why context matters in the study of racial disproportionality in special education: Toward a critical disability education policy approach. *Equity & Excellence in Education, 53*(4), 433–448.

Thompson, R. G. (1997). *Extraordinary bodies: Figuring physical disability in American literature and culture.* Columbia University Press.

Thompson, V. (2016). #DisabilityTooWhite, Twitter. https://twitter.com/search?q=%23DisabilityTooWhite&src=hashtag_click

Thompson, V. (2018, March 16). *The overlooked history of Black disabled people*. Rewire News Group. https://rewirenewsgroup.com/article/2018/03/16/overlooked-history-black-disabled-people/

Thorius, K. A. K. (2015, July). *Addressing "Equity Traps" in school & district transformation efforts: Centering race and ability*. Christina School District Summer Leadership Conference.

Thorius, K. A. K. (2016). Stimulating artifact-mediated tensions in special education teachers' figured world: An approach toward inclusive education. *International Journal of Inclusive Education, 20*, 1326–1343.

Thorius, K. A. K. (2017, October). *Countering problematic legacies of the practice of psychology in schools: From "gatekeeper" to "inclusive education activist."* Idaho Association of School Psychologists Annual Meeting.

Thorius, K. A. K. (2019). Facilitating en/counters with legacies of white supremacy and ableism through teacher learning to eliminate special education disproportionality. *International Journal of Qualitative Studies in Education, 32*, 323–340.

Thorius, K. A. K. (2021). Traditional and innovative assessment techniques for students from culturally and linguistically diverse backgrounds: Problematic histories and transformative futures. In J. Bakken, & F. Obiakor (Eds.), *Advances in special education (Vol. 35): Special education for young learners with disabilities* (pp. 197–208). Emerald.

Thorius, K. A. K., & Artiles, A. J. (in press). Accountability elasticity in relation to U.S.Federal legislation at the intersection of race and disability. In G. A. Postiglione, C. J. Johnstone, & W. R. Teter (Eds.), *Elgar handbook of educational policy*. Edward Elgar Publishing.

Thorius, K. A. K., & Kyser, T. S. (2021). Developing anti-racist leaders through equity-expansive TA. In S. Diem, & A. J. Welton (Eds.), *Strengthening anti-racist educational leaders* (pp. 207–218). Bloomsbury.

Thorius, K. A. K., Maxcy, B. D., Macey, E., & Cox, A. (2014). A critical practice analysis of response to intervention appropriation in an urban school. *Remedial and Special Education, 35*(5), 287–299.

Thorius, K. A. K., Novak, B., Fausuamallie, E., Bischoff, J., Skelton, S. M., & Coomer, M. N. (under review). Equity-expansive learning in a technical assistance partnership at the intersections of literacy, disability, and race.

Thorius, K. A. K., Waitoller, F., Cannon, M., & Moore, T. (2018). Responsive to what? Conceptualizations of "culture" and "culturally responsive" in "Multiple Voices." *Multiple Voices: Ethnically Diverse Exceptional Learners, 18*(1), 3–21.

Thorius, K. A. K., & Waitoller, F. R. (2017). Strategic coalitions against exclusion at the intersection of race and disability—A rejoinder. *Harvard Educational Review, 87*, 251–257.

Titchkosky, T. (2011). *The question of access: Disability, space, meaning*. University of Toronto Press.

Traxler, C. B. (2000). The Stanford achievement test: National norming and performance standards for deaf and hard-of-hearing students. *Journal of Deaf Studies and Deaf Education, 5*(4), 337–348.

Triano, S. (2000). Categorical eligibility for special education: The enshrinement of the medical model in disability policy. *Disability Studies Quarterly, 20*(4). http://dx.doi.org/10.18061/dsq.v20i4.263

References

Tronto, J. (1993). *Moral boundaries: A political argument for an ethic of care.* Routledge.

Tucker, B. P. (1998). Deaf culture, cochlear implants, and elective disability. *Hastings Center Report, 28*(4), 6–14.

Tyack, D., & Cuban, L. (1995). *Tinkering toward Utopia: A century of public-school reform.* Harvard University Press.

Union of the Physically Impaired Against Segregation (UPIAS). (1975). *Fundamental principles of Disability.* Author

Urrieta, L. (2010). *Working from within: Chicana and Chicano activist educators in whitestream schools.* University of Arizona Press.

U.S. Department of Education. (2011, October 26). *Teach special education* [Video]. YouTube. https://www.youtube.com/watch?v=2XsaK3pWyII

U.S. Department of Education. (2019). *2015–16 Civil rights data collection: school climate and safety.* https://www2.ed.gov/about/offices/list/ocr/docs/school-climate-and-safety.pdf

U.S. Department of Education, National Archives and Records Administration, §300.306. (2006, August 14). Federal Register, Part II: Assistance to states for the education of children with disabilities and preschool grants for children with disabilities, final rule. *Federal Register.* https://www.govinfo.gov/content/pkg/FR-2006-08-14/pdf/06-6656.pdf

U.S. Equal Employment Opportunity Commission. (2021). *The Americans with Disabilities Act Amendments Act of 2008.* https://www.eeoc.gov/statutes/americans-disabilities-act-amendments-act-2008

Valeras, A. (2010). "We don't have a box": Understanding hidden disability identity utilizing narrative research methodology. *Disability Studies Quarterly, 30*(3/4).

Valle, J., & Connor, D. J. (2019). *Rethinking disability: A disability studies guide to inclusive practices* (2nd ed.). Routledge.

Van Cleve, J. V., & Crouch, B. A. (1989). *A place of their own: Creating the deaf community in America.* Gallaudet University Press.

Veditz, G. (1997). The preservation of sign language (Video). Burtonsville, MD: Sign Media. (Original work published in 1913)

Vidal Gutiérrez, M., & Acevedo, S. M. (n.d.). Autismo, liberación y orgullo [Autism, liberation and pride]. https://autismoliberacionyorgulloblog.wordpress.com/

Voulgarides, C. K., Fergus, E., & Thorius, K. A. K. (2017). Pursuing equity: Disproportionality in special education and the reframing of technical solutions to address systemic inequities. *Review of Research in Education, 41,* 61–87.

Vowell, S. (2011). *Unfamiliar fishes.* Riverhead Books.

Vygodskaya, G. L. (1999). Vygotsky and problems of special education. *Remedial and Special Education, 20*(6), 330–332.

Vygotsky, L. S. (1978). *Mind in society: The development of higher psychological processes.* Harvard University Press.

Vygotsky, L. S. (1993). *The fundamentals of defectology. The collected works of L. S. Vygotsky, vol. 2.* Plenum Press.

Waitoller, F., & Annamma, S. (2017). Taking a spatial turn in inclusive education: Seeking justice at the intersections of multiple markers of difference. In M. Hughes, & E. Talbott (Eds.), *The Wiley handbook of diversity in special education* (pp. 23–44). John Wiley & Sons.

Waitoller, F. R., & Artiles, A. J. (2013). A decade of professional development research for inclusive education: A critical review and notes for a research program. *Review of Educational Research, 83*(3), 319–356.

Waitoller, F. R., Artiles, A. J., & Cheney, D. A. (2010). The miner's canary: A review of overrepresentation research and explanations. *The Journal of Special Education, 44*(1), 29–49.

Waitoller, F. R., & Kozleski, E. B. (2013). Working in boundary practices: Identity development and learning in partnerships for inclusive education. *Teaching and Teacher Education, 31,* 35–45.

Waitoller, F. R., & Thorius, K. A. K. (2016). Cross-pollinating culturally sustaining pedagogy with universal design for learning: Toward an inclusive pedagogy that accounts for student dis/ability. *Harvard Educational Review, 86,* 366–389.

Ware, L. (2010). Disability studies in education. In S. Tozer, B. Gallegos, A. Henry, M. Bushnell Greiner, & P. Groves Price (Eds.), *The handbook of research in the social foundations of education* (pp. 244–59). Routledge.

Ware, L. (2013). Special education teacher preparation: Growing disability studies in the absence of resistance. In G. Wilgus (Ed.), *Knowledge, pedagogy, and postmulticulturalism: Shifting the locus of learning in urban teacher education* (pp. 153–176). Palgrave.

Ware, L. (Ed.). (2020). *Critical readings in inter-disciplinary disability studies, an international reader.* Springer.

Ware, L., & Nusbaum, E. A. (Eds.). (2020). *The strong poet: Essays in honor of Lous Heshusius.* Brill.

Ware, L., & Sauer, J. S. (Eds.). (2021). *Blue man living in a red world: Essays in honor of Steven J. Taylor.* Brill.

Ware, L., & Slee, R. (Eds.). (2020). *Ellen A. Brantlinger: When meaning falters and words fail, ideology matters.* Brill.

Ware, L., & Valle, J. (2010). How do we begin a conversation on disability in urban education? In S. R. Steinberg (Ed.), *19 urban questions: Teaching in the city* (pp. 113–130). Peter Lang.

Watkins, W. H. (1993). Black curriculum orientations: A preliminary inquiry. *Harvard Education Review, 63*(3), 321–338.

Weinberg, A. E., Sebald, A., Stevenson, C. A., & Wakefield, W. (2020). Toward conceptual clarity: A scoping review of coteaching in teacher education. *The Teacher Educator, 55*(2), 190–213.

Wendell, S. (1996). *The rejected body: Feminist philosophical reflections on disability.* Routledge.

Werstch, J. V. (1985). *Vygotsky and the social formation of mind.* Harvard University Press.

White, G. W., Lloyd Simpson, J., Gonda, C., Ravesloot, C., & Coble, Z. (2010). Moving from independence to interdependence: A conceptual model for better understanding community participation of centers for independent living consumers. *Journal of Disability Policy Studies, 20*(4), 233–240.

Whitney, C. (2006). Intersections in identity–identity development among queer women with disabilities. *Sexuality and Disability, 24*(1), 39–52.

Whitney, E. (2018). *Writing as worldmaking.* Language Arts.

Wilgus, G. (Ed.). (2013). *Knowledge, pedagogy, and postmulticulturalism: Shifting the locus of learning in urban teacher education.* Palgrave.

References

Wilkinson, M. (2014). The concept of the absent curriculum: The case of the Muslim contribution and the English National Curriculum for history, *Journal of Curriculum Studies, 46*(4), 419–440.

Williams, E. (2012). Encouraging discussion between teacher candidates and families with exceptional children. *Education, 133*(2), 239–247.

Williams, R. M. (2018). Autonomously autistic. *Canadian Journal of Disability Studies, 7*(2), 60–82. https://doi.org/10.15353/cjds.v7i2.423

Wong, A. (Ed.). (2020). *Disability visibility*. Vintage.

Woodward, J. (1975). *How you gonna get to heaven if you can't talk with Jesus: The educational establishment vs the deaf community*. Paper presented at the Annual Meeting of the Society for Applied Anthropology, Amsterdam, The Netherlands.

Wright, S. J., Lawyer, G., & Bart, E. (2021). *Redrawing the boundaries of audism*. Paper presented at Deaf Studies 360 2021 Virtual Conference, Utah Valley University, Provo, UT.

Yell, M. L., Katsiyannis, A., Rose, C. A., & Houchins, D. E. (2016). Bullying and harassment of students with disabilities in schools: Legal considerations and policy formation. *Remedial and Special Education, 37*(5), 274–284. DOI: 10.1177/0741932515614967

Yergeau, M. (2018). *Authoring autism: On rhetoric and neurological queerness*. Duke University Press.

Yosso, T. J. (2005). Whose culture has capital? A critical race theory discussion of community cultural wealth. *Race Ethnicity and Education, 8*(1), 69–91.

Young-Bruehl, E. (2012). *Childism: Confronting prejudice against children*. Yale University Press.

Yukhymenko, M. A., Brown, S. W., Lawless, K. A., Brodowinska, K., & Mullin, G. (2014). Thematic analysis of teacher instructional practices and student responses to middle school classrooms with problem-based learning environment. *Global Educational Review, 1*(3), 93–110.

Zames-Fleischer, D., & Zames, F. (2001). *The disability rights movement: From charity to confrontation*. Temple University Press.

About the Editors and the Contributors

Dr. Sara M. Acevedo is an autistic Mestiza, critical educator, and disability studies scholar-activist born and raised in Colombia. She is an assistant professor in disability studies at Miami University, Ohio, and serves on the editorial boards of *Disability, The Global South: The International Journal,* and *Ought: The Journal of Autistic Culture*. Her formal training is in historical linguistics, action anthropology, and disability studies. Dr. Acevedo uses emancipatory research methods such as activist ethnography and collaborative research and draws from a variety of critical traditions, including plural feminisms, social movement theory, spatial theory and analysis, geographies of disability, critical autism studies, queer studies, postmodern theory, posthumanist philosophy, and others. Overall, her work is rooted in anti-racist, anti-ableist, decolonial, anti-capitalist, disability justice praxis. Her activist research agenda focuses on grassroots disabled leadership, horizontal organizing, the politics of self-direction and self-governance, and the creation of liberated communities and autonomous spaces by and for neurodivergent people living at the intersection of other minoritized identities.

Prior to her doctoral studies, **Subini Ancy Annamma** was a special education teacher in public schools and youth prisons. Currently, she is an associate professor at Stanford University. Her research critically examines the mutually constitutive nature of racism and ableism by positioning multiply marginalized students as knowledge generators, exploring how they experience and resist intersectional injustice, and imagine a liberatory education.

Brittany Aronson earned her doctorate in 2014 in cultural studies in education. She is currently working as an associate professor of sociocultural studies at Miami University, Ohio, and teaching classes in sociocultural foundations, sociology of education, and multicultural education. Her research interests include critical teacher preparation, social justice education, critical race theory, critical whiteness studies, and critical educational policy.

Midred Boveda is associate professor of special education at the Pennsylvania State University and honorary visiting professor at Teachers College,

Columbia University. Her interests include teacher education, intersectionality, and Black feminist epistemology. She uses the terms "intersectional competence" and "intersectional consciousness" to refer to educators' understanding of sociocultural differences and how students, families, and colleagues navigate multiple systems of oppression.

David J. Connor, Ed.D., is professor emeritus of the School of Education at Hunter College, and the Graduate Center of the City University of New York. He has published numerous books, book chapters, and articles on inclusive education, learning disabilities, disability studies in education, and—with his colleagues Subini Annamma and Beth Ferri—disability critical race theory (DisCrit).

Beth A. Ferri, PhD, is a professor of education at Syracuse University. She has published widely on the intersection of race, gender, and disability, including her two most recent coedited books, *How Teaching Shapes Our Thinking about Dis/Ability: Stories from the Field* (2021, Peter Lang, with D. J. Connor) and *DisCrit Expanded: Inquiries, Reverberations & Ruptures* (2022, Teachers College Press, with S. A. Annamma & D. J. Connor).

Dr. Cristina Santamaría Graff is an associate professor of special education, Urban Teacher Education at IUPUI. She has expertise in bilingual/multicultural special education and applies her skills in working alongside Latinx immigrant families of children with dis/abilities in family-centered projects. Her scholarship focuses on families' epistemic wisdom and knowledge-making as central to the process of transforming educational systems.

Keith Jones is President and CEO of SoulTouchin' Experiences LLC, an organization aimed at bringing perspective to issues of access, inclusion, and empowerment, which affect him as well as others who are persons with and without disabilities. His multicultural, cross-disability education and outreach efforts include collaboration and trainings to provide services and information for people with disabilities. He tackles wide ranging issues including immigration, criminal justice reform, health care and environmental justice. Jones, along with Leroy Moore and Rob Temple, founded Krip-Hop Nation: an international collection of artists with disabilities. Krip-Hop Nation is currently celebrating 13 years with the recent Emmy Award winning success of their title song for the Netflix documentary of the Paralympic Games, Rising Phoenix, and its critically acclaimed sound track.

Gloshanda Lawyer, PhD, is a community-based disability justice and language justice practitioner. She does research and advocacy internationally on issues of social justice; colonization; Deaf education and Deaf studies analyzing systems of power; and multilingualism for Deaf, DeafBlind, DeafDisabled and Hard of Hearing populations. She is an assistant professor in ASL and Deaf studies at Utah Valley University.

Bradley Minotti is a doctoral student in school psychology at the University of Florida. He identifies as a person with a physical disability. His research focuses on improving mental health and well-being for students with disabilities, as well as disability identity. Additionally, he has taught a course on diversity and social justice in education for future teachers.

Anjali J. Forber-Pratt, PhD, is a disability activist, a two-time Paralympian and the director of the National Institute on Disability, Independent Living and Rehabilitation Research (NIDILRR) in the Administration for Community Living. As a researcher, her primary area of work relates to disability identity development. As a wheelchair user, Dr. Forber-Pratt is nationally and internationally recognized as a disability leader.

David Mitchell and Sharon Snyder's work in disability studies includes extensive published scholarship: six books (*The Body and Physical Difference: Discourses of Disability* [Ann Arbor: U of Michigan P, 1997]; *Narrative Prosthesis: Disability and the Dependencies of Discourse* [Ann Arbor: U of Michigan P, 2000]; *Volume 5: An Encyclopedia of Disability in Primary Sources* [Thousand Oaks: Sage P, 2005]; *Cultural Locations of Disability* [Chicago: U of Chicago P, 2006]; *The Biopolitics of Disability: Neoliberalism, Ablenationalism, and Peripheral Embodiment* [Ann Arbor: U of Michigan P, 2015]; *The Matter of Disability: Materiality, Biopolitics, Crip Affect* [U of Michigan P, 2019]), more than 65 journal articles and chapters, curated museum exhibits on disability history at the Chicago-based National Vietnam Veterans Memorial Museum, disability film and arts programming for festivals and conferences, the longest running academic book series on disability studies in the humanities with the University of Michigan Press, and four award-winning documentary films—*Vital Signs: Crip Culture Talks Back* (1995); *A World Without Bodies* (2002); *Self Preservation: The Art of Riva Lehrer* (2005); and *Disability Takes on the Arts* (2006). Together their work stands as some of the most influential and guiding innovations in disability studies and the contemporary understanding of disability as a critical facet of human embodiment. Their work is routinely taught on syllabi across the country and the world, and Mitchell and Snyder are actively sought out for international lectures of noteworthiness. In 2007 their film work on disability arts, history, and culture was honored by the Munich Film Museum for its transformative influence on contemporary media portrayals of disabled people.

2021 Emmy award–winning **Leroy F. Moore Jr.** is the founder of the Krip-Hop Nation. Since the 1990s, Moore has been a key member of POOR Magazine, starting with the column "Illin-N-Chillin" and then as a founding member of the magazine's school, the Homefulness and Decolonize Academy. Moore is one of the founding members of the National Black Disability Coalition and an activist around police brutality against people with disabilities. Leroy has started and helped start organizations, including Disability Advocates of Minorities Organization, Sins Invalid, and Krip-Hop Nation. His cultural work includes the film documentary *Where Is Hope: Police Brutality Against People with Disabilities*, and the children's book *Black Disabled Art History 101*, published by Xochitl Justice Press. In fall 2021, Leroy started his PhD in anthropology at UCLA. Leroy Moore with Krip-Hop Nation is working to open the Krip-Hop Institute in LA.

Srikala Naraian is professor of education in the Department of Curriculum and Teaching at Teachers College, Columbia University. Her interests are qualitative inquiry in inclusive education and teacher preparation for inclusive education. Alongside research in U.S. public schools, she has prepared teachers for inclusive education in international contexts; she has served as a Fulbright Specialist in Germany and in India.

Dr. Onudeah "Oni" Nicolarakis is an assistant professor at Gallaudet University's Department of Education. She has been an educator for 15 years and used multimodal approaches to provide access to academic and social content. Her areas of interest are in producing counter narratives of the writing experience for the DDBDDHH community and redirecting attention to the advantages of the intersectional experiences from people within marginalized communities.

Akilah English is a deaf and hard of hearing specialist for a public school system in Washington, DC Akilah is currently attending the University of Maryland-College Park where she is pursuing a PhD in teaching and learning, policy, and leadership with a specialty in minority and urban education. Her research examines teaching pedagogy and curriculum violence through an antiracist and anti-audist lens and creating spaces for liberatory deaf education.

Robin Roscigno is a PhD candidate at the Rutgers University Graduate School of Education. Her research focuses on ethical, affirming education for autistic and otherwise neurodivergent children and eradicating school-based forms of curative violence such as restraint and seclusion. She also runs a successful TikTok account about autism, education, and advocacy under the name AuTeach, and her work can be seen in *Ms. Magazine*, TEDx, *Rolling Stone*, Tilt Parenting, and other high-visibility media.

Seena M. Skelton, PhD, brings 24 years of extensive training in principles of learning, teaching, and assessment, and broad professional experience working in the areas of school improvement and educational equity. As a Black woman with a dis/ability, and with professional experiences as an educational consultant for a special educational regional resource center, project lead for statewide special and general education reform initiatives, and former school psychologist, she brings into her scholarship and praxis the intersectional experiences of her own K–12 educational history, and her history as a practitioner, which enable a particular perspective and a personal awareness of the intended and unintended consequences of being a student of color with a dis/ability. In her capacity as director of operations at the Midwest and Plains (MAP) Equity Assistance Center, one of four federally funded equity assistance centers in the United States, she has worked extensively with educators engaged in professional learning around such issues as disproportionality, cultural responsiveness, response to intervention, early intervening, and positive behavior support.

Minhye Son is an assistant professor of teacher education at California State University, Dominguez Hills. Grounded in sociocultural theories, her scholarly interests focus on the intersections of language and power in the areas of teacher education and bilingualism. At CSUDH, she has the privilege of serving future teachers to support their practice in developing critical and humanizing pedagogy.

Kathleen A. King Thorius is an associate professor in the Urban Teacher Education Department of Indiana University School of Education–IUPUI. She is founder and executive director of the *Great Lakes Equity Center*, a hub for educational justice-focused research, technical assistance, and resource development projects, including the *Midwest and Plains Equity Assistance Center*. Her scholarship focuses on critical and systemic approaches for remediating education practices and policies that sort youth into race/disability hierarchies.

Patricia Martínez-Álvarez is an associate professor of bilingual/bicultural education at Teachers College, Columbia University. Employing cultural historical and disability studies in education theories, her research exposes the educational inequities that bilingual children with a disability experience in schools and prepares teachers for enacting inclusive education in bilingual programs. Among other contributions, she has authored *Teacher Education for Inclusive Bilingual Contexts*.

Federico R. Waitoller is an associate professor at the department of special education at the University of Illinois at Chicago. His research agenda has two strands: teacher learning and pedagogies for inclusive education, and the experience of students with disabilities with market-driven educational policies. He is the author of *Excluded by Choice: Urban Students with Disabilities in the Education Marketplace.*

Linda Ware, PhD, recently retired from a lengthy career of teaching in universities from New Mexico to New York. Her research and scholarship appeared in national and international journals, and numerous book chapters. She has published several edited volumes: *(Dis)Assemblages: An International Critical Disability Studies Reader* (Springer, 2020), *Ideology and the Politics of (In)Exclusion* (Peter Lang, 2004), and most recently a multi-volume series, *Critical Leaders and the Foundation of Disability Studies in Education* (Brill, 2020–continuing). She now resides in New Mexico.

Index

Ableism, 7, 9–11, 148
Absent curriculum, 77
Acceptance, disability identity development, 19
Acevedo, Sara M., 33
Achievement, indices of, 29
Achondroplasia, 6
Activity system, 171
Adoption, disability identity development, 20
Agency, 98
Alim, H. S., 65, 86
Allyship, 15
American Educational Research Association Conference, 2016, 159
American Sign Language (ASL), 60
Americans with Disabilities Act (ADA), 9
Americans with Disabilities Act Amendments Act (ADAAA), 9
Analyzing power relations, 132–133
Andrews, E. E., 15
Annamma, S. A., 74, 75, 84
Annual performance report (APR), 172–173
Anti-Blackness, 160
Anti-Black racism, 62, 160
Artiles, A., 75
Asset-based approach, 12–16
Asset-based learning and teaching, 121
Asset pedagogy (AP), 35–36, 37, 75, 130
   and DDBDDHHLD/CI community, 65–68
   disability critical race theory as (see Disability critical race theory (DisCrit))
   and disability studies in education, 46–56
   extending, 51–54
   radical inclusive pedagogy and, 96–97
   to remediate underpinnings of race/disability injustices, 174–175
   supporting positive ethnic-racial-disability identity development with, 27
Assets, children's and families', 136–141
   children's behaviors, contextualizing/reframing, 138–139
   educators' misinterpretations, 139–141
   naming, 136–138
Attitudinal injustice, 7
Autism scholarship
   critical disability studies and, 34–35
Autistic lived body, 32–34
Autistic Self Advocacy Network (ASAN), 41, 43
Autistic Women and Nonbinary Network (AWN), 41, 43

Biklen, D., 120
Bilingual children with disability, 95–96
   children's volitional actions, 100–106
   theoretical constructs, 96–100
Black ASL (BASL), 67, 68, 69, 70–71
Black Deaf Gain, 67–68
   from theory to application, 68–72
Black Power movement, 18
Blanchett, W., 75
Boda, P., 82
Bogard, W., 38
Bogart, K. R., 8, 9
Bullying, 16

Index   229

Centering Diverse Bodyminds in Critical Qualitative Inquiry, 121
Centrality, ethnic-racial identity dimension, 20
Chicano movement, 18
Children's behaviors, contextualizing/ reframing, 138–139
Clark, N. M., 83, 84
Coherent disability identity, 8
Collaborations
  curriculum theorizing through, 161–162
Collaborative partnership, 158–160
Collective impact, 84
Collins, P. H., 75
Color-evasiveness, 25
Compensation, 50
Consciousness, 69–71
Cooper, A. J., 75
COVID-19 pandemic, 11
Crenshaw, K. W., 75
Critical autism studies (CAS), 35
Critical disability studies (CDS), 32, 34
  and autism scholarship, 34–35
Critical pedagogy, 41–42
Cultural artifacts, 51
Cultural competence, disability as form of, 15
Cultural-historical activity theory (CHAT), 46, 51–56, 97, 170–171
Cultural modeling, 46, 52
Culturally responsive, relevant, and sustaining pedagogy (CRRSP), 79, 80
Culturally sustaining pedagogy (CSP), 27, 65–66
  principles, 28
  recommendations for disabled youth, 28–30
Culture, 52–53
  disability as, 18–19, 132–133
  as dynamic and intersectional, 130–131
Curricular cripistemologies, 114–117, 124
Curriculum, 77–79
  framing, 162–167
  theorizing, 157–158, 161–162

D'Ardenne, C., 83, 84
Deaf, DeafBlind, DeafDisabled, Hard of Hearing, and Cochlear Implant Users (DDBDDHHCI), 60
Deaf, DeafBlind, DeafDisabled, Hard of Hearing, and Late-Deafened (DDBDDHHLD) community, 59–62
  asset pedagogies and, 65–68
  Black Deaf Gain from theory to application, 68–72
  children, educating, 64–65
  tensions and resistance in, 62–64
Defectology, 48
Deleuze, G., 36, 37, 38
Dickens, B., 121–122
Direct challenge literatures, 121–123
Disability
  bio-cultural understanding of, 55–56
  as cultural phenomenon, 113–114
  history of, 116
  positive images of, 115
  social model(s) of, 54–56
  as sociocultural phenomenon, 48
Disability critical race theory (DisCrit), 74–85, 164
  classroom ecology, 75–82
  curriculum, 77–79
  overview, 74–75
  pedagogy, 79–81
  solidarity, 81–82
  and teacher education, 82–85
Disability identity, 7–8, 19–20
  asset-based approach to foster, 12–16
Disability Identity Circle, 12–13
Disability movement, history of, 3
Disability pride, 3, 8
  asset-based approach to foster, 12–16
Disability Rights movement, 18
Disability studies in education (DSE), 34
  asset pedagogy and, 46–56
  developmental and learning science in education, 54–56
Discourse of specialness, 116–117
Diversity model of disability, 7
Double stimulation, 98–100, 106
Dual language bilingual program (DLBP), 99–100

DuBois, W. E. B., 75, 76
Dumas, M. J., 62
Dunn, D. S., 9

Educational sovereignty, 130
Education policy, 15–16
Educators' misinterpretations, 139–141
Ellis-Robinson, T., 83
Engagement, disability identity development, 20
Epistemology of the Closet (Sedgwick), 44
Equity Assistance Center (EAC), 170
Equity-expansive TA, 170–172, 175–182
Erevelles, N., 75, 163, 164
Erickson, K. A., 83, 84
Escobar syndrome, 21
Essential understandings (EUs), 127, 129
  analyzing power relations, 132–133
  examining positionality, 131–132
  families are experts, 130–131
Ethnic-racial identity, 20–21
  cultivating, by centering race in hidden curriculum, 26–27
  positive, 25–26, 27
Eugenics movement, 5–7
Exploration, ethnic-racial identity dimension, 20

Family as faculty (FAF), 127–128
  assets, children's and families', 136–141
  centering children's and families' assets in, 136–141
  describing, 133–136
  implications, 142–143
  interacting frameworks, 129–133, 142
  interweaving, 128–133
  overview, 126–127
Forber-Pratt, A. J., 4, 19
Foucault, M., 116
Free and appropriate public education (FAPE), 118
The Fundamentals of Defectology (Vygotsky), 48, 56
Funds of knowledge (FofK), 52

Gallaudet, Thomas Hopkins, 64
Gift theory, 76
Gindis, B., 56
Goffman, E., 19
Graduation rate for students with disabilities, 10
Guattari, F., 31, 36, 37, 38

Haraway, D., 33
Hehir, T., 9
A Hero Ain't Nothin' but a Sandwich (film), 25, 30
Heshusius, L., 120
Hip-hop culture, 27, 86–87. See also Krip-Hop Nation
Hipolito-Delgado, C. P., 15
Human agency, 98
Human development principles, 49
Hunt, P., 121
Husserl, E., 32
Hybrid learning spaces, 97–98

Ideologies, 69–71
Ideology, ethnic-racial identity dimension, 20
Incorporation, 38
Indices of achievement, 29
Individualization, 117–118
Individualized education programs (IEP), 23, 118, 126
Individuals with Disabilities Education Act (IDEA), 8, 11, 18, 161, 172–173
Individuals with Disabilities Improvement Act (IDEIA), 118
Intellectual disability, 131
Intersectionality, 59–60, 68–69

Jones, K., 53

Kemerling, A. A., 12
Koppenhaver, D. A., 83, 84
Krip-Hop Nation, 86–94
  education toward liberation, 93–94
  foundations of, 87–89
  politics, 89–94
  reclaiming language and reframing disability, 91–93
Kulkarni, S. S., 82

Index

Lalor, M., 117
Leary, J. D., 90
Least restrictive environment (LRE), 118, 119
Lester, J., 121, 122
Life in the Sick Room (Martineau), 116
Lived body, 32–34
Lorde, A., 75
Loutzenheiser, L. W., 163, 164
Lund, E. M., 8
Lyew, D. A., 19

Martineau, H., 116
Medical model of disability, 5–7
Mehan, H., 120
Memories, 23–27
Merleau-Ponty, M., 32, 33
Miller et al. v. Board of Education of District of Columbia et al., 70
Minh-Ha, T., 148
Minotti, B., 4–5
Moges, R. T., 70
Mohanty, C. T., 148
Moll, L., 130
Moore, L., 53
Morgan, J., 84
Morrison, D., 74, 75
Mueller, C., 19
Mukhopadhyay, T. R., 123, 124
Multiplicity, 147

Nario-Redmond, M. R., 9, 12
Narrative stance toward teachers, 152–154
National Endowment for the Humanities (NEH), 112
NCCRESt, 173
Neurodiver-agency, 32
Noblit, G. W., 83, 84
Nomadic philosophy, 31
Nomadology, 36–38
Nonce taxonomy, 44
#NothingAboutUsWithoutUs, 3
Nusbaum, E., 82, 121, 122

Paris, D., 65, 86
Pearson, H., 122–123

People of color (POC), 18
Philosophy of movement and flow, 31
Plankton Dreams: What I Learned in Special-Ed (Mukhopadhyay), 123, 125
Politics, Krip-Hop Nation, 89–94
Positionality, 131–132
Positionality statements, 4–5
Positive ethnic-racial identity development, 25–26
Post Modern Audism (PMA), 66–67
Power of norm, 119–121
Power relations, analyzing, 132–133
Pre-service special education teachers (PSETs), 127, 128, 131–132
  teaching through stories, 141–142
Principles of human development, 49
Private regard, ethnic-racial identity dimension, 20
Psychosocial Disability Identity Development (PDID) model, 19–20, 23–24
Public education plankton, 123–125
Public regard, ethnic-racial identity dimension, 20

Rabaka, R., 76
Race
  disability as culture at intersection of, 18–19
Race/disability inequities
  contributions and challenges with TA responses to, 173–174
Race/disability injustices
  leveraging asset pedagogies to remediate underpinnings of, 174–175
Race-linked stressors, 30
Racial identity, 22
Radical Accessibility, 29
Radical inclusive pedagogy, 96–97
Relationship, disability identity development, 19
Remediation approach, 112–113
Resistance, in DDBDDHHLD community, 62–64

Ritualistic procedural performative compliance, 117–119
Roberts, E., 7
Roscigno, R., 33
ross k. m., 62
Rottenstein, A., 8
Ruderman Family Foundation, 10
Ruíz, R., 130

Samples, L. B., 19
Schools as powerful socializing agents, 21
Schult, A., 36
Sedgwick, Eve Kosofsky, 44
Silverman, A., 12
Skrtic, T., 120
Sleeter, C., 120
Smoothness, 38–39
Social injustice, 7
Socializing agents, schools as, 21
Social model of disability, 7, 63
Solidarity, DisCrit, 81–82, 84
Specialized education, and teacher education, 160–161
Specialness, discourse of, 116–117
State performance plan (SPP), 172–173
Sterilizations, 6
Stornaioulo, A., 81
Storytelling, 71–72
Stressors, race-linked, 30
Striation, 38–39

Taylor, S., 120
Teacher education, 144–155
  becoming of teachers/continual (re)making of inclusion, 151–155
  collaborations in, 158–159
  content-focused considerations, 165–166
  diversification, 147–148
  inclusion from teachers' practice, 149–151
  inclusive research and practice, 162–167
  narrative stance toward teachers, 152–154
  process-centered considerations, 166–167
  specialized education and, 160–161
  theoretical assumptions, 163–165
  theorizing practice in order to practice theory, 145–147
Teacher training programs, 119–120
Technical assistance (TA), 169–170
  contributions and challenges with, 173–174
  equity-expansive, 170–172, 175–182
  legislative foundations and center history, 172–173
Tensions, in DDBDDHHLD community, 62–64
Theoretical constructs, 96–100
Theory of human cognition, 47–48
Third Space, 46, 52
Third World, 147
Thorius, K. A. K., 65, 82, 129
Trent, S. C., 75

Universal Design for Learning (UDL), 29–30, 54, 83

Victimization, of crime, 9–10
Volitional act, 95
Vowell, S., 125
Vygotsky, L. E., 46–56, 97, 106
  and disabled youth, 47–50

Waitoller, F. R., 65, 82, 129
Whitney, E., 81
Woodward, J., 59
Worthiness, asset-based approach to foster, 12–16

Youth of color (YOC), 17
  culturally sustaining pedagogy for, 28–30
  disabled, 20–21